THE UNIVERSITY OF CHICAGO

RAIL TRANSPORTATION AND THE ECONOMIC DEVELOPMENT OF SOVIET CENTRAL ASIA

DEPARTMENT OF GEOGRAPHY
RESEARCH PAPER NO. 64

By
Robert Taaffe

CHICAGO · ILLINOIS
1960

 PUBLISHED 1960. PRINTED BY
THE UNIVERSITY OF CHICAGO PRESS
CHICAGO, ILLINOIS, U.S.A.

ACKNOWLEDGMENTS

I wish to express my appreciation to Professors Chauncy D. Harris and Harold M. Mayer for their invaluable assistance in the preparation of this study. The generous donation of time and experience by Professor Harris was the major impetus for the completion of this monograph, while Professor Mayer provided helpful guidance not only during the difficult formative stages of this study, but also during innumerable classroom lectures and discussions.

I wish to thank the Inter-University Committee on Travel Grants for making possible a visit to Soviet Central Asia during the summer of 1957 and, also, a year of post-graduate study and research at Moscow University during the academic year 1958-59. Thanks are also due to Professor Edward J. Taaffe, my brother, who, among other things, handled the details of the publication of this study during my return visit to the Soviet Union. I am also grateful to Holland Hunter for ideas imparted by correspondence during the planning stages. For cartographic assistance, I am indebted to J. Indans, a graduate student at the University of Chicago, who prepared the finished versions of all the maps used in this study.

It is difficult to find words suitable for an expression of my deeply felt gratitude to my mother, whose enthusiasm for learning and whose endless sacrifices have made this study possible.

TABLE OF CONTENTS

		Page
ACKNOWLEDGMENTS		iii
LIST OF TABLES		ix
LIST OF ILLUSTRATIONS		xi
Chapter		
I.	INTRODUCTION	1

Methods and Purposes of Study
Relation of Study to Geography
Limitations of the Study

II. THE REGIONAL AND HISTORICAL SETTING OF RAIL TRANSPORTATION IN CENTRAL ASIA 4

Definition of Area
The Regional Setting
The Natural Environment
The lowland desert zone
The zone of mountains
The loessial piedmont plains
Effects on transport problems and costs
Population
The Regional Economy
Agriculture
Industry
Industries relying directly on cotton and other agricultural commodities for raw materials
Industries serving the cotton-growing areas
Other industries
Transport Implications of Economic Development
The Evolution of the Central Asian Rail Net in the Pre-Soviet Era
Historical Background
The Evolution of the Rail Net

III. THE DEVELOPMENT OF THE RAIL PATTERN OF CENTRAL ASIA DURING THE SOVIET ERA 39

The Development of the Rail Pattern Within the Central Asian Republics
Tadzhikstan and Southern Uzbekistan
The Rail Pattern of the Kirghiz Republic
The Rail Pattern of the Fergana Basin and Approaches
Other Feeder Lines
The Rail Pattern of the Lower Amu-Darya
Summary of the Internal Pattern of Soviet Central Asia
The Interregional Rail Pattern
The Turkestan-Siberian Railroad
Feeder Lines on the Turk-Sib Route
The Trans-Kazakhstan Magistral

TABLE OF CONTENTS--Continued

Chapter Page

Other Lines on the Approaches to Central Asia
Competition from the Caspian-Volga Route
The Projected Interregional Rail Pattern
Summary

IV. THE TECHNICAL RENOVATION OF THE RAIL PATTERN OF SOVIET CENTRAL ASIA 75

Measures to Increase Train Speed and Frequency
Double-tracking
Signaling
Measures Designed to Increase Train Weight As Well As Speed and Frequency
Ruling grades
Rails
Dieselization
Length of classification tracks
Conclusions

V. THE INTERREGIONAL TRADE OF SELECTED COMMODITIES . . 101

Cotton
Grain and Lumber
Grain
Lumber
Coal
Petroleum
Other Commodities
Mineral fertilizers
Ferrous metals
Summary

VI. THE EXTRA COSTS OF CENTRAL ASIAN INTERREGIONAL RAIL TRADE AND ATTEMPTS TO REDUCE THEM 129

The Extra Costs of Central Asian Interregional Trade
Extra Costs Associated with the Regional Average Distance of Haul
Interregional exports
Interregional imports
Extra Transportation Costs Associated with the Regional Imbalance in Movement
Attempts to Reduce the Average Distance of Haul of Rail Freight Terminated in Central Asia
Increasing the Trade Ties between Central Asia and Kazakhstan through the Construction of the Mointy-Chu Line
Increasing the Degree of Regional Self-Sufficiency
Changes in the degree of regional self-sufficiency in the Soviet Union
Changes in the degree of regional self-sufficiency in Central Asia

TABLE OF CONTENTS--Continued

Chapter Page

VII. SUMMARY AND CONCLUSIONS 156

The Construction of the Central Asian Rail Pattern
The Technical Renovation of the Central Asian Rail Pattern
Commodity Movement and Regional Economic Development
Future

APPENDIXES 163

BIBLIOGRAPHY 181

LIST OF TABLES

Table		Page
1.	Population of Central Asia	14
2.	Population of the Leading Cities of Central Asia	14
3.	The Irrigated Cotton Area of Central Asia and Kazakhstan--1913 to 1956	18
4.	The Production of Ginned Cotton	21
5.	Energy Balance of the Uzbek Republic--1953	26
6.	Operating Length of Rail Lines in Central Asia	52
7.	Distance to Moscow by Selected Routes	69
8.	Freight-Density of the Soviet Rail Net	75
9.	The Growth of Central Asian Rail Freight, 1913-1956	77
10.	Central Asian Originations and Terminations by Rail	101
11.	Relative Share of Domestic Ginned Cotton in Total Consumption	109
12.	Irrigated Acreage of Selected Crops in Central Asia	109
13.	Rail Originations and Terminations of Grain in Central Asia	113
14.	Central Asian Grain Imports by Rail--1937	114
15.	Central Asian Lumber Imports by Rail--1937	116
16.	Rail Originations and Terminations of Forest Products in Central Asia	117
17.	Rail Originations and Terminations of Coal and Coke in Central Asia	118
18.	Rail Originations and Terminations of Petroleum and Petroleum Products in Central Asia	121
19.	Maritime Petroleum Trade of the Turkmen Republic	123
20.	Average Length of Haul of Goods Terminated on Central Asian Railroads--1952	131
21.	Central Asian Rail Terminations--by Railroad Administration	133
22.	Ton-Kilometer Rail Terminations of Central Asia--1952	133
23.	Average Length of Haul of Terminated Commodities in the Basic Economic Regions--1952	135
24.	Density of Empty Freight Car Flow on the Turk-Sib--1940	137
25.	Per Cent of Total Terminations by Region of Origin--1952	139
26.	Coal Imports of Central Asia and Southern Kazakhstan South of Alma-Ata--1940-1955	143

LIST OF TABLES--Continued

Table		Page
27.	Savings in Distance by Use of Karaganda Coal in Central Asia	144
28.	Relation of Central Asian Rail Terminations by Area of Origin to Average for Basic Economic Regions .	152
29.	Estimated Percentage of Terminations on Individual Railroads in Union Republics	163
30.	Average Length of Haul of Terminated Commodities on Railroads Within Basic Economic Regions--1952 . .	164
31.	Interregional Rail Trade of Central Asia	165
32.	Rail Exports of the Kazakh Republic in 1952 and 1955.	166
33.	Rail Exports of Grain from Kazakhstan--1955	167
34.	Per Cent of Local Originations in the Total Terminated Rail Tonnage of the Basic Economic Regions in 1940 and 1952	168
35.	Per Cent of Terminations from Neighboring and "Distant" Regions in the Terminated Rail Tonnage of the Basic Economic Regions in 1940 and 1952 . . .	169
36.	Sources of Electricity in the Uzbek Republic in 1958 and 1965	172

LIST OF ILLUSTRATIONS

Figure		Page
1.	Land Use in Central Asia and Approaches (Map) Facing	4
2.	Natural Regions of Central Asia (Map)	6
3.	Average Annual Precipitation in Central Asia and Approaches (Map)	8
4.	The Snow-Capped Peaks of the Kara-Tau Southwest of Dzhambul as Viewed from the Turk-Sib (Photo) . . .	10
5.	A Sprawling Belt of Dry Farming in Southern Kazakhstan Near Dzhambul (Photo)	10
6.	A View of the Old Section of Samarkand (Photo) . . .	15
7.	A "Showpiece" Boulevard in the Old Section of Tashkent (Photo)	15
8.	The Zeravshan River Just Outside of Samarkand (Photo)	17
9.	The Cultivation of a Cotton Field in the 2,000 Hectare Engel's Kolkhoz West of Samarkand (Photo) . .	19
10.	Officials of the Engel's Kolkhoz Proudly Inspect a Modern Irrigation Canal (Photo)	19
11.	Entrance to the Tashkent Textile Combine (Photo) . .	24
12.	The Tomb of Timur in Samarkand (Photo)	30
13.	Rail Pattern of Eastern Central Asia (Map)	45
14.	An Asphalt Highway Leading into Samarkand from the East (Photo)	54
15.	A Coal-Burning Locomotive on the Ust-Kamenogorsk-Zyryanovsk Line (Photo)	59
16.	Caspian Sea Routes (Map)	66
17.	Projected Rail Pattern of Central Asia and Approaches (Map)	70
18.	Transit Divides for Freight Moving to Central Asia (Map)	73
19.	Double Tracks on the Central Asian Rail Pattern (Map)	78
20.	Scheduled Passenger Trains: Summer--1957 (Map) . . .	80
21.	Signaling on the Rail Pattern of Central Asia and Approaches (Map)	82
22.	Diesel Traction on the Rail Pattern of Central Asia and Approaches (Map)	90
23.	The TE-3 Diesel-Electric Locomotive (Photo)	92
24.	Railroad Systems in Central Asia and Approaches--1957 (Map)	95
25.	Railroad Freight Originations in the Central Asian Republics--1940 (Map)	103

LIST OF ILLUSTRATIONS--Continued

Figure		Page
26.	Railroad Freight Originations in the Central Asian Republics--1956 (Map)	104
27.	Railroad Freight Terminations in the Central Asian Republics--1940 (Map)	105
28.	Railroad Freight Terminations in the Central Asian Republics--1956 (Map)	106
29.	Minimum Surpluses and Deficits of Selected Rail-Borne Commodities--1940 (Map)	126
30.	Minimum Surpluses and Deficits of Selected Rail-Borne Commodities--1956 (Map)	127
31.	Area in the Soviet Union with an Average Distance of Haul for Terminated Rail Freight Longer Than That of Central Asia--1952 (Map)	136
32.	The Relative Share of Neighboring Regions in the Rail Exports of Kazakhstan--1952 (Map)	141
33.	The Relative Share of Neighboring Regions in the Rail Exports of Kazakhstan--1955 (Map)	141
34.	The Relative Share of Neighboring Regions in the Grain Exports of Kazakhstan by Rail--1955 (Map) .	145
35.	Rail Terminations Within the Basic Economic Regions of the Soviet Union by Area of Origin--1940 (Map).	149
36.	Rail Terminations Within the Basic Economic Regions of the Soviet Union by Area of Origin--1952 (Map).	150
37.	The Rail Pattern of Central Asia and Approaches (Map) . . . . Facing	163
38.	Date of the Completion of the Rail Lines of Central Asia and Approaches (Map) . . . . Facing	163

CHAPTER I

INTRODUCTION

Methods and Purposes of Study

One of the fundamental problems in the utilization of the natural and cultural resources of the underdeveloped, outlying regions of a country is the creation of efficient transport links between these areas and the major existing centers of economic activity. This problem is of particular significance to the Soviet Union, which not only occupies one-sixth of the land area of the earth's surface, but also has most of its territory in the deep continental interior of Eurasia far from the reaches of maritime transport.

This paper is a case study in the role of rail transportation in the transformation of one of the outlying areas in the Soviet Union, Central Asia, into a zone of highly specialized economic activity. This region focuses upon the production of commodities destined for distant market and, in turn, relies, to a considerable extent, upon distant sources of supply of food, raw materials, and manufactured goods. In examining the interaction of transportation and economic development in Central Asia particular attention will be paid to the following topics:

1. The scale and direction of economic growth in this region in relation to the evolution of the rail pattern. The first rail line into Central Asia, the Trans-Caspian, was an adjunct to a short-lived military campaign but the railroad became a powerful weapon of economic and social development in this region.

2. The relation between the growth of Central Asian rail freight and the technical renovation of the rail pattern serving this region. The results of Soviet efforts to handle increasingly larger increments of freight traffic while simultaneously attempting to minimize the allocation of capital investment for the renovation of the rail lines of Central Asia and Kazakhstan deserves careful study because of the implications of this cost-economizing approach for other capital-scarce countries now embarking upon programs of regional development.

3. The impact of economic growth in Central Asia upon the regional average distance of haul for rail-borne freight. One of the criteria that must be considered in appraising the real costs of economic development in Central Asia is the extra distance, by comparison with the rest of the country as a whole, involved in the interregional exchange of commodities between this relatively remote region and the other areas of the Soviet Union.

4. The forces of regional specialization and self-sufficiency in relation to interregional commodity movement. Although the relation of these forces to transportation has frequently been described in general terms, this study will attempt to utilize a measure of regional self-sufficiency which will be comparable for different regions and different periods of time. Although the contrasting forces of specialization and self-sufficiency are persistently operative in regional economic growth, their relative importance in the economic regions of the Soviet Union will be examined in particular detail for the period since 1939, when the intensification of the degree of regional autarky became the ostensible motif of Soviet regional planning. Central Asia provides a particularly interesting study of efforts to reduce regional transport inputs by expanding "comprehensive" (autarkic) regional economic development because of the enormous distances involved in the movement of goods to and from this region.

Relation of Study to Geography

An important component of geographic regional investigation is the study of the complex interrelationships between areas. The addition of a dynamic element to static patterns of distribution adds a perspective which not only results in a better understanding of the role of a particular region in the national economy, but also gives deeper meaning to the patterns of activity within homogeneous regions. An examination of the patterns of interregional commodity flows, thus, is basic to a geographic understanding of a particular region.

In this paper, rail transportation in Central Asia will not be considered as an autonomous segment of the economy, artificially isolated from its natural and cultural environment for the purposes of analysis, but rather, it will be viewed as a primary integrating force, grouping specialized foci of economic activity into coherent patterns of spatial organization. The linking of homogeneous patterns of land use in Central Asia with dynamic patterns of spatial organization based upon the interrelations of this region with the rest of the country will be reinforced by the use of the concept of regional specialization as an organizing theme in this study.

Limitations of the Study

In selecting the topics to be examined many promising themes were omitted because they did not seem to be directly pertinent to the goals of the study. For example, the emphasis is on the movement of goods rather than people. For this reason, the scheduled movement of passenger trains is considered only in relation to the carrying capacity of Central Asian rail lines, while air transportation is mentioned only in connection with freight service to some of the areas in Central Asia isolated from the main rail net. Another topic barely touched upon in this study is the highway trade between Central Asia and neighboring countries.

Other omissions reflect a lack of recent information. Detailed flow maps for individual rail lines, for example, are unavailable, just as are recent regional origin-destination tables of commodity movement. In several instances, estimates have been used to fill in some of the gaps in statistical coverage. Data limitations have also resulted in an uneven coverage in terms of time even when relatively recent information is available. The most recent data about rail facilities, freight flow, and regional average distances of haul used in this study are for the years 1957, 1956, and 1952 respectively.

This study will be based on the boundaries of the four union republics of Central Asia as they existed on January 1, 1956. The incorporation of a portion of the South Kazakhstan Oblast into the Uzbek Republic in March, 1956 was not shown on base maps because nearly all the Central Asian statistical data used in this paper are based on the older boundaries.

The reading of this paper will be facilitated immeasurably if Figures 1, 37 and 38 (fold-out maps showing land use, the rail pattern, and the date of rail construction) are kept folded out. Constant reference to these maps will help overcome the formidable Russian place-name barrier and make the text considerably more intelligible. The reader is also urged to consult Appendix H, which describes some of the most recent changes in the characteristics and prospects of transportation and economic growth in Soviet Central Asia. The data in this Appendix were obtained in the period between the initial completion of this study and its publication.

CHAPTER II

THE REGIONAL AND HISTORICAL SETTING OF RAIL TRANSPORTATION IN CENTRAL ASIA

Definition of Area

In this study, the designation "Central Asia" will refer to a group of four union republics of the Soviet Union: the Uzbek S.S.R., the Turkmen S.S.R., the Tadzhik S.S.R., and the Kirghiz S.S.R. The total territory occupied by these republics in 1956 was 477,606 square kilometers[1]--an area slightly smaller than the combined territory of Texas, New Mexico, and Arizona. Since the interregional railroads linking Central Asia with the rest of the country pass through Kazakhstan, more extensive regional boundaries have been adopted for the study of the evolution of the rail pattern serving Central Asia. The examination of rail construction and renovation in Central Asia and its approaches through Kazakhstan will focus on the rail pattern south of an imaginary line curving through the junctions of Chkalov, Karaganda, and Semipalatinsk.

An understanding of some of the broader patterns of economic activity in Central Asia, viewed in their natural setting, as well as a survey of the pre-Soviet rail pattern, is requisite to an appraisal of the interaction of rail transportation and economic development in this region during the Soviet era. Rather than attempt a comprehensive survey of the regional economy of Central Asia, the next section of this chapter will focus upon certain characteristics of the natural environment, settlement, and economic activity which seem to have the greatest pertinence to rail transportation. The last portion of this chapter will be concerned with the evolution of the rail pattern of this region prior to the October Revolution.

---

[1]U.S.S.R., Tsentral'noye Statisticheskoye Upravleniye pri Sovete Ministrov SSR, Narodnoye Khozyaistvo SSSR v 1956 Godu: Statisticheskiy Yezhegodnik (Moscow: Gosstatizdat, 1957), pp. 22-23. Cited hereafter as Narodnoye Khozyaistvo SSSR v 1956 Godu.

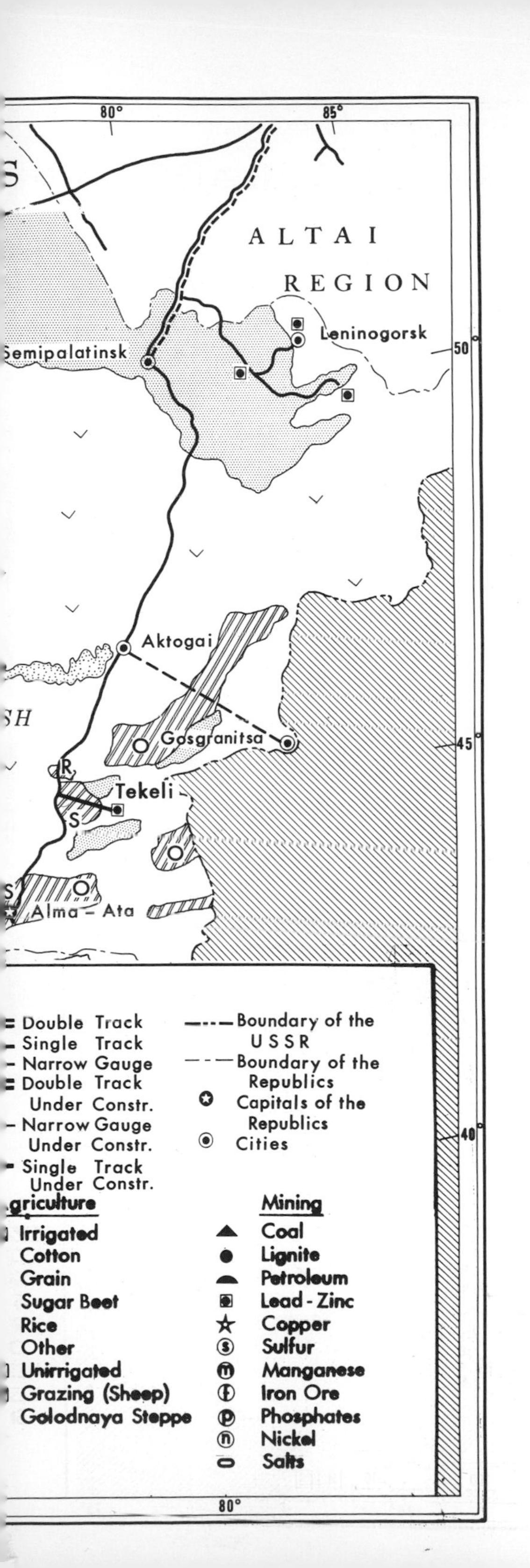

80°
85°
ALTAI
REGION
Leninogorsk
Semipalatinsk
50°
Aktogai
SH
Gosgranitsa
45°
R
Tekeli
S
S
Alma - Ata
40°
Double Track
Single Track
Narrow Gauge
Double Track Under Constr.
Narrow Gauge Under Constr.
Single Track Under Constr.
Boundary of the USSR
Boundary of the Republics
Capitals of the Republics
Cities
griculture
Irrigated
Cotton
Grain
Sugar Beet
Rice
Other
Unirrigated
Grazing (Sheep)
Golodnaya Steppe
Mining
Coal
Lignite
Petroleum
Lead - Zinc
Copper
Sulfur
Manganese
Iron Ore
Phosphates
Nickel
Salts
80°

USE in CENTRAL ASIA and APPROACHE
65°
70°
75°
A Z A K H
S. S. R.
Karaganda
Kazalinsk
LAKE BALKHA
CHU
SYR-DARYA
Achisai
Chu
Dzhambul
Frunze
Lenger
K I R G H I Z
Tashkent
St
Chirchik
Tashkumyr
Angren
Uzgen
E K
S. R.
khara
Kagan
Samarkand
Begovat
Margelan
S. S. R.
ZERAVSHAN
Stalinabad
T A D Z H I K
S. S. R.
Kugitang
UM CANAL
Constr.
50 0 100 200 MILES
C
G
S
R
O
St

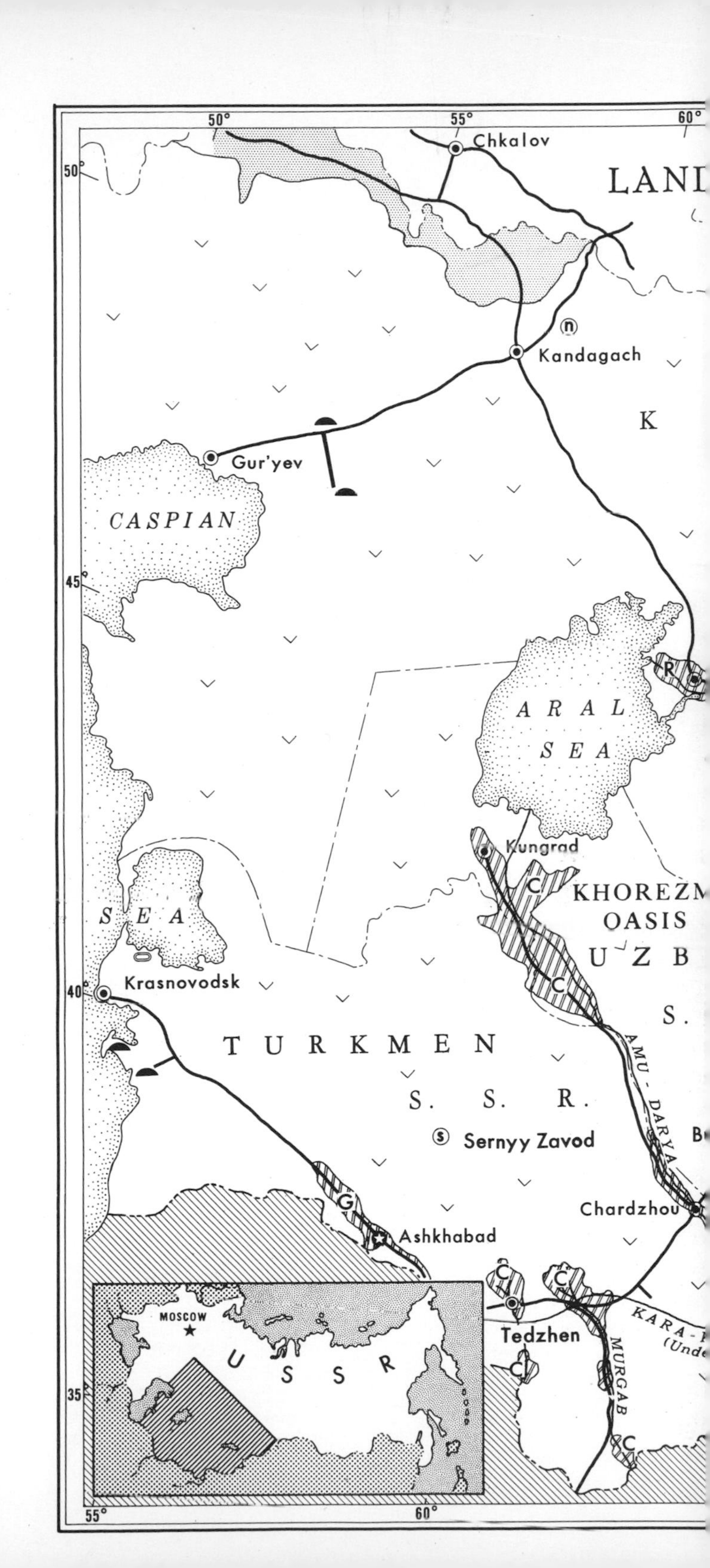

Chkalov
LAND
Kandagach
K
Gur'yev
CASPIAN
SEA
ARAL
SEA
Kungrad
KHOREZM
OASIS
UZB
S.
Krasnovodsk
TURKMEN
S. S. R.
Sernyy Zavod
AMU-DARYA
Chardzhou
Ashkhabad
Tedzhen
MURGAB
KARA-
MOSCOW
USSR
50°
55°
60°
45°
40°
35°

The Regional Setting

The Natural Environment

The lowland desert zone.--The most striking characteristic of the natural setting of Central Asia and its approaches through Kazakhstan is the existence of a vast zone of deserts occupying the largest portion of the territory of this region (Fig. 2). The lowland zone of deserts contains the driest area in the Soviet Union. As Figure 3 reveals, this zone consists of an elongated area in the sands of the Kara-Kum and Kyzyl Kum stretching from the Amu-Darya to the north of the Syr-Darya in which the yearly precipitation averages less than four inches. Most of the desert area in the western half of Central Asia and Kazakhstan, including the clay-stony desert atop the virtually uninhabited Ust-Urt (Ustyurt) Plateau, receives from three to eight inches of rainfall annually. The arid regions in the eastern half of Kazakhstan receive eight to eleven inches of precipitation yearly. This amount of precipitation, however, does not go far because the rate of evaporation is extremely high as a result of high temperatures and low relative humidity. Other important characteristics of the desert climates of Central Asia are the extreme seasonality of precipitation, with maximum rainfall occurring during spring and almost no rainfall during summer, and the extreme seasonal temperature ranges characteristic of continental climates.

If the lack of precipitation were not a serious enough impediment to agriculture, vast areas in the desert zone are occupied by either salt-encrusted solonchaks, or the compact, clay fragments of salinized takyrs (similar to playas). Nonetheless, a few delta oases in the desert zone, such as the Khorezm oasis in the delta region of the Amu-Darya, are densely settled and have intensive forms of agriculture, in contrast to the nomadic sheep herding practiced over much of the desert zone.

The zone of mountains.--Another region dominated by either extensive forms of agriculture, particularly the summer grazing of sheep, or no agriculture at all, is the broad belt of high, snow-capped mountains and intermontaine plateaus of the Pamir and Tyan'-Shan', as well as the Kopet-Dag in Southern Turkmeniya (see Figs. 2 and 4). The highest elevations in the Soviet Union are found in the Pamir group of mountains, where Stalin Peak rises to a height of 24,595 feet above sea-level, which is not much higher than the maximum elevation in the Tyan'-Shan' group of 24,400 feet at Pobeda (victory) Peak, located near the Soviet-Chinese border.

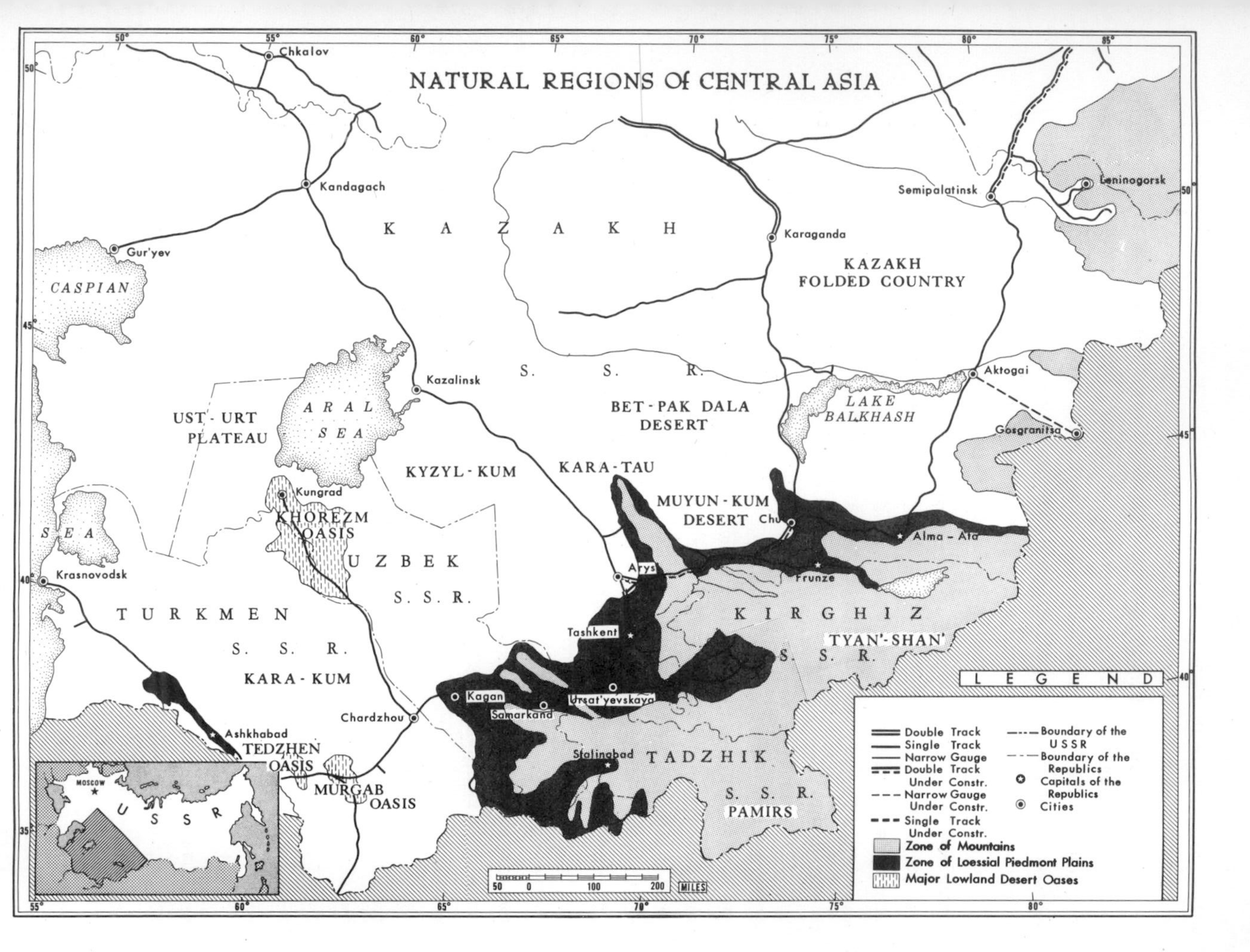

NATURAL REGIONS OF CENTRAL ASIA
KAZAKH S. S. R.
KAZAKH FOLDED COUNTRY
BET-PAK DALA DESERT
MUYUN-KUM DESERT
KARA-TAU
KYZYL-KUM
UZBEK S. S. R.
KHOREZM OASIS
ARAL SEA
UST-URT PLATEAU
TURKMEN S. S. R.
KARA-KUM
TEDZHEN OASIS
MURGAB OASIS
CASPIAN SEA
LAKE BALKHASH
KIRGHIZ S. S. R.
TYAN'-SHAN'
TADZHIK S. S. R.
PAMIRS
Chkalov
Kandagach
Gur'yev
Kazalinsk
Karaganda
Semipalatinsk
Leninogorsk
Aktogai
Gosgranitsa
Kungrad
Krasnovodsk
Arys
Chu
Alma-Ata
Frunze
Tashkent
Kagan
Samarkand
Ursat'yevskaya
Chardzhou
Ashkhabad
Stalinabad
LEGEND
Double Track
Single Track
Narrow Gauge
Double Track Under Constr.
Narrow Gauge Under Constr.
Single Track Under Constr.
Boundary of the USSR
Boundary of the Republics
Capitals of the Republics
Cities
Zone of Mountains
Zone of Loessial Piedmont Plains
Major Lowland Desert Oases
50 0 100 200
MILES
MOSCOW
U S S R

Fig. 2

The existence of this massive barrier of mountains separating Soviet Central Asia from Chinese Turkestan and Afghanistan has greatly increased the significance of the mountain passes linking these regions. Although the Central Asian republics at present rely exclusively upon highways for their overland trade with Sinkiang Province, a rail line is presently being constructed which will pass through the famed Dzhungarian Gate (Gosgranitsa) and establish an overland rail link with China.

The loessial piedmont plains.--Nestled between the vast, sandy deserts and snow-capped mountains is the winding, discontinuous core region of Central Asia--the loessial piedmont plains. Every area of dense settlement in Central Asia, with the exception of the relatively few lowland, desert oases, is found on these gently rising plains, which, for the most part, have fertile sierozem soils overlying thick beds of loess. Average yearly precipitation in the loessial piedmont plains increases from eight inches in the lowland fringes to 24 inches on the slopes of the Kirghiz Range, south of Frunze. At the major centers of settlement, such as Tashkent and Samarkand, the average yearly precipitation ranges from eleven to fifteen inches. However, annual averages of precipitation are less revealing than data about the seasonal variation in rainfall. The most important feature of the annual march of precipitation in the piedmont plains, as well as in the desert zone, is the prolonged summer drought, which is accompanied by an unusually high percentage of cloudless days and frequent dust storms.

The production of cotton in this zone is never undertaken without the aid of irrigation. This, in turn, has given the rivers of Central Asia a vital role in the localization of cotton production on the fertile oases within the zone of loessial piedmont plains. The major rivers in the Central Asian interior drainage basin, including the Amu-Darya, Syr-Darya, and Zeravshan, have two maximum periods of flow. One of these is in the spring, when the melting snows combine with the spring rains, while a summer maximum (June-July) occurs when water from the melting mountain glaciers descends to the plains. In addition to the presence of water for irrigation, the production of cotton and other crops is aided by the long growing season in Central Asia. Although temperatures in the loessial piedmont plains are marked by a high degree of continentality, including freezing temperatures in winter and temperatures over 100 degrees in summer, the long hot summer in this zone, coupled with a mild spring and autumn, provides a growing

AVERAGE ANNUAL PRECIPITATION of CENTRAL
ASIA and APPROACHES
K A Z A K H
S. S. R.
U Z B E K
S. S. R.
T U R K M E N
S. S. R.
K I R G H I Z
S. S. R.
T A D Z H I K
S. S. R.
CASPIAN
SEA
A R A L
S E A
LAKE
BALKHASH
Chkalov
Kandagach
Gur'yev
Kazalinsk
Kungrad
Krasnovodsk
Ashkhabad
Chardzhou
Kagan
Samarkand
Ursat'yevskaya
Tashkent
Arys'
Chu
Frunze
Alma Ata
Karaganda
Semipalatinsk
Leninogorsk
Aktogai
Gosgranitsa
Stalinabad
4"
8"
16"
24"
40"
U S S R
MOSCOW
50
0
100
200
MILES
L E G E N D
Double Track
Single Track
Narrow Gauge
Double Track
Under Constr.
Narrow Gauge
Under Constr.
Single Track
Under Constr.
Isohyets
Boundary of the
U S S R
Boundary of the
Republics
Capitals of the
Republics
Cities
1958
50°
55°
60°
65°
70°
75°
80°
85°
45°
40°
35°

Fig. 3

season of 150 to 190 days, which is suitable for the production of cotton.[1] The upper limit of this growing season is reached in the southern portions of the Turkmen Republic and the southwestern valleys of Tadzhikstan, where long-staple, Egyptian-type cotton predominates. In both republics, which are the leading producers of long-staple cotton in the Soviet Union, approximately one-third the total cotton acreage is planted in Egyptian-type cotton.[2]

Another subdivision of the loessial piedmont plains, which is considerably less important than the irrigated areas in this zone, is the belt of dry-farming land, found on the higher slopes of the piedmont plains in the eastern half of Central Asia as well as in southern Kazakhstan (see Figs. 1 and 5). Just as the irrigated lands on the gently rising portions of the piedmont plains are focused primarily on the production of cotton, the dry-farming lands of Central Asia are even more specialized on the production of grain and, in particular, wheat. For example, approximately 90 per cent of the sown acreage in the dry-farming belt of the Uzbek Republic is planted in grain crops.[3]

Effects on transport problems and costs.--Central Asia and its approaches through Kazkhstan can be subdivided into three major natural regions, which are zoned vertically as well as horizontally. The largest amount of territory is occupied by either barren desert or difficult, mountainous terrain. Although several important nodes of settlement have developed around the deltas of desert rivers, the major center of settlement and economic activity is found in the narrow, piedmont plains adjacent to the numerous mountain ranges in Central Asia and southern Kazakhstan.

The natural setting of economic activity in this region, as outlined above, has important implications for rail transporta-

---

[1] Sredneaziatskiy Gosudarstvennyy Universitet imeni V. I. Lenin, Geograficheskiy Fakul'tet, Uzbekskaya SSR (Moscow: Geografgiz, 1956), p. 223. Cited hereafter as Uzbekskaya SSR.

[2] I. K. Narzikulov and S. N. Ryazantsev (eds.), Tadzhikskaya SSR: Ekonomiko-Geograficheskaya Kharakeristika, Akademiya Nauk Tadzhikskoi SSR and the Institut Geografii Akademii Nauk SSR (Moscow: Geografgiz, 1956), p. 94.

Z. G. Freikin, Turkmenskaya SSR: Ekonomiko-Geograficheskaya Kharakteristika (2d ed. rev.; Moscow: Geografgiz, 1957), p. 216.

[3] G. N. Cherdantsev, N. P. Nitin, and B. A. Tutykhin (eds.), Ekonomicheskaya Geografiya SSSR: Rossiiskaya Sovetskaya Federativnaya Sotsialisticheskaya Respublika (Moscow: Uchpedgiz, 1956), p. 289.

Fig. 4.--The Snow-Capped Peaks of the Kara-Tau Southwest of Dzhambul as Viewed from the Turk-Sib.

Fig. 5.--A Sprawling Belt of Dry Farming in Southern Kazakhstan Near Dzhambul.

tion. The concentration of economic activity in the elongated and fragmented core region of Central Asia, the loessial piedmont plains, and the sparse habitation of the surrounding desert and mountainous regions indicates that there is no need at present for a dense rail pattern in Central Asia and its approaches, such as that found in the Ukraine. The linear orientation of the zone of intensive settlement also means that many of the major areas of economic activity in Central Asia, such as the Tashkent and Zeravshan oases, can be served by one rail line, the Trans-Caspian, as well as by relatively short spurs leading off this route to other important agricultural and industrial regions in the piedmont zone.

However, it should be noted that many of the major cotton-growing regions in the piedmont plains, such as in southwestern Tadzhikstan, are located at considerable distances from the Trans-Caspian main-line. This problem is intensified by the extreme route circuity involved in by-passing mountainous terrain in order to provide rail access to cotton-growing kolkhozes previously isolated from the mainstream of Central Asian intra-regional commerce. The costs of constructing more direct rail lines through most of the winding mountain passes of the Pamir and Tyan'-Shan' ranges are virtually prohibitive. Although the high cost of rail construction in areas with steep gradients and sharp curves can be lessened by the laying of narrow-gauge rail lines, construction costs in difficult terrain still remain extremely high. For example, in the Second Five-Year Plan (1933-1937), the estimated cost of the 131 kilometer narrow-gauge line from Stalinabad to Kurgan-Tyube, which would have a 2.7 per cent ruling grade, was 610,000 rubles per kilometer, while the cost of laying a broad-gauge line from Karaganda to Balkhash during the same period was estimated at 167,000 rubles per kilometer, or only about one-fourth as much.[1]

The transport costs imposed by mountainous terrain are considerably less than those associated with the existence of an enormous zone of lowland desert in Central Asia and Kazakhstan. One of the major problems, of course, is that of water supply. This is a problem, however, which has been mitigated, to a certain extent, by the widespread use of Diesel traction in this region.

---

[1] U.S.S.R., Gosplan pri Sovete Narodnykh Komissarov SSSR, _Osnovnyye Ob'yekty Kapital'nogo Stroitel'stva vo Vtorom Pyatiletii_ (Moscow: Partizdat, 1934), pp. 132-33.

Another feature increasing the cost of rail construction and operations in the lowland desert zone is the persistent shifting of the unstabilized sand dunes (barkhans) in the southern portions of the Kara-Kum. Repeated attempts to stabilize these sands with the planting of saxaul vegetation and other measures have met with only a limited amount of success.

The major transport costs associated with the natural setting of Central Asia and Kazakhstan, however, are those incurred in overcoming the time-cost barrier to overland movement imposed by the insulation of the primary traffic-generating centers of Central Asia, concentrated on the loessial piedmont plains, from their interregional markets and sources of supply by a vast belt of relatively unproductive, arid land. Even within Central Asia, the major agricultural and industrial areas located, for the most part, in the eastern half of this region must travel over 1,500 kilometers through the Kyzyl-Kum and Kara-Kum just to reach the Caspian Sea port of Krasnovodsk. Thus, not only has the lowland desert zone of Central Asia and Kazkhstan contributed to an extremely high regional average distance of haul, but has also helped reinforce the dominance of the interregional rail routes, as opposed to Caspian Sea routes, in the exchange of commodities between Central Asia and the rest of the country.

Population

Most of the peoples of Soviet Central Asia, including the Uzbeks, Turkmen, and Kirghiz, are of Turkic-Mongol origin and are also classified as Sunni Moslems. These groups speak Turkic languages. The Tadzhiks, however, differ from the other Sunni Moslem groups of Central Asia in that they are of Iranian origin and speak a language similar to modern Persian. According to the 1926 census, the indigenous population in each of the Central Asian republics constituted at least two-thirds of the total population, while the proportion of Russians in the population of these republics ranged from less than 1 per cent in Tadzhikstan (then the Tadzhik A.S.S.R.) to 12 per cent in Kirghiziya (then the Kirghiz A.S.S.R.).[1] In the Uzbek and Turkmen republics, Russians accounted for 6 per cent and 8 per cent respectively of the total population.[2]

---

[1]Frank Lorimer, The Population of the Soviet Union: History and Prospects (Geneva: League of Nations, 1946), p. 64.

[2]Ibid.

For the most part, Russian settlement in Central Asia has been concentrated in newly laid-out sections of ancient trade centers, such as Tashkent and Samarkand. In Samarkand, Slavs account for 36.9 per cent of the population, which is just slightly less than the 39.5 per cent of the total accounted for by Uzbeks and Tadzhiks (Fig. 6).[1] Even more striking is the dominance of Russian population in cities which sprang up after the coming of the railroad. Ashkhabad, the capital of the Turkmen Republic, was founded by the Russians as a military outpost in 1881--the year construction began on the Trans-Caspian rail line.[2] In 1901, Russians comprised 43.1 per cent of the population of this city,[3] while by 1939, the relative share of Russians in the Ashkhabad population had reached 61.9 per cent.[4] The capital of the Tadzhik Republic, Stalinabad, and the Kirghiz capital of Frunze are other Russian cities which were developed in conjunction with the establishment of rail access (in 1931 and 1924 respectively). According to the 1939 census, Russians comprised 57 per cent of the population of Stalinabad, while Tadzhiks accounted for only 12 per cent.[5]

The inflow of Russians and other groups into Central Asia and the natural increases of the indigenous ethnic groups led to the growth of the Central Asian population from 8.1 million persons in 1926 to 12.4 million in 1956. The changes in the population totals of the Central Asian union republics are shown in Table 1, which reveals the role of the Uzbek Republic as the primary zone of settlement in Central Asia. In 1956, for example, 59 per cent of the inhabitants of Central Asia resided in this republic. The population change with the most important transport implications, however, has been the growth of the relative share of urban population from 19 per cent of the Central Asian total in 1926 to 37 per cent in 1956. During the 1926-1956 period, the rural population of the Central Asian republics increased by 1.2 million people, or by 18 per cent, while the urban centers of this region received an additional 3.1 million inhabitants, which represented a 250 per cent increase.

Changes in the population of the five largest cities of Central Asia are shown in Table 2. Perhaps the most striking

---

[1] I. I. Umnyakov, Yu. N. Aleskerov, and K. M. Mikhailov, _Samarkand: Kratkiy Spravochnik-Putevoditel'_ (Tashkent: Gosizdat Uzbekskoi SSR, 1956), p. 66.

[2] Freikin, p. 317. [3] _Ibid._, p. 319. [4] _Ibid._, p. 333.

[5] Narzikulov and Ryazantsev, p. 173.

TABLE 1

POPULATION OF CENTRAL ASIA[a]
(Millions and Per Cent Urban)

Political Unit	1926		1956	
	Total (Million)	Per Cent Urban	Total (Million)	Per Cent Urban
Central Asia	8.1	19	12.4	37
Uzbek S.S.R.[b]	5.3	24	7.3	32
Turkmen S.S.R.	1.0	14	1.4	45
Tadzhik S.S.R.[c]	0.8	5	1.8	31
Kirghiz S.S.R.[d]	1.0	12	1.9	31

[a]Lorimer, p. 70; Narodnoye Khozyaistvo SSSR v 1956 Godu, p. 74.

[b]Excluding the Tadzhik A.S.S.R. in 1926.

[c]Tadzhik A.S.S.R. in 1926. [d]Kirghiz A.S.S.R. in 1926.

feature of Central Asian urbanization brought out by Table 2 is the rapid growth of Frunze and Stalinabad, which as mentioned earlier, were transformed into relatively large cities after they received rail access in 1924 and 1931 respectively. But the most important urban characteristic of Soviet Central Asia revealed by the table is the unchallenged role of Tashkent as the primate city of this region (Fig. 7).

TABLE 2

POPULATION OF THE LEADING CITIES OF CENTRAL ASIA[a]
(Thousands of Inhabitants)

City	1926	1956
Tashkent	324	778
Stalinabad[b]	6	191
Frunze	37	190
Samarkand	105	170
Ashkhabad	52	142

[a]S. Balzak, V. Vasyutin, and Ya Feigin (eds.), Economic Geography of the USSR, American edition edited by Chauncy D. Harris (New York: The Macmillan Company, 1949), pp. 527-31; Narodnoye Khozyaistvo SSSR v 1956 Godu, pp. 30-31.

[b]In 1926 Stalinabad was known as Dyushambe.

Fig. 6.--A View of the Old Section of Samarkand

Fig. 7.--A "Showpiece" Boulevard in the Old Section of Tashkent

In summary, the most important transport effect of the population changes of Central Asia during the Soviet era has been the growth of cities, made possible, to a considerable degree, by the settlement of Russians in the urban areas of this region. The growing urbanization of Central Asia has not only resulted in an expanded volume of intra-regional trade based on the interchange of goods between urban and rural areas, but has also been associated with a growing volume of interregional rail imports and exports. The railroad, in turn, has played a key role in the growth of urbanization in Central Asia by lowering the time and cost of passenger and commodity movement. One of the major results of rail construction in Central Asia has been a sharp rise in the population of many Central Asian urban centers. Another major contribution of the railroads to urban growth has been the funneling of all the rail-borne trade of Central Asia (with the exception of northern Kirghiziya) through the metropolis of Tashkent. The location of Tashkent at the convergence of the Central Asian interregional rail routes has contributed greatly to the primacy of this city in the urban life of Central Asia.

The Regional Economy

Agriculture.--Although Central Asia produces a variety of products, such as silk, wool, and diversified fruits, which are destined for markets in other regions of the Soviet Union, the primary contribution of this region to the national economy is the supply of cotton fiber to textile mills concentrated in and around the city of Moscow. Central Asia utilizes a climatic endowment characterized by a long, hot, and almost cloudless growing season and the water provided by the rivers originating in the mountainous fringes of this region primarily to produce cotton. Other crops such as alfalfa, rice, and sugar beets, however, are also grown with the aid of irrigation.

Since it is virtually impossible to grow commercial types of cotton in Central Asia without irrigation, cotton production has been concentrated, to a considerable degree, in the areas of loessial piedmont plain drained by the major Central Asian rivers and their tributaries (see Fig. 1). The most important of these areas are those obtaining irrigation water from the upper Syr-Darya and its tributaries. Among the oases relying on water from the Syr-Darya are the fertile enclave of irrigated agriculture in the Fergana Basin, which alone produces 30 per cent of all the raw

Fig. 8.--The Zeravshan River Just Outside of Samarkand

cotton produced in the Soviet Union,[1] the Tashkent oasis, and the Golodnaya (Hungry) Steppe. The Zeravshan is another of the rivers flowing through the loessial piedmont plains which is used to support intensive cotton farming, particularly around the ancient trade centers of Samarkand and Bukhara (Fig. 8). The Amu-Darya and its tributaries provide water to irrigated areas in southern Uzbekistan and southwestern Tadzhikstan, and also supply the water used in the largest area of irrigated farming in the lowland deserts of Central Asia--the Khorezm Oasis. Among the other areas in the lowland desert utilized for the production are the oases located on the upper reaches of the Murgab and Tedzhen rivers.

During the Soviet era, the amount of irrigated cotton land in the Central Asian republics and the southern portions of Kazakhstan has more than tripled, as Table 3 reveals:

TABLE 3

THE IRRIGATED COTTON AREA OF CENTRAL ASIA AND KAZAKHSTAN, 1913-1956[a]
(Thousands of Hectares)

Region	1913	1940	1950	1955	1956
Soviet Union					
Total cotton area . .	688.0	2,076.2	2,316.5	2,198.5	2,065.4
Irrigated area alone	688.0	1,550.0	1,710.0	2,074.4	2,060.2
Central Asia and Kazakhstan	562.0	1,345.9	1,539.4	1,855.6	1,842.0
Uzbek SSR[b]	424.6	923.5	1,098.5	1,317.9	1,304.3
Turkmen SSR	69.4	150.4	153.0	181.6	191.2
Kirghiz SSR	21.6	64.1	65.0	79.9	72.5
Tadzhik SSR	26.7	106.1	126.0	161.8	164.9
Kazakh SSR[b]	19.7	101.8	96.9	114.4	109.9

[a]Narodnoye Khozyaistvo SSSR v 1956 Godu, p. 121.

[b]In 1956, a portion of the major cotton producing region of Kazakhstan, the South-Kazakhstan Oblast, was incorporated into the Uzbek Republic.

Much of the vast increase in the extent of irrigated cotton cultivation in Central Asia can be attributed to the modernization and expansion of the irrigation network as well as other water reform measures (see Figs. 9 and 10). One of the most dramatic of these changes was the construction of the Great Fergana Canal in

[1]Uzbekskaya SSR, p. 299.

Fig. 9.--The Cultivation of a Cotton Field in the 2,000 Hec-
e Engel's Kolkhoz West of Samarkand.

Fig. 10.--Officials of the Engel's Kolkhoz Proudly Inspect a
Modern Irrigation Canal.

the southern portions of the Fergana Basin during the summer of 1939, when 180,000 collective farmers in the Uzbek and the Tadzhik republics joined forces with other workers to complete the most ambitious of the "peoples projects" undertaken in Central Asia.[1] At present, the opening up of additional irrigated lands for the production of cotton is receiving particular emphasis in two areas the Golodnaya Steppe, southwest of Tashkent, and the southern oase of the Turkmen Republic on the route of the Kara-Kum Canal, which is scheduled to begin diverting water from the Amu-Darya to the Murgab Oasis by the year 1958.[2]

Accompanying the expansion of the area devoted to cotton in Central Asia has been an even greater percentage increase in the production of raw cotton because of the sharply rising productivit per unit of land. This has been made possible by the more efficient utilization of water resources, the enrichment of soil by th intensive application of mineral fertilizers and the expansion of the cotton-alfalfa rotation system, the introduction of improved strains of seed, and many other measures. In the Uzbek Republic, for example, the average yield of raw cotton increased from 9.4 centners per hectare in 1928[3] to 22 centners per hectare in 1956.[4]

The best available set of comparable data covering the changes in Central Asian cotton production during the Soviet era are those dealing with the production of ginned cotton as shown in Table 4. From these data it can be seen that the production of ginned cotton in Central Asia and the neighboring portions of Kazakhstan increased 6.7 times from 1913 to 1955. The relative shar of this region in the total volume of ginned cotton production in the Soviet Union in the latter year was 89.5 per cent, or one-half per cent greater than in 1913. However, the role of Central Asia in supplying the nation with ginned cotton declined in relative importance during the pre-war era when the Soviet Union launched a vigorous program to increase cotton fiber production by opening up vast areas of low-yield, unirrigated cotton land in the Ukraine, the Trans-Volga region, and the Northern Caucasus. In 1937, these

---

[1] _Ibid._, p. 220.

[2] Freikin, p. 414.

[3] A. E. Gaister (ed.), _Srednyaya Aziya_, Vol. VII: _Trudy Pervoi Vsesoyuznoi Konferentsii po Razmeshcheniyu Proizvoditel'nykh Sil Soyuza SSR_ (Moscow: Izdatel'stvo Obshchestva Izucheniya Sovetskoi Azii, 1933), p. 9.

[4] _Yezhegodnik Bol'shoi Sovetskoi Entsiklopedii: 1957_, ed. B. A. Vvedenskiy (Moscow: Gosnaukizdat, 1957), p. 202.

TABLE 4

THE PRODUCTION OF GINNED COTTON[a]
(Thousands of Tons and Per Cent of Total)

Region	1913 Volume	1913 Per Cent	1932 Volume	1932 Per Cent	1940 Volume	1940 Per Cent	1950[b] Volume	1950[b] Per Cent	1955 Volume	1955 Per Cent
Soviet Union	223	100.0	395	100.0	849	100.0	953	100.0	1,487	100.0
Central Asia and Kazakhstan[c]	198	89.0	322	81.5	734	85.7	849	89.0	1,332	89.5

[a]U.S.S.R. Tsentral'noye Statisticheskoye Upravleniye pri Sovete Ministrov SSSR, Promyshlennost' SSSR: Statisticheskiy Sbornik (Moscow: Gosstatizdat, 1957), p. 146. Cited hereafter as Promyshlennost' SSSR.

[b]The slow rate of growth from 1940 to 1950, to a large extent, reflects the sharp decline of cotton production during World War II.

[c]All the raw cotton produced in Central Asia and Kazakhstan is ginned within this region.

regions accounted for 24.3 per cent of total Soviet cotton acreage, but supplied only 9.2 per cent of total raw cotton production.[1] Since the early 1950's, Soviet policy has de-emphasized the growing of cotton on the unirrigated lands west of the Urals-Caspian divide in favor of intensifying production on the irrigated lands of Central Asia, Kazakhstan, and Azerbaidzhian. The area devoted to the growing of cotton without the aid of irrigation in the European portions of the Soviet Union (including the Trans-Volga region) declined sharply from 607,500 hectares in 1950 to only 5,200 hectares in 1956, while during the same period, the irrigated cotton land in Central Asia and southern Kazakhstan increased by 302,600 hectares (see Table 3).

The continued dominance of Central Asia in the production of cotton fiber, together with the concentration of over 80 per cent of the cotton textile production of the Soviet Union in the Center (the region in which Moscow is located), is primarily responsible for an extremely high national average distance of haul for

[1]Balzak, Vasyutin, and Feigin, p. 392.

ginned cotton. In the year 1954, for example, the average distance of ginned cotton movement on the Soviet rail net reached the figure of 3,327 kilometers.[1]

Industry.--The high priority attached by Soviet planners to the transformation of Central Asia into a highly specialized zone of commercial agriculture focusing on the production of commodities destined, to a large extent, for distant markets, has had a far-reaching effect on the scale and direction of industrial activity in this region. The development of industries linked closely to the cotton-growing areas of Central Asia, in turn, has played a key role in the rapid industrial growth of this region. According to Soviet figures, from 1913 to 1937 the gross output of large-scale industry in the Uzbek Republic, the dominant industrial area of Central Asia, increased 5.4 times,[2] with most of the increase occurring after 1928, while from 1940 to 1955, the gross industrial output of this republic expanded 2.9 times.[3] Although the rate of growth in the latter period slowed down somewhat, the absolute increments of production were considerably greater than in the prewar era. The rapid industrialization of Central Asia during the Soviet era is reflected in the increase of the urban population of this region from 19 per cent of the total Central Asian population in 1926 to 37 per cent of the total in 1956.

A classification of the types of Central Asian industrial activity which is pertinent to the approach of this study is one based on the ties of local industries to the cotton-growing kolkhozes and sovkhozes of this region. Although most of the industries of Central Asia rely either directly or indirectly on local agriculture as a market or source of raw materials, needless to say, certain types of industrial activity, such as the production of equipment for the motion picture industry in Samarkand, have little to do with the function of Central Asia as a supplier of cotton fiber and other agricultural products to the nation.

1. Industries relying directly on cotton and other agricultural commodities for raw materials.--The most ubiquitous forms of industrial activity in Central Asia are the ginning of cotton and the production of a wide variety of cotton by-products, such

---

[1] E. D. Khanukov, Transport i Razmeshcheniye Proizvodstva (Moscow: Transzheldorizdat, 1956), p. 122.

[2] Balzak, Vasyutin, and Feigin, p. 206.

[3] Narodnoye Khozyaistvo SSSR v 1956 Godu, p. 55.

as cottonseed oil and cake. For example, the Uzbek Republic alone has 62 relatively large-scale cotton ginneries.[1] Approximately 4 to 5 per cent of the ginned cotton produced in the republics of Central Asia is consumed by local cotton textile mills; particularly those located in Tashkent, Fergana, and Stalinabad. The largest of the textile plants in Central Asia is the Tashkent Textile Combine, which employs 20,000 workers and carries on the spinning and weaving of cotton as an integrated industrial process (Fig. 11).[2]

Other agricultural commodities have also given rise to the development of local cleaning, packing, and processing industries. Among the products included in this category are silk, which is derived from silkworms feeding on the leaves of the mulberry trees usually found bordering irrigated cotton fields; wool, including that obtained from karakul sheep; diversified fruits, such as grapes and apricots; and the sugar beets grown in the northern portions of the Kirghiz Republic. Many of these products are not only processed locally to reduce their bulk or, in the case of many of the fruits, to decrease their perishability, but also serve as raw materials for the local manufacture of finished consumer goods. For example, in the Uzbek Republic, which is the leading producer of natural silk in the Soviet Union, silk weaving is carried on in two large plants. One of these is located in the Fergana Basin (Margelan), while the other is found in Samarkand and employs 2,200 workers to make it the largest factory in this city.[3]

2. Industries serving the cotton-growing areas.--The most striking change in the industrial development of Central Asia during the Soviet era has been the growth of industries geared closely to meeting the needs of the cotton-growing kolkhozes and sovkhozes for raw materials and machinery. One of the most important types of industrial activity falling into this category is the production of mineral fertilizers. At present, the largest nitrogen fertilizer plant in the Soviet Union is the Chirchik Electro-Chemical Combine, which is located on a branch line running northeastwards from Tashkent.[4] By 1960, however, an enormous nitrogen fertilizer works will

---

[1] Uzbekskaya SSR, p. 183.

[2] Interview with an official of the Tashkent Textile Combine, July 12, 1957.

[3] Interview with the Manager of the Samarkand silk-weaving factory, July 10, 1957.

[4] Uzbekskaya SSR, p. 177.

Fig. 11 Entrance to the Tashkent Textile Combine

be constructed at the lignite-mining center of Angren, east of Tashkent. This plant will produce twice as much fertilizer as is presently produced at the Chirchik plant.[1] Superphosphate fertilizers are supplied to the agricultural regions of Central Asia from plants in Samarkand, Kokand, which is located at the western convergence of the rail lines encircling the Fergana Basin, and in the city of Dzhambul in southern Kazakhstan.

Another example of market-oriented manufacturing activity in Central Asia which facilitates the growing of cotton is the production of agricultural machinery. The primary center for the manufacture of agricultural machinery, as well as other types of machinery, in Central Asia is Tashkent. Among other things, the machinery industries of this city produce a large volume of equipment to aid the sowing, cultivation, and harvesting of raw cotton. Additional examples of local industries with a market in the rural areas of Central Asia are provided by industries producing: building materials, insecticides for use against cotton pests; and tractor fuel, which is obtained from petroleum refineries in the Fergana Basin and Krasnovodsk. However, it should be mentioned that the rapid expansion of petroleum production in the western portions of the Turkmen Republic since World War II has led to a large volume of interregional exports, which apparently overshadows the importance of intra-regional petroleum movement.

3. Other industries.--This section will focus on two industries, coal and steel. The production of coal in Central Asia (including the small Lenger deposit in southern Kazakhstan) increased from 248,000 tons in 1913 to 6,333,000 tons in 1955, to a large extent, as a result of the opening up of new areas of coal production rather than by the intensification of mining at sites which were in use in 1913.[2] At present, the most important coal mining areas of Central Asia are located around Angren, which produces lignite and, also, at several sites in the Fergana Basin and its western approaches (see Fig. 1). One of the main problems connected with the utilization of Central Asian coals is their relatively low quality. In 1955, for example, 84.5 per cent of these coals consisted of lignites or brown coals.[3] Nonetheless, coal

---

[1] Ibid., p. 78.

[2] U.S.S.R. Ministerstvo Ugol'noi Promyshlennosti, Ugol'naya Promyshlennost' SSSR: Statisticheskiy Spravochnik (Moscow: Ugletekhizdat, 1957), p. 84. Cited hereafter as Ugol'naya Promyshlennost' SSSR.

[3] Ibid., pp. 48-49.

occupies a vital position in the Central Asian economy, as can be seen in Table 5, which shows the relative importance of coal in the energy consumption balance of the Uzbek Republic. As this table indicates, coal is by far the most important source of energy in the Uzbek Republic--the major energy consuming region of Central Asia. Of even greater significance is the fact that coal imported from the Kuznetsk and Karaganda basins over extremely long distances accounted for more than 16 per cent of the energy consumed by this republic in 1953.

TABLE 5

ENERGY BALANCE OF THE UZBEK REPUBLIC, 1953[a]
(Per cent of Total Consumption)

Source of Energy	Per Cent of Consumption
Coal	44.5
Including coal produced in:	
Central Asia	28.1
The Kuznetsk and Karaganda basins .	16.4
Waterpower	23.1
Petroleum	16.5
Guza-Paya[b]	13.0
Other	2.9

[a]A. M. Vasil'nitskiy, "Voprosy Gasifikatsii Narodnogo Khozyaistvo i Kompleksnogo Ispol'zovaniya Tverdogo Topliva v Uzbekskoi SSR i Tyagoteishchikh Raionakh," Voprosy Ekonomiki Promyshlennosti Uzbekskoi SSR, Akademiya Nauk Uzbekskoi SSR, Institut Ekonomiki (Tashkent: Izdatel'stvo Akademiya Nauk Uzbekskoi SSR, 1957), p. 38.

[b]Guza-Paya is the term for the stems of the cotton plant. The surprisingly high percentage this primitive fuel occupies in the energy balance of the Uzbek Republic reflects the widespread use of this fuel in the rural areas of the republic.

The only steel plant in Central Asia is the converter works at Begovat, which is located on the rail line linking the Fergana Basin with the main rail net. In 1955, this plant produced approximately 200,000 tons of steel.[1] Although plans to enlarge the Begovat works by the addition of blast furnaces have been discussed frequently in Soviet journals, there are no plans to implement these proposals until at least 1970.

---

[1]Narodnoye Khozyaistvo SSSR v 1956 Godu, p. 69.

Transport Implications of Economic Development

Although succeeding chapters will examine the interaction of transportation and economic development in Central Asia during the Soviet era at considerably greater length, a few initial generalizations based on the preceding discussion will at least isolate some of the threads interwoven in the subsequent portions of this study.

1. The high priority given the production of cotton, and certain other commodities, on the irrigated plains of Central Asia has not only resulted in the rapid growth of the agricultural sector of the Central Asian economy but has also had a decisive effect on the pace and direction of industrial development in this region. One of the consequences of the persistently rising regional income has been a sharp increase in the tonnage of rail freight originating on the railroads of this region from 2.7 million tons in 1913 to 26.5 million tons in 1956 and the even more rapid expansion of freight terminations from 2.2 million tons to 36.1 million tons during the same period.[1]

2. The concept of an agricultural and industrial complex in Central Asia based either directly or indirectly on the growing of cotton embodies the forces of regional specialization and self-sufficiency, which have opposite traffic effects. The degree of regional specialization is reflected in the relative volume of interregional exports, expressed either in physical or monetary units, in the total freight originations of a region, while the share of interregional imports in the total terminations of a particular region is a measure of the relative importance of the forces of self-sufficiency at a given moment. In Central Asia, as in every other region of the Soviet Union, these two forces are in operation simultaneously. The expansion of ginned cotton production in Central Asia, as well as many other products, has resulted in large-scale exports to textile mills located in other regions of the country. At the same time the export functions of the Central Asian republics were being emphasized, the development of many types of local industrial activity, such as the production of low-grade coal and the manufacture of cotton machinery, has tended to reduce the relative volume of interregional imports or, in other words, to increase the degree of regional self-sufficiency.

---

[1]U.S.S.R., Tsentral'noye Statisticheskoye Upravleniye pri Sovete Ministrov SSSR, Transport i Svyaz' SSSR: Statisticheskiy Sbornik (Moscow: Gosstatizdat, 1957), p. 67. Cited hereafter as Transport i Svyaz' SSSR.

The Evolution of the Central Asian Rail Net in the Pre-Soviet Era

Historical Background

The most striking characteristic of the historical evolution of the area now known as Soviet Central Asia is the traditional role of this region as a gateway between the peoples of the East and West. Several historic routes crossed the mountains bordering this area and then were channeled through major trading centers, such as Samarkand and Bukhara along the Zeravshan River, and Merv (Mary) on the Murgab River. One of these routes ran from Kashgar, in present-day Chinese Turkestan, to Samarkand by way of the Fergana Basin. This route then followed a path quite similar to that used by the Trans-Caspian railroad today to Merv, whence it veered to the south of the Caspian Sea and eventually reached the Black Sea in present-day Turkey.[1] Another important historic route ran from Bukhara to the north of the Caspian Sea by way of the Khorezm Oasis. Perhaps the most famous of the historic routes leading into Central Asia was the one passing through the Dzhungarian Gate (Gosgranitsa) in the area of present-day Kazakhstan, which was used, among other times, during the Mongol invasions of Russia in the thirteenth century. At present, the Dzhungarian Gate is scheduled to become the meeting point of a rail line now under construction simultaneously from the Soviet Union and China. The primary beast of burden on these routes, the camel, has still not disappeared from Central Asian commerce, although it is now used primarily for local movement in the Kara-Kum of western Turkmenistan.

The role of Central Asia as a crossroads between East and West not only led to the development of numerous local trade centers which handled silks, spices, and dyestuffs, among other products, but also made this region particularly vulnerable to invasion. Among the groups who succeeded in establishing hegemony over various portions of this region prior to the fourteenth century were: the Persians, the Greeks under Alexander the Great, the Chinese, various Turkic forces, the Arabs, and the Mongol hordes of Genghiz Khan. Central Asia reached its apex of power, relatively speaking, during the second half of the fourteenth century, when Tamerlane, the son of a Central Asian Mongol lord, created a new

---

[1] Peter I. Lyashchenko, History of the National Economy of Russia: To the 1917 Revolution, trans. L. M. Herman (New York: The Macmillan Company, 1949), inset map No. 2.

Mongol Empire with Samarkand serving as the political and economic capital (Fig. 12). By the beginning of the sixteenth century, the Mongol Empire founded by Tamerlane was replaced by two states--Khiva, centered in the Khorezm Oasis, and Bukhara. At the beginning of the nineteenth century, a third major political unit was formed when the Kokand Khanate, including the Fergana Basin and the Tashkent region, was carved out of the Bukhara Emirate.[1] This political organization persisted until Central Asia fell under Russian domination in the last half of the nineteenth century. Russian armed forces moved into Central Asia from a line of fortifications in present-day Kazakhstan and succeeded in capturing Tashkent in 1865, and Samarkand three years later. Shortly afterwards, the Bukhara Emirate and the Khiva Khanate became Russian protectorates, while in 1876, the last independent state in Central Asia, the Kokand Khanate, was directly absorbed into the Russian state.[2]

The Evolution of the Rail Net

Although the necessity of linking Central Asia with European Russia by an overland rail route had been widely discussed after the establishment of Russian hegemony in Central Asia, the first rail line in this area came about primarily as a result of a stunning military reversal inflicted upon a Russian military expedition by a group of belligerent Turkic tribesmen.

With the fall of the Kokand Khanate in 1876, the Russian conquerors began the subjugation of hostile Turkic settlements concentrated in the oases of Turkestan. One of the most troublesome of these groups was the Tekkes of the Akhal and Merv oases. The Tekkes comprised a large and well-organized tribe, who frequently raided Russian caravans bringing Chinese teas and silks to Russia. In the summer of 1879, the Governor of Transcaspia received orders to attack the Tekke stronghold of Geok Teppe in the Akhal oasis, just northwest of the present Ashkhabad. This expedition suffered a humiliating defeat and was forced to retreat.[3] Russian officials then appointed a new commander-in-chief, General

---

[1]George Vernadsky, _A History of Russia_ (3d ed. rev.; New Haven: Yale University Press, 1944), p. 164.

[2]_Ibid._

[3]George N. Curzon, _Russia in Central Asia_ (London: Longmans, Green, and Company, 1889), pp. 37-38.

Fig. 12.--The Tomb of Timur in Samarkand

Skobelev, to head an expeditionary force to crush the troublesome Tekkes. Since the previous expedition had failed primarily as a result of a critical logistic deficiency caused by the loss of 8,377 camels out of the total of 12,273 used to transport supplies,[1] it was decided to construct a rail line from the Caspian Sea to Kizyl-Arvat, a desert outpost on the edge of the Akhal oasis to insure the success of Skobelev's expedition. Thus, the Trans-Caspian line was not the product of careful, long-range planning, but rather was designed to meet an immediate military need. Skobelev himself was more skeptical about the contribution the Trans-Caspian Railroad could make to the pacification of the Akhal Tekkes. He still intended to rely primarily on camels to carry supplies for his forces in the forthcoming campaign.[2]

Nonetheless, construction began on the Trans-Caspian in 1881 from the shallow-water port of Michailovsk on the Caspian through the Kara-Kum to Kizyl-Arvat.[3] The builders of the Trans-Caspian were presented with many problems. Among the most pressing were: the shortage of water, disease, windstorms, and the shifting sands of the Kara-Kum. Of these problems the one that gave General Annenkov, the builder of the Trans-Caspian, the greatest difficulty was the periodic destruction of the roadbed by the migration of the unstable barkhans of the Kara-Kum. Several methods were employed to protect the roadbed from the devastation of wind and sand. In some regions sand fences three to four feet high were set up to halt the migration of sand, while in other areas, the roadbed was built up to the level of the barkhans. However, the most effective means of preventing the desert from encroaching upon the rail line was to stabilize the sand dunes contiguous to the route by planting these areas with tamarisk, saksaul and other types of desert vegetation. However, even today this problem has not been fully resolved.

The first locomotive steamed into Kizyl-Arvat in September 1881, nine months after the start of construction.[4] However, in January of the same year, Skobelev had finally crushed the re-

---

[1] Ibid.

[2] Ibid., p. 40.

[3] Russia. Pereselencheskago Upravleniye Glavnago Upravleniya Zemleustroistva i Zemledeliya, Aziatskaya Rossiya, II (Saint Petersburg: Izdaniye Pereselencheskago Upravleniya Glavnago Upravleniya Zemleustroistva i Zemledeliya, 1914), p. 547. Cited hereafter as Aziatskaya Rossiya.

[4] Ibid.

sistance of the Akhal Tekkes by capturing their stronghold of Geok Teppe. Thus, Skobelev's pessimism was justified. The Trans-Caspian rail line contributed little if anything to the pacification of the Akhal oasis. By the time Kizyl Arvat had been reached by rail, the immediate motivation of construction had lost its former significance. Although the terminus of the line Kizyl-Arvat was linked to Persia by two caravan routes, there was little prospect of transforming the line as it then existed into an important freight route since it did not extend into the most productive agricultural regions of Central Asia. But changing political and military events in Central Asia rejuvenated the Trans-Caspian project.

The Russians, continuing to consolidate political power, annexed the oases of Merv and Kushka in 1884 and 1885, respectively. This action increased British fears of Russian expansion into Asia, and particularly into Afghanistan and British India. British protests, in turn, only intensified Russian efforts to colonize Central Asia. To achieve this goal, the Russians envisaged a new role for the Trans-Caspian line. In the words of Lord Curzon,"No longer the prudent auxiliary to a single campaign, it became the mark of a definite policy, imperial in its quality and dimensions. Till then the Russians had regarded the line as an isolated and limited undertaking, rather than part of a great design. It now emerged as a warning to England and a warning to Asia."[1]

In July of 1885, the extension of the Trans-Caspian from Kizyl-Arvat to Merv began. By December of that year the line was completed to Ashkhabad, 136 miles from Kizyl-Arvat, and approximately one year from the start of construction at Kizyl-Arvat, the Merv oasis was reached.[2] But Merv was only a temporary resting-place and after a pause of only six weeks the Trans-Caspian was pushed on through the most difficult stretch of shifting Kara-Kum sands to Chardzhou, on the banks of the Amu-Darya. Annenkov decided to span the Amu-Darya with a wooden bridge over 2,000 yards long which was designed for temporary use but which actually was in service fourteen years. In May 1888, five months after the Amu-Darya bridge was completed, the rail line had been laid to Samarkand.[3] The Russians were not content to stop at Samarkand,

---

[1]Curzon, p. 44.

[2]Aziatskaya Rossiya, II, 547. [3]Ibid., p. 548.

particularly since the most productive agricultural regions of Central Asia, the densely settled Fergana Basin and the Tashkent Oasis, were still not served by rail. In 1895, construction began on the line running from Samarkand to Tashkent, with a branch extending to Andizhan in the Fergana Basin. After the completion of this line in 1898, through rail movement was possible from the shores of the Caspian Sea to Tashkent--a distance of 1,862 kilometers.[1]

Shortly before the completion of the main line of the Trans-Caspian, a branch paralleling the Murgab and Kushka rivers from Merv to Kushka on the Afghanistan border was completed. This line was designed primarily to strengthen Russian military positions along the Russian-Afghanistan border. During World War I, another important branch line from the Trans-Caspian to the vicinity of the Afghanistan border was completed from Kagan on the mainline to Samsonovo on the upper Amu-Darya.

Thus, the first rail line in the Asiatic portions of the Russian empire was originally constructed to facilitate a short-lived military campaign. Although Czarist colonial expansion revived plans for the transformation of the Trans-Caspian into a major magistral, economic as well as strategic considerations seem to have played an important role in the decision to extend the rail line to the east of the Amu-Darya.

The Trans-Caspian provided a link between the densely settled oases of Central Asia. Since ancient times these oases served as centers of irrigated agriculture, producing cotton, rice, wheat, and many additional commodities. As mentioned earlier, many of the towns which developed on these oases, such as Samarkand and Bukhara, derived much of their importance from their position astride historic trade routes linking the East and the West.

However, there were serious doubts about the wisdom of giving the Trans-Caspian line priority over other possible routes between Central Asia and European Russia. In the first place, the Trans-Caspian was not connected directly to the rail net of European Russia. Cotton, moving from the Fergana Basin to the textile mills of Moscow, for example, was shipped in two directions--by a rail-sea-river route via the Caspian Sea and the Volga or by a rail-sea-rail route with transshipments at Krasnovodsk and Petrovsk Port (now Makhach-Kala) in the northern Caucasus. Both of these

---

[1] Ibid.

routes were slow and costly. Another problem was that the Volga was closed to navigation approximately five-and-one-half months a year. After the construction of a direct rail route between Central Asia and European Russia, the relative importance of the Krasnovodsk-Moscow route declined sharply.

Apart from the failure to envisage the limited transit capabilities of the Trans-Caspian, other aspects of the short-range nature of the planning of this line resulted in added costs. In the first phase of construction, the shallow water port of Mikhailovsk on an inlet of the Caspian served as the origin of the Trans-Caspian route. By the time the line had been extended to the Amu-Darya in 1886, the starting point had been shifted to the island port of Uzun-Ada, fifteen miles northwest of Mikhailovsk.[1] However, Uzun-Ada served as the port of the Trans-Caspian only about three years longer than its predecessor. The penetration of the rail line across the Amu-Darya into the productive oases of eastern Turkestan and the concomitant increase in the demand for transportation rendered the shallow-water facilities of Uzun-Ada obsolete. In 1894, Krasnovodsk was selected as the basic port of the Trans-Caspian route, primarily because it possessed a relatively deep harbor.[2]

The construction of the Trans-Caspian did not solve the transport problems of Central Asia. This line had been operating only about a year when construction started on a direct rail route between Central Asia and European Russia. The importance of establishing a direct rail link between the compact centers of agricultural production in Central Asia and the industries of European Russia had long been recognized by Russian planners. This project was brought to the attention of the energetic French engineer, Ferdinand de Lesseps, in 1873. De Lesseps immediately drafted a plan in which he envisaged the route from Tashkent to Orenburg (now Chkalov) as part of a super-magistral extending from Calais to Calcutta.[3] Two other routes in Russia were proposed in this plan as possible alternatives to the Orenburg route. One of these routes ran to the west of the Aral Sea, then paralleled the Amu-Darya and Zeravshan to Bukhara, and finally terminated in Tashkent. A third proposed route linked Tashkent with the main rail net by

---

[1] Ibid., p. 547. [2] Ibid., p. 548.

[3] A. Stuart, Les Traces du Chemins de Fer Central-Asiatique Projetes par Mm. F. de Lesseps et Cotard (Paris: Aux Bureaux de L'Exploreteur, 1875), inset map.

way of Akmolinsk and Yekaterinaberg (now Sverdlovsk).[1] However, de Lesseps' project did not succeed in generating much enthusiasm among the western powers and soon passed into obscurity.

Proposals to build a direct rail line to Central Asia became prominent once more around the turn of the nineteenth century. One of these alternatives called for the construction of a line from the town of Chardzhou on the Amu-Darya to the railhead of Alexandrov-Gai, a plan which incidentally was revived during the first post-World War II Five Year Plan. The second proposal, which was adopted, embodied a plan to build a rail line from Tashkent to Orenburg, paralleling both the Syr-Darya and an important post road.[2] Construction on this route began from both terminii in the year 1901. The physical obstacles to rail construction were relatively insignificant since most of the track was laid on level desert-steppe land. The 1,736 kilometers between Tashkent and Orenburg were joined by rail in 1906 and it thus became possible to establish all-rail freight communication between Central Asia and European Russia.[3]

This railway, which hereafter will be referred to as the Kazalinsk route, was a more efficient route for the shipment of many of the commodities interchanged between Central Asia and the industrial areas of the country in terms of speed, cost, and dependability. In addition, the real costs of construction of this line were much lower than those incurred in laying the rails of the Trans-Caspian route since the physical obstacles to the construction of a rail line across the flat takyrs of the floodplain of the Syr-Darya were considerably less imposing than those presented by the shifting sands of the Kara-Kum. In 1914, the Kazalinsk route shipped 76 per cent of the grain and 69 per cent of the lumber imported by Central Asia, as well as 61 per cent of the cotton-fiber exports of this region.[4] The Caspian Sea route, however, handled 90 per cent of the petroleum imported by Central Asia in the same year.[5]

Apart from the diversion of freight from the Caspian Sea route, the Kazalinsk route also reinforced the position of Tashkent as the gateway for the overland commerce of Central Asia. Even

---

[1]Ibid. [2]Aziatskaya Rossiya, II, 549. [3]Ibid.

[4]N. B. Arkhipov, Sredne-Aziatskiye Respubliki (3d ed.; Moscow: Gosizdat, 1930), p. 132.

[5]Ibid.

today, all the interregional rail freight of this region, with the exception of northern Kirghiziya, must be channeled through the Tashkent junction.

The emergence of a new and efficient form of transportation in Central Asia proved to be a powerful weapon of economic and social change. With the help of the railroad the diverse regions of Central Asia--including the old, compact centers of sedentary agriculture in the irrigated oases, the sprawling areas of nomadic herding in the lowland deserts and sloping mountain pastures, and the elongated belt of dry farming on the rolling foothills--were incorporated more fully into the economic life of Russia. Some of the changes associated with the coming of the railroad to the Central Asian domains of Russia were: (1) the intensified commercialization of agriculture; (2) the development of an industrial base in this region oriented around the processing of cotton; and (3) the expansion of urbanization. These changes were made possible, in large part, by the influx of Russian settlers to the ancient cities of this region.

The linking of Central Asia to the textile mills concentrated in the Moscow region and in Leningrad by an efficient form of overland communication had a far-reaching impact on the growing of cotton. For one thing, the cultivated area devoted to cotton in Central Asia increased from approximately 45.1 thousand hectares in 1885 to 590.7 thousand hectares in 1915.[1] The growth of irrigated cotton acreage was accompanied by an even more rapid percentage increase in the volume of cotton lint exported to European Russia. In 1888, Central Asia shipped only 15.7 thousand tons of cotton lint to European Russia, while by 1912 this figure had risen to 247.3 thousand tons, which represented more than a fifteenfold increase in 24 years.[2]

Not the least of the changes occurring after the laying of steel rails in Central Asia and the sharply increased demand in European Russia for high quality domestic cotton was the replacement of the coarse, short-fiber, indigenous types of cotton by American upland varieties. The initial appearance of American varieties of cotton in Central Asia took place in the early 1880's, when an experimental plantation was set up just outside Tashkent to test the adaptability of American types to Central Asian conditions. This experiment proved so successful that by the year

---

[1]Lyashchenko, p. 611. [2]Aziatskaya Rossiya, p. 278.

1900 the indigenous types of cotton had all but disappeared from the irrigated fields of Central Asia.[1]

The growth of factory-type industry in this region also increased sharply after the arrival of rail transportation. In 1887, only 1,571 persons were employed in factory-type industries,[2] while by 1914 this figure had risen to 20,925.[3] The ginning of cotton and the production of cottonseed oil and cake in the latter year accounted for 81 per cent of the total value of local industrial production.[4] Although Central Asia did not possess a large or diversified industrial base on the eve of the October Revolution, the development of numerous, small-scale, raw material-oriented industries processing cotton represented a considerable advance over earlier years, such as 1884, when the initial harvests of American varieties of cotton in this region were sent to the United States to be ginned and then returned to Russian textile mills.[5]

One of the most striking features of the settlement of Russians in Central Asia after the opening of rail communication to this region, which set Central Asia apart from the other frontier areas in Russia located to the east of the Urals-Caspian divide, was the relatively modest share of Russians in the total regional population. Another distinguishing characteristic was the settlement of nearly all the Russians coming to Central Asia in cities, rather than in the irrigated rural areas. The relatively few Russians settling in the rural areas engaged in the growing of grain rather than in unfamiliar cotton farming.

Although the total Slavic population of Central Asia in 1911 comprised only 6.3 per cent of the total, this group accounted for a considerably larger share of the urban population.[6] For example, Russians, Ukrainians, and Belorussians comprised 20 per cent of the population of Tashkent.[7] The influx of Russians and other Slavic peoples into the newly laid-out portions of the ancient

---

[1] _Ibid._, p. 276.

[2] R. S. Livshits, _Razmeshcheniye Promyshlennosti v Dorevolyutsionnoi Rossii_, Akademiya Nauk SSSR, Institut Ekonomiki (Moscow: Izdatel'stvo Akademii Nauk SSSR, 1955), p. 150.

[3] _Ibid._, p. 227.

[4] _Ibid._

[5] Lyashchenko, p. 610.

[6] _Aziatskaya Rossiya_, I, 82.

[7] _Ibid._, p. 331.

trade centers of Central Asia, as mentioned earlier, led to a sharp dichotomy between the old native sections and the new European sections of these cities. This contrast still persists, although in less striking form. The urban-oriented Russian settlement of Central Asia not only rejuvenated the old cities of this region, but also contributed greatly to a strengthening of the trade ties between Central Asia and distant markets and sources of supply in European Russia.

CHAPTER III

THE DEVELOPMENT OF THE RAIL PATTERN OF CENTRAL ASIA DURING THE SOVIET ERA

The discussion of the evolution of the rail pattern of Central Asia during the Soviet era will center around an examination of the construction of rail lines in relation to changing patterns of production, commodity movement, and the interaction of competitive forms of transportation.

This chapter is divided into the following major divisions: (1) The development of the rail pattern within the Central Asian republics, or the internal pattern. (2) The development of the rail pattern on the approaches to Central Asia through Kazkhstan, or the interregional pattern.

The Development of the Rail Pattern Within the Central Asian Republics

Tadzhikstan and Southern Uzbekistan

Prior to the October Revolution, the area of present-day Tadzhikstan was served by only one rail route; the Ursat'yevskaya-Andizhan line, which linked the Fergana Basin with the main-line of the Trans-Caspian route. Since this line traversed only the northern extremities of the present-day republic, most of Tadzhikstan did not have rail access until 1931, when the construction of a circuitous line from Samsonovo to Stalinabad was completed (see back foldout maps--Figs. 37 and 38). The line from Samsonovo, hugging the right bank of the Amu-Darya, veers sharply to the north after reaching the Uzbek town of Termez and passes through the fertile valley of the Surkhan-Darya en route to the Tadzhik border. This route thus avoids the difficult terrain of the Gissar ranges, which impedes direct access to southwestern Tadzhikstan from the north and northwest. This rail line continues on to Stalinabad through the productive Gissar Valley, the leading area of cotton production in the Tadzhik Republic, and terminates at the rail-highway junction of Ordzhonikidzeabad (Yangi-Bazar), 23 kilometers east of Stalinabad.

The bringing of a rail line to Stalinabad has transformed this center into a major entrepot for the cotton, fruit, and silk of the rich irrigated valleys of southwestern Tadzhikstan. An inherent characteristic of this rail route, however, which greatly impedes its utility is extreme circuity. The straight line distance from Stalinabad to Samarkand is approximately 220 kilometers. By rail, this distance is 963 kilometers, or over four times as long. This is not a problem which is likely to be remedied in the near future since the costs of building a rail line, even a narrow-gauge route, across the Gissar and Zeravshan ranges would be prohibitive.

Another characteristic of this route is the relatively light volume of traffic it handles. In 1932, the density of freight flow on the approaches to Stalinabad was only 189,000 ton-kilometers per kilometer of route, or 9 per cent of the national average density.[1] In 1940, the entire Tadzhik Republic originated only 1.8 million tons of freight, while terminating 0.9 million tons. Even in 1956 this republic originated only 2.7 million tons, while terminating 4.0 million tons.[2] It should be remembered that the largest portion of this freight was handled by the rail line to the Fergana Basin which crosses a northern projection of Tadzhikstan isolated from the rest of the republic by mountains. In 1956, 44 per cent of the total freight loadings of the Tadzhik Republic was accounted for by lignite from the Shurab deposits in northern Tadzhikstan, leaving only 1.5 million tons of diversified freight originations.[3] However, the Stalinabad route handles a relatively large-scale passenger movement, although the volume of through passenger trains handled on this line in 1957 was the same as in 1934. In both years, three trains daily in each direction traversed the 715 kilometers separating Stalinabad from Kagan on the Trans-Caspian line.[4]

---

[1]U.S.S.R., Narodnyy Komissariat Putey Soobshcheniya, Otdel Ucheta, Materialy po Statistike Putey Soobshcheniya, CXXXIX (Moscow: Transzheldorizdat, 1935), 92. Cited hereafter as Materialy po Statistike Putey Soobshcheniya.

[2]Transport i Svyaz' SSSR, p. 67. [3]Ibid., p. 70.

[4]U.S.S.R., Narodnyy Komissariat Putey Soobshcheniya, Ofitsial'nyy Ukazetel' Zheleznodorozhnykh, Vodnykh i Drugikh Passazhirshikh Soobshcheniy: Zimneye Dvizheniye--1934-35 Godu (Moscow: Transzheldorizdat, 1934), p. 263; U.S.S.R., Ministerstvo Putey Soobshcheniya SSSR, Glavnoye Passazhirskoye Upravleniye, Ofitsial'nyy Ukazatel' Passazhirshikh Soobshcheniy: Leto 1957 Goda (Moscow: Transzheldorizdat, 1957), p. 205. Cited hereafter as Ofitsial'nyy Ukazatel' Passazhirskih Soobshcheniy: Leto 1957 Goda.

Despite the many shortcomings of the Stalinabad route which could be cited, such as its circuity and relatively light volume of traffic, this line has played a key role in the development of Tadzhikstan, and, in particular, has contributed to the specialization of the Tadzhik economy. In 1955, by comparison with 1913, the sown area under cotton in the republic increased more than five times, while the gross harvest of cotton was thirteen times greater.[1] Also associated with the coming of the railroad was the rapid growth of Stalinabad (formerly Dyushambe). In 1926, the population of Stalinabad (then Dyushambe) was only 5,607, while just thirteen years later this figure reached 82,540--almost a fourteenfold increase. At the beginning of 1956, Stalinabad had 191,000 inhabitants.[2]

However, in order to utilize effectively the natural locational advantages of Stalinabad a great deal of investment had to be channeled into the construction of narrow-gauge rail lines and highways linking Stalinabad with its productive hinterland. One of the most noteworthy of these projects was the laying in 1941 of an extremely expensive narrow-gauge rail line with a 2.7 per cent ruling grade from Stalinabad to Kurgan-Tyube in the Vakhsh Valley--the primary center of long-staple cotton production in the Tadzhik Republic.[3] This line connected with another narrow-gauge line running from Kurgan-Tyube to Nizhniy-Pyandzh to form a north-south through route. In 1950, the Stalinabad-Kurgan Tyube line handled a light freight volume of 700,000 tons.[4] Another cotton-hauling narrow-gauge line is now under construction from Kurgan-Tyube to the town of Kulyab, directly to the east. In 1946, Soviet sources reported that narrow-gauge lines handled approximately two-thirds of all the goods shipped in Tadzhikstan (presumably tonnage) by all forms of transport, except broad-gauge railways.[5] However, in recent years, the rapid growth of highway transportation has reduced the freight share of the Tadzhik narrow-gauge lines to 16 per cent of the total intra-Republic freight volume.[6]

Thus, a hierarchy of transportation forms has evolved in Tadzhikstan. At the apex is broad-gauge rail communication, which

---

[1]Tadzhikskaya SSR, p. 94. [2]Ibid., p. 173.

[3]Ibid., p. 129; M. M. Gel'fman, "Novoye Zheleznodorozhnoye Stroitel'stvo vo Vtorom Pyatiletke," Sotsialisticheskiy Transport, No. 12 (December, 1934), p. 57.

[4]Narzikulov and Ryazantsev, p. 129. [5]Ibid. [6]Ibid.

handles the bulk of interregional traffic. At the next levels are narrow-gauge railroads and improved highways, which primarily handle intra-republic movement. River transportation in the Tadzhik Republic, just as in most of Central Asia, plays a relatively insignificant role in the interchange of freight, although regular service has been established from Nizhniy-Pyandzh to Termez on the shallow and swift-flowing Amu-Darya. From 1913 to 1956, the relative importance of Tadzhik river-borne trade has decreased significantly, and even the absolute volume of river loadings has declined. In 1913, the river ports of present-day Tadzhikstan loaded 21,000 tons and unloaded 50,000 tons.[1] In that year, river loadings were equal to 21 per cent of rail loadings, while river terminations were actually 25 per cent greater than the volume of rail terminations. In 1956, Tadzhik ports loaded only 12,000 tons of freight, or 9,000 tons less than in 1913, while terminating 131,000 tons.[2] By this year, river originations were equal to only 0.5 per cent of the volume of freight originating by broad-gauge rail line, and river terminations were equal to 3 per cent of broad-gauge rail terminations.

A year before the Kagan-Samsonovo line had been extended to Termez, in 1925, a 122-kilometer rail line was laid from Karshi to Kitab, on the upper reaches of the Kashka-Darya. Kitab is the center of an enclave of irrigated cotton production based upon the meager water resources of the Kashka-Darya. The town itself, as well as nearby towns, contains cotton ginneries and numerous other small-scale plants processing local agricultural raw materials. At present, the irrigated cotton acreage of this region amounts to only about 5 per cent of the Uzbek total. If a plan to divert some of the waters of the Zeravshan River to the Kashka-Darya is implemented, this lightly loaded branch line should acquire much greater importance.

The Rail Pattern of the Kirghiz Republic

The Kirghiz SSR has concentrated zones of settlement in the northern and western extremities of the republic. The high ranges of Tyan-Shan, which occupy most of Kirghizstan, have thus far prevented the establishment of direct rail communication between the two primary zones of habitation. Discussion of the spurs from the mining centers on the western fringes of the republic to

---

[1] Transport i Svyaz' SSSR, p. 127. [2] Ibid.

the Fergana Basin will be deferred until the section of this chapter dealing with the rail pattern of the Fergana region.

One of the most ambitious projects undertaken in Central Asia before the First Five-Year Plan was the completion in 1924 of a 332-kilometer railroad from the town of Burnoye, 59 kilometers to the west of Dzhambul, to Frunze, the capital of the present-day Kirghiz SSR, through the rich sugar-beet, grain, and fiber-producing areas of the Chu Valley. In many respects this line is similar to the Stalinabad route. Both rail lines were designed to link the regional capitals of productive hinterlands to the main rail net. Another similarity is that both lines have a light freight load. In 1956, the Kirghiz Republic originated 3.6 million tons and terminated 3.7 million tons for a combined total of 7.3 million tons of freight as compared to a figure of 6.7 million tons in the Tadzhik Republic.[1] However, just as in the case of Tadzhikstan, a large share of the total traffic originations consisted of coal and lignite moving from mines located at the terminii of short spurs into the Fergana Basin. Excluding the 2.1 million tons of coal loadings, the Kirghiz Republic originated only 1.5 million tons of other commodities--a figure identical to a comparable measuro of Tadzhik freight originations.

A handicap restricting the efficiency of the rail access of both Stalinabad and Frunze is their location on branch lines off the path of the major freight flows; although this is not as serious a problem for Frunze since it has more direct access to the main rail net than its Tadzhik counterpart. But for a last-minute decision, in the late 1930's, Frunze would have had direct access to the main rail net. In the initial directions outlining the route of the Turkestan-Siberian railroad issued in the middle 1920's, Frunze and the settlements in the Chu Valley were scheduled to be located on the main line. This was to be accomplished by channeling the main line through the Kurdai Pass in the Kendyktas (see Fig. 13). However, after construction of the Turk-Sib began, Soviet engineers resurrected a survey carried out in 1907 which showed that the present route of the Turk-Sib, far to the north of the Kurdai Pass variant, would require smaller sums to construct and, also, could be laid in a shorter period of time. The government of the Kirghiz Republic urged that the Turk-Sib be constructed through the Kurdai Pass, but to no avail. The planners of the Turk-

---

[1] Ibid., p. 67.

Sib determined that the Kurdai Pass route would cost an additional 23 million rubles, which would raise the cost of building the entire line by approximately 14 per cent.[1] As a result, Frunze was left on a branch line, 156 kilometers from the tracks of the main line.

It was not until 1950, 26 years after the first locomotive steamed into Frunze, that the Chu Valley line was extended to the town of Rybach'ye on the western edge of Issyk-Kul' (lake). Rybach'ye is located at the junction of three highways; two of which encircle Issyk-Kul', while the third leads to the town of Kashgar in Sinkiang Province. Rybach'ye is also linked with the grain-producing areas east of the lake by steamship service. This town, incidentally, was originally scheduled to receive rail access by 1937.[2] The long delay between the planned and actual completion of rail lines has been a characteristic feature of the evolution of the Soviet rail net.

The Rail Pattern of the Fergana Basin and Approaches

The Fergana Basin is a fertile enclave of irrigated lowland surrounded by snow-capped mountains and linked to the rest of the country by a single-track rail line. Among other things, this region produces about 30 per cent of all the cotton grown in the Soviet Union and accounts for 31 per cent of the gross industrial production of the Uzbek Republic.[3]

By 1917, the Fergana Basin had a relatively dense rail pattern. The main line went from Kokand to Andizhan and terminated at Dzhalal-Abad. Another branch line went from Kokand to Namangan in the north-central portion of the basin (see Figs. 13 and 38). In addition, narrow-gauge spurs reached out from the main line to lignite mines at Sulyutka and Kizyl-Kiya. During the Bashmakh Insurrection in the early 1920's, most of the rail lines in the Fergana Basin were destroyed. However, by the start of the First Five-Year Plan in 1928, the previously existing pattern had been restored.[4]

---

[1]Z. Ostrovsky, The Great Trunk-Line (Moscow: Centrizdat, 1931), p. 30.

[2]Gel'fman, Sotialisticheskiy Transport (November, 1934), p. 56.

[3]Uzbekskaya SSR, p. 303. [4]Arkhipov, p. 132.

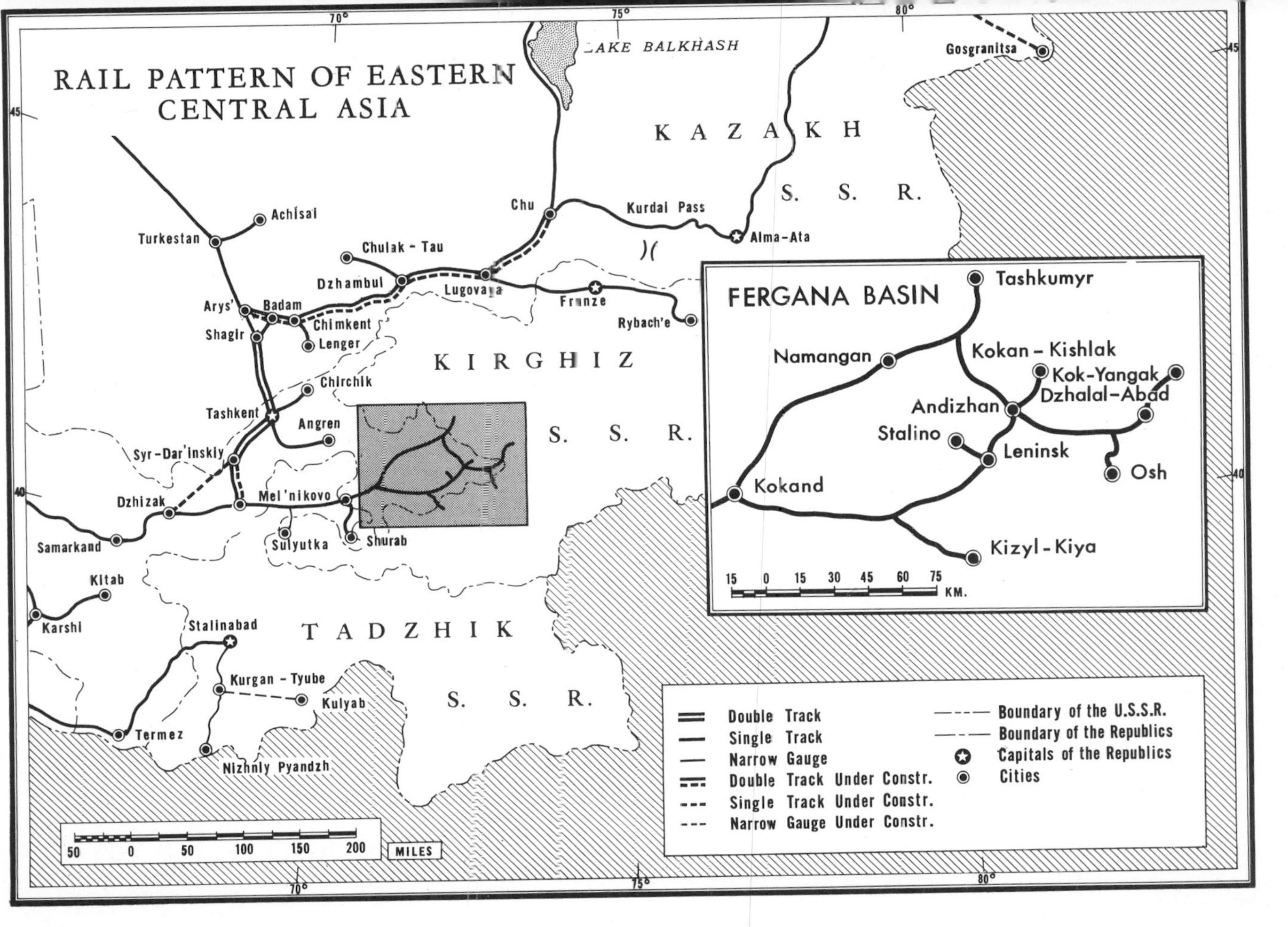
RAIL PATTERN OF EASTERN CENTRAL ASIA
LAKE BALKHASH
KAZAKH S. S. R.
KIRGHIZ S. S. R.
TADZHIK S. S. R.
Gosgranitsa
Chu
Kurdai Pass
Alma-Ata
Turkestan
Achisai
Chulak - Tau
Dzhambul
Lugovaya
Frunze
Rybach'e
Arys'
Badam
Chimkent
Shagir
Lenger
Chirchik
Tashkent
Angren
Syr-Dar'inskiy
Dzhizak
Mel'nikovo
Samarkand
Sulyutka
Shurab
Kitab
Karshi
Stalinabad
Kurgan - Tyube
Kulyab
Termez
Nizhniy Pyandzh
50 0 50 100 150 200 MILES
70°
75°
80°
45
40
FERGANA BASIN
Tashkumyr
Namangan
Kokan - Kishlak
Kok-Yangak
Dzhalal-Abad
Andizhan
Stalino
Leninsk
Osh
Kokand
Kizyl-Kiya
15 0 15 30 45 60 75 KM.
Double Track
Single Track
Narrow Gauge
Double Track Under Constr.
Single Track Under Constr.
Narrow Gauge Under Constr.
Boundary of the U.S.S.R.
Boundary of the Republics
Capitals of the Republics
Cities

Fig. 13

Additions to the rail pattern of this region since 1923 have been guided by three objectives: to develop a circular line around the basin, to construct feeder lines to centers of mining, and to develop short spurs to centers of cotton ginning. The first of these goals was achieved when the existing route from Kokand to Namangan was extended to Andizhan in 1924. In addition to providing rail service for the densely settled cotton-growing areas of the basin, the circular railway has also greatly increased the flexibility of rail operations. The only area in the Fergana Basin not within easy access of this line is the barren Karakalpak Steppe in the center of the basin. After the completion of the circular railway, the renovation and construction of rail spurs to centers of coal, lignite, and petroleum production began in earnest. One of the initial projects was the replacement of the narrow-gauge track on the spur to the lignite and petroleum producing regions in the vicinity of Kizyl-Kiya by broad gauge track in 1928. In 1931, the branch line to Dzhalal-Abad was extended 16 kilometers northward to the coal-mining center of Kok-Yangak, while, at the same time, another spur from the Andizhan-Dzhalal-Abad line was being laid to the highway junction of Osh. Two other feeder lines constructed in the 1930's tapped the coal resources of Tashkumyr in the Kirghiz Republic (see Fig. 1), and the brown coal and oil reserves in the vicinity of Shurab. Some indication of the mineral traffic on these spurs and the role of the railroad in developing mineral resources is revealed by the volume of coal and lignite production in the Kirghiz and Tadzhik republics, most of which is produced in the oblasts of these republics economically tributary to the Fergana Basin. Coal production in these republics increased from only 99,000 tons in 1928 to 3,619,000 tons in 1956.[1] However, the net of feeder lines providing mineral fuels to the consuming centers of the Fergana Basin is still not adequate since many sources of raw materials are isolated from the main rail net. One of the most important of these is in the Uzgen area, southeast of Dzhalal-Abad, which has large reserves of coal apparently suitable for coking. Still other spurs in the Fergana Basin link cotton-ginning centers with the circular railway. Included in this category are the 15-kilometer line from Leninsk to Stalino and the 18-kilometer spur from Andizhan to the town of Kokan-Kishlak.

---

[1] Promyshlennost' SSSR, p. 146; Narodnoye Khozyaistvo SSSR v 1956 Godu, p. 74.

The Fergana Basin originates more freight than any region in the Uzbek Republic. The basin exports ginned cotton, silk, fruit, petroleum, cement, and many other products while importing large quantities of lumber and grain in addition to diversified manufactured goods. One of the most striking features of the interregional exchange of commodities originating or terminating in the Fergana Basin is that traffic moving to Tashkent or areas outside Central Asia by rail must follow a circuitous right-angle route on one of the most congested sections of track in Central Asia--between Ursat'yevskaya and Tashkent. In an attempt to remedy this situation, the Second Five-Year Plan scheduled the construction of a rail line from Tashkent directly to Mel'nikovo (see Fig. 13), which was to be completed by 1936. The total cost of this line was estimated at 30 million rubles. By January 1, 1933, 11 per cent of this figure had already been expended.[1] However, at the end of 1933, this project was placed in "conservation" and as yet has not been revived.[2] At present, efforts to relieve the traffic congestion of the crowded Ursat'yevskaya junction, center around the construction of a line from Dzhizak to Syr-Dar'inskiy, which will pass through the Golodnaya Steppe. In addition to lightening the traffic burden of the Ursat'yevskaya-Syr-Dar'inskaya route, this line will shorten the distance between Tashkent and the areas to the west of Dzhizak by 50 kilometers.[3] If this were not enough, the Dzhizak line will also contribute to the achievement of the goal to expand the area of irrigated land in the Golodnaya Steppe by 741,000 acres from 1950 to 1962.[4]

Other Feeder Lines

In 1933, a 25-kilometer rail line was laid from Nebit-Dag, on the main line of the Trans-Caspian, to the desolate oil-producing region of Vyshka. The Nebit-Dag-Vyshka region is not only the main petroleum producing area in the Turkmen Republic but, also, in all Central Asia. From 1940 to 1955, the production of petroleum in the Turkmen Republic jumped from 587,000 tons to 3,126,000

---

[1] Osnovnyye Ob'yekty Kapital'nogo Stroitel'stva vo Vtorom Pyatiletti, p. 133.

[2] Gel'fman, Sotsialisticheskiy Transport, No. 11 (November, 1934), p. 53.

[3] Gudok, August 19, July 19, 1956.

[4] Ob Oroshenii i Osvoyenii Golodnoi Stepi: Sbornik Materialov (Tashkent: Gosizdat Uzbekskoi SST, 1956), p. 10.

tons.[1] One of the most important functions of this line is to handle the movement of workers from their residences in Nebit-Dag to the oil wells of Vyshka. The commuting nature of passenger movement along this line can be verified by the fact that the 1957 summer schedule of passenger-train movement lists three trains daily in each direction which are spaced to provide transportation for three shifts of workers.[2]

Two of the most important rail spurs in Soviet Central Asia originate in Tashkent and were completed in the same year, 1944. One of these lines links the Uzbek capital with the huge Chirchik Electro-Chemical Combine, which produces nitrogen fertilizers for the cotton-growing areas of Central Asia. The second of these lines was laid over the 119 kilometers separating Tashkent from the lignite-producing region around Angren. This line also provides access to the large copper reserves at Almalyk, which as of 1955, were not being exploited. In 1940, before the Angren lignites were being mined, the Uzbek Republic produced only 3.4 thousand tons of coal and lignite. However, by 1955, the Angren area alone produced an estimated 2.34 million tons of lignite, or 40 per cent of the total volume of coal and lignite mined in Central Asia.[3] The importance of the Angren branch line is scheduled to increase significantly from 1955 to 1960, when the ambitious "Great Angren" project is implemented. Among other things, this program calls for the rapid expansion of lignite mining and processing, the construction of a huge nitrogen fertilizer plant, and an aluminum plant based on local kaolin clay and cheap power in Angren; and, also, the construction of a copper-smelting plant in Almalyk.[4]

The Rail Pattern of the Lower Amu-Darya

The most ambitious rail project carried out by the Soviet Union within Central Asia has been the construction of a 629-kilometer line from Chardzhou, at the intersection of the Amu-Darya

---

[1] Promyshlennost' SSSR, p. 155.

[2] Ofitsial'nyy Ukazatel' Passazhirshikh Soobshcheniy: Leto 1957 Goda, p. 487.

[3] Uzbekskaya SSR, p. 167.

[4] T. M. Kalashnikova, "Perspektivy Kompleksnogo Razvitiya Angrenskogo Ygol'nogo Promyshlennogo Tsentra," Voprosy Ekonomiki Promyshlennosti Uzbekskoi SSR, pp. 30-34.

and the Trans-Caspian, to Kungrad in the lower reaches of the Amu-Darya. This line, which was completed in 1956, is scheduled to be extended to Alexandrov-Gai, at the head of a branch line southeast of Saratov (and north of the Caspian Sea) to form another interregional trunkline between Central Asia and the European portions of the Soviet Union. This line follows a route originally surveyed by Ferdinand de Lesseps as part of a Calais to Calcutta rail line (Fig. 37).

Although it was originally anticipated that the line from Chardzhou to Alexandrov-Gai would reach Makat by 1955, construction had proceeded only as far as Kungrad by the year 1956. The extension of this line to Makat is not included in the list of rail lines to be constructed during the period from 1956 to 1960. In part, this can be attributed to the abandonment of the ambitious plans announced in 1950 to build the Main Turkmen Canal from the lower Amu-Darya to the vicinity of Krasnovodsk, which, among other things, was planned to provide an additional 3.2 million acres of irrigated lands. Even though the rail line from Chardzhou to Kungrad does not handle transit traffic, it does perform the important function of linking the cotton-producing lands of the lower Amu-Darya to the main rail net.

The region of the lower Amu-Darya (Khorezm Oasis) is the most important cotton-growing area in the lowland deserts of Central Asia. In 1954, the Khorezm Oblast has 106 thousand hectares planted in cotton and produced approximately 9 per cent of the gross harvest of raw cotton in the Uzbek Republic while, in 1955, the Karakalpak ASSR, with almost the same acreage, harvested 6.8 per cent of the total Uzbek harvest.[1] In addition, the areas of the Turkmen Republic served by this line are important cotton-producing regions.

Prior to the coming of the railroad, the lower Amu-Darya region relied primarily upon the river for the shipment of commodities to the rest of the country. Most of the river-borne commerce of this region was transshipped to rail at the junction of Chardzhou. However, the Amu-Darya is an extremely expensive and uncertain route. Among the disadvantages of this river are its swift currents, shifting channels, and numerous shoals; quite often the color of the water is the only guide to the changing channel depths and, thus, navigation is restricted to daytime hours. Still another handicap to navigation is that most of the goods shipped on

[1]Uzbekskaya SSR, pp. 427 and 438.

this river have to move in flat-bottomed vessels with a draught of only 2 feet 3 1/2 inches (70 centimeters).[1] Another alternative utilized before the construction of the railroad was highway transportation. But the dirt road linking the Khorezm Oasis with Chardzhou was even more expensive and less reliable than the Amu-Darya. A third possible method of providing transportation for the cotton-growing areas of the lower Amu-Darya would be to reorient trade toward the north via the Aral Sea. However, this route is also quite inefficient, in part, because of the extremely expensive 200-kilometer haul across the treacherous delta of the Amu-Darya needed to reach the Aral Sea port of Muinak from the cotton-producing regions. The freezing of the Aral Sea for 140-160 days a year and the inadequate port facilities of Muinak are also responsible for the relative unimportance of movement on the Aral Sea.[2] The net result of the inadequate transportation provided the fertile oases of the Amu-Darya prior to the Fifth Five-Year Plan was that quite often the cotton harvest was unable to reach its major markets. In describing the transport dilemma of this region a Soviet source mentions that during the navigation season, the Amu-Darya was often unable to handle one-half of the transport needs of this region. Occasionally, it was even necessary to ship bulky cotton fiber by air.[3] In addition, liquid fuels had to be brought in by air even though the airplane consumed the equivalent of one-half this fuel in making the round trip.

Thus despite the postponement of the extension of the Chardzhou-Kungrad line to Makat until some time between 1961 and 1970, construction of the line to Kungrad filled an important need. This is true even though the traffic volume is presumably rather low. Although current flow data for this route are unavailable, in 1947 it was estimated that the freight volume on this line immediately after its opening would be only 1.5 million tons a year.[4] Passenger movement is also on a rather modest scale

---

[1] S. P. Suslov, Fizicheskaya Geografiya SSSR: Aziatskaya Chast' (2d ed. rev.; Moscow: Uchpedgiz, 1954), p. 585.

[2] Akademiya Nauk SSSR, Sovet po Izucheniyu Prirodnikh Resursov Turkmenskoi SSR, Problemy Turkmenii, I, Trudy Pervoi Konferentsii po Izucheniyu Proizvoditel'nykh Sil Turkmenskoi SSR (Leningrad: Izdatel'stvo Akademiya Nauk SSSR, 1934), pp. 341-43.

[3] Uzbekskaya SSR, p. 436.

[4] G. Khodzhayev, "Zheleznaya Doroga Chardzhou-Kungrad," Zheleznodorozhnyy Transport, XXVIII (July, 1947), 19.

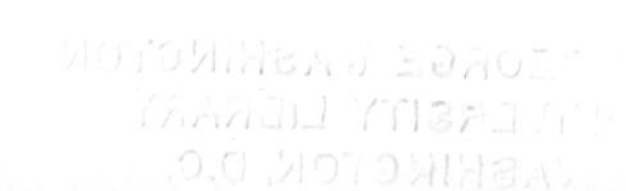

as can be evidenced by the scheduling of only one train daily in each direction in 1957.[1] However, even taking the light traffic load into consideration, Soviet planners estimated that the amortization period of this line would be only four to five years because of the great reduction in the existing transportation expenditures of this region.[2] Perhaps the most surprising feature of the development of this badly needed line is that a crash program, which was subsequently abandoned, to build the Main Turkmen Canal had to be the initial motivating force for its construction.

Summary of the Internal Pattern of Soviet Central Asia

The most ambitious rail projects undertaken in Central Asia during the Soviet era have been those designed to link regional agricultural centers with the main rail net. Two of these lines, to Stalinabad and Frunze, have the additional justification of serving regional political capitals. The longest rail line built by the Soviets entirely within Central Asia, from Chardzhou to Kungrad, has the added potential advantage of serving eventually as part of an interregional rail route. Another type of rail line emphasized by Soviet planners, has been the short feeder line from mining centers, primarily producing mineral fuels, to local centers of consumption. By 1956, the internal rail pattern of Central Asia accounted for almost 5 per cent of the total rail mileage of the Soviet Union, as Table 6 shows.

From 1933 to 1950, the relative share of the Central Asian rail pattern in the total rail mileage of the Soviet Union declined somewhat despite a large absolute increase in route kilometers. With the construction of the Kungrad line in 1956 the Central Asian percentage of total rail mileage increased somewhat, although it was still below the 1933 percentage. The density of the rail pattern of Central Asia in 1956 was 4.0 kilometers of route per 1,000 square kilometers of territory, while the all-union figure was 5.3 kilometer per 1,000 square kilometers. A comparable figure for the Ukraine was 34.3 kilometers, or eight times the density of Central Asia.

However, aggregate statistics of rail line density are quite misleading. The important considerations are whether the major

---

[1] Ofitsial'nyy Ukazatel' Passazhirskikh Soobshcheniy: Leto 1957 Goda, p. 487.

[2] Khodzhayev, Zheleznodorozhnyy Transport, XXVIII (July, 1947), 19.

existing centers of economic activity are served by rail; whether areas of important undeveloped raw materials are without rail access; and whether the rail pattern is efficient in terms of route directness.

TABLE 6

OPERATING LENGTH OF RAIL LINES IN CENTRAL ASIA[a]
(Thousands of Route Kilometers)[b]

Region	1933	1940	1950	1956
Uzbek Republic	1.89	1.91	2.07	2.25
Turkmen Republic	1.70	1.75	1.74	2.10
Kirghiz Republic	0.18	0.22	0.37	0.38
Tadzhik Republic	0.19	0.25	0.26	0.26
Total Central Asia	3.96	4.13	4.44	4.99
Total Soviet Union	81.8	106.1	116.9	120.7
Central Asia per cent of national total	4.9	3.8	3.8	4.1

[a]Transport i Svyaz' SSR, p. 30; A. Yakobi, Zheleznyye Dorogi SSSR v Tsifrakh (Moscow: Tsunkhu Gosplana SSSR, 1935), pp. 110-11.

[b]Data include broad-gauge and narrow-gauge lines.

With the completion of the line to Kungrad, the first of these questions can be answered in the affirmative. Despite the relatively low rail coverage per 1,000 square kilometers, the most important existing center of economic activity in Central Asia now have rail access (see Fig. 1). An exception is the old, sulfur-mining area of Sernyy Zavod in the Kara-Kum about 200 kilometers north of Ashkhabad; it relies upon the odd combination of camel caravans and airplanes. Many of the newly developing raw material sites, such as the coal-producing areas of Kugitang in the Turkmen Republic and the Uzgen region in the eastern slopes of the Fergana Basin, however, are still isolated from the rail net.

An equally great problem is that of route circuity. Although much of the circuity in the rail pattern of Central Asia induced by difficult terrain is unavoidable because of the economic limit imposed by prohibitive construction costs through mountains, Soviet planners are now turning toward rail projects which can increase route directness without enormous capital outlays. One of the examples of this type line is the Dzhizak-Syr-Dar'inskaya bypass, which is now under construction. In recent publications,

Soviet authors have stressed the need for additional by-pass lines in Central Asia, including a possible line from Kitab to Samarkand, which would shorten the average haul of commodities moving on the Stalinabad route, and the once-abandoned proposal for a direct rail link between Tashkent and the Fergana Basin.[1]

The railroad is by far the dominant form of transportation in Central Asia. River movement on the Amu-Darya is costly, slow and unreliable, while most sections of the Syr-Darya are not navigable. Highway transportation is important primarily for the movement of goods from cotton-growing kolkhozes and sovkhozes to local collection and trade centers and, secondarily, because it provides access to the remote mountainous and desert regions of Central Asia (Fig. 14). Truck transportation is also used in the international trade of Central Asia with Afghanistan and China. In some of the nodes of settlement in the sandy Kara-Kum, the camel serves as the major vehicle of bulk commodity movement. Air transportation in Central Asia is not only used to move passengers, but also handles a considerable share of the freight of the portions of this region isolated from the rail net.

Although the evolution of the internal pattern of Central Asia has been associated with the rapid economic growth of this region, the intensity of regional specialization and the orientation of the interregional trade of this region during the Soviet era have been altered more by the development of the interregional trunk-lines.

The Interregional Rail Pattern

The Turkestan-Siberian Railroad

Until the middle of the First Five-Year Plan, Central Asia was linked to the major industrial areas of European Russia by two routes. The Caspian Sea route was virtually non-competitive because it was slow, costly, and inconvenient. On the other hand, the all-rail route by way of Kazalinsk was strained almost beyond its rather limited capacity. In 1927-28, the single-track Kazalinsk route north of Chkalov handled a density of two million ton-kilometers per kilometer of route, or a density 65 per cent greater

---

[1]U. Tulyaganov, "Zheleznyye Dorogi i Razvitiye Ekonomiki Respublik Sredney Azii," Zheleznodorozhnyy Transport, XXXVIII (September, 1957), 6.

Fig. 14.--An Asphalt Highway Leading into Samarkand from

than the national average density.[1] Large quantities of lumber, grain, and manufactured goods were shipped into Central Asia via this line in exchange for cotton and other diversified agricultural products. At this time, Central Asia had no direct rail connection with the extensive grain and forest lands of Siberia.

The need for a rail line to re-orient the interregional ties of Central Asia to new supply areas became particularly acute in the late 1920's, when the Soviet Union, attempting to reduce its dependence on imported cotton, intensified the production of cotton in Central Asia. This, in turn, generated a greater demand in that region for such bulky imports as grain and lumber, which could be supplied from Siberia. Among the methods proposed during this period to expand the production of cotton in Central Asia were the shifting of a large percentage of the irrigated lands in Central Asia used to grow grain into the production of cotton and, also, the opening up of extensive areas to irrigation. The Turkestan-Siberian rail line, hereafter referred to as the Turk-Sib, was expected to handle the movement of Siberian grain to Central Asia to fill the anticipated increase in the grain deficit of this region. At the same time, the Turk-Sib was scheduled to relieve the traffic pressure on the Kazalinsk route; not only by shipping grain, but also by handling the entire movement of lumber to Central Asia. According to Soviet estimates, construction of the Turk-Sib would also provide an immediate impetus to the expansion of grain production and forestry in Siberia.[2] The actual contributions of the Turk-Sib to the intensified specialization of Central Asian agriculture will be examined in a later chapter.

Preliminary surveys of the route of the Turk-Sib were first carried out in 1887 and, in greater detail, in 1907 and 1914. The laying of a branch line from Novosibirsk to Semipalatinsk in 1915 was viewed by Tsarist planners as the beginning of a trunk-line route to Central Asia. The coming of the war and the subsequent revolution curtailed these plans. The first phase of the Soviet attempts to develop the Turk-Sib magistral was the construction of a rail line from Burnoye to Frunze in 1924. Two years later, in December, 1926, a decree was issued by the Council of Labor and

---

[1] Materialy po Statistike Putey Soobshcheniya, CV, 243.

[2] U.S.S.R. Komitet Sodeistviya Postroiki Turkestano-Sibirskoi Zheleznoi Dorogi pri SNK, RSFSR, Turkestano-Sibirskaya Magistral': Sbornik Statey (Moscow, 1929), p. 16.

Defense of the USSR calling for the construction of the Turk-Sib magistral between Frunze and Semipalatinsk--a distance of 1,500 kilometers.[1] On August 1, 1927, tracks of the Turk-Sib route began to be laid from Semipalatinsk toward the south. The line was pushed through the relatively flat western edge of the Kazakh folded uplands, and then, after traversing the sandy desert south of Lake Balkhash, paralleled the foothills of the Tyan'-Shan' through southern Kazakhstan. After reaching Alma-Ata, as mentioned above, the original route was altered and Frunze was by-passed in favor of a less costly route to the north. By the end of 1930, a year ahead of schedule, the Turk-Sib line had been placed in permanent operation.[2]

Soviet planners believed that the inherent importance of the Turk-Sib as the only direct rail link between Central Asia and Siberia would ensure an enormous volume of freight almost immediately. Much to their dismay, however, in the initial years of operation, traffic on this line fell far below the planned goals. In 1933, which was the year of a general "transport crisis" on the Soviet rail system, the density of freight movement on the section of track approaching Alma-Ata from the north was only 895,000 ton-kilometers per kilometer of route, or approximately one-third the density of the Kazalinsk route north of Chkalov (Orenburg) in the same year.[3] The reasons behind the failure of the Turk-Sib to meet the Central Asian demand for grain and lumber in the early 1930's will be examined in a later chapter.

By 1937, traffic on the Turk-Sib rose to 7.3 million tons, or more than triple the 1933 tonnage.[4] Despite the considerable increases in traffic, in 1937, the Turk-Sib ranked thirty-ninth among the forty railroads of the country in terms of total freight originations and terminations, and thirty-seventh in terms of the total volume of transit traffic.[5] However, during the postwar era, the Turk-Sib has experienced an even more rapid upsurge of traffic. To a large extent, this is based upon the opening up of

---

[1] Ibid., p. 237. [2] Ostrovskiy, p. 5.

[3] Materialy po Statistike Putey Soobshcheniya, CXXXIX, 96.

[4] D. Chernomordik, "Rol' Transporta v Razvitii Proizvoditel'nykh Sil Strany," Zheleznodrozhnyy Transport, XXVIII (December, 1947), 29.

[5] L. Ya. Vol'fson, V. I. Ledovskoi, and N. S. Shil'nikov, Ekonomika Transporta (Moscow: Transzheldorizdat, 1941), pp. 275-77.

the virgin and idle lands of the black-earth Altai, northeast of Semipalatinsk and, also, to the increased consumption of grain, lumber, coal, building materials, and other products in Central Asia. By 1956, freight traffic on the Turk-Sib Railroad (including the line from Mointy to Chu, the branch line to Frunze, and other shorter lines) reached 28.5 billion ton-kilometers,[1] as compared to 1.9 billion ton-kilometers on the less-extensive Turk-Sib of 1932. From 1932 to 1956, the average density of freight flow increased from 0.93 billion ton-kilometers per kilometer of route to 8.12 billion ton-kilometers per route kilometer,[2] which would still be below the 1956 national average freight density of 9.0 ton-kilometers per kilometer of route. It should be remembered, however, that the 1956 average density figure undoubtedly understates the actual density of freight flow on the main line of the Turk-Sib, since this figure is based upon the entire route mileage of the Turk-Sib system, which includes such lightly loaded branches as the rail line leading to Frunze. Nonetheless, the Turk-Sib and the other main lines of Central Asia handle less traffic than the major Soviet trunk-lines. But when one considers that the Central Asian interregional lines are single-track routes, they handle a great deal of traffic. The accelerated evolution of the Turk-Sib into a major trunk-line in recent years seems to be justifying, at long last, the sanguine expectations of the early planners of this route.

Feeder Lines on the Turk-Sib Route

The creation of a through route from Novosibirsk to Tashkent has been accompanied by the development of numerous feeder lines funneling diverse mineral products into the main transportation artery. Many of these feeder lines have been constructed in order to develop the polymetallic ores of Kazakhstan. In 1939, the longest and most important rail line linking the Turk-Sib with a major center of polymetallic ore production was laid from the village of Lokot', 120 kilometers northeast of Semipalatinsk, to Ust-Kamenogorsk in the heart of the "Altai Complex" (Figs. 37 and 38). In the same year, a narrow-gauge rail line from Ust-Kamenogorsk

---

[1]U.S.S.R. Statisticheskoye Upravleniye Kazakhskoi SSR, Narodnoye Khozyaistvo Kazakhskoi SSR: Statisticheskiy Sbornik (Alma-Ata: Kazakhskoye Gosudarstvennoye Izdatel'stvo, 1957), p. 245.

[2]Ibid., pp. 240-45.

to the smelting-center of Leninogorsk (Ridder) was converted to broad-gauge. By 1953, the line from Lokot' to Ust-Kamenogorsk had been extended to the mining center of Zyryanovsk in the west (Fig. 15). The "Altai Complex" specialized in the mining, enriching, and smelting of lead and zinc. The major mining and processing centers in and around Leninogorsk, Ust-Kamenogorsk, and Zyryanovsk are all now served by rail.

Other feeder lines in Southern Kazakhstan are related directly to the construction of the largest lead smelter in the Soviet Union at Chimkent in 1934. The principal ore bases of the Chimkent plant were the scattered deposits of lead in the nearby Kara-Tau (mountains) at Achisai and surrounding areas, which are located on a narrow-gauge branch line leading into the village of Turkestan (near Borisovka) on the Kazalinsk route. In the same year the Chimkent smelter was placed in operation, 1934, a 29-kilometer spur line was completed from Chimkent to the lignite mines at Lenger. The Chimkent Lead Combine alone accounted for 49 per cent of all the lead smelted in the Soviet Union in 1937. Even though it is still the largest lead smelting plant in the country, production has persistently been far below plant capacity because of a chronic shortage of ore.[1] By 1946, the Achisai ores, formerly the leading supplier, were no longer able to meet the ore needs of the Chimkent plant.[2] The shortage of ore led to the construction of yet another feeder line to a center of polymetallic ore production in 1943 when the branch line to Tekeli, east of Lake Balkhash was completed. This area evidently is now filling a large part of the ore needs of the Chimkent plant.

Another example of a mineral feeder line branching off the Turk-Sib is the 90-kilometer line from Dzhambul to the mining center of Chulak-Tau, which taps the enormous reserves of phosphate rock in the eastern slopes of the Kara-Tau. A superphosphate combine has been constructed in Dzhambul to utilize these ores.

The Trans-Kazakhstan Magistral

By far the single most important rail project carried out on the approaches to Central Asia in the postwar period has been the completion in 1953 of a 441-kilometer line from Mointy, which

---

[1] Demitri B. Shimkin, Minerals: A Key to Soviet Power (Cambridge: Harvard University Press, 1953), p. 122.

[2] *Ibid.*, p. 123.

Fig. 15.--A Coal Burning Locomotive on the Ust-Kamenogorsk-Zyryanovsk Line.

is located on the rail line to Karaganda, to the village of Chu on the Turk-Sib, through the barren Bet-Pak-Dala Desert. The obvious lack of local traffic opportunity along this route emphasizes the function of the Mointy-Chu line as a bridge line forging the last link in a north-south through route, usually referred to as the Trans-Kazakhstan Magistral or Trunk-line, between the wheat lands of northern Kazakhstan, on the one hand, and Southern Kazakhstan and Central Asia, on the other. Among the reasons cited for the development of the Trans-Kazakhstan line were the following:

1. To replace long-haul Kuzbass coal in Central Asia and Southern Kazakhstan by the closer coal of the Karaganda Basin.

2. To shorten the distance required to ship freight from the Urals to southern Kazakhstan and Central Asia.

3. To divert traffic from the other interregional trunk lines.

4. To increase the flow of grain from Northern Kazakhstan to Southern Kazakhstan and Central Asia.[1] The opening up of the virgin and idle lands of Kazakhstan and Western Siberia in 1954 has given this function of the Trans-Kazakhstan Trunk-line an importance far beyond that envisaged in the original plans for this route. In a later chapter, traffic movement of this line will be examined in greater detail, but it should be mentioned at this point that this line has succeeded in providing Central Asia with more efficient access to the grain and coal producing areas of Northern and Central Kazakhstan. This, in turn, has resulted in a partial realignment of the imported raw material supply base of Central Asia from Western Siberia to Northern Kazakhstan. In 1955, Central Asia (and the portions of southern Kazakhstan south of Alma-Ata) imported approximately 1.9 million tons of coal and 141,000 tons of grain from Kazakhstan, primarily by way of the Trans-Kazakhstan magistral.[2]

The role of the Trans-Kazakhstan line as a through route to

---

[1] Gudok, November 4, 1953.

[2] Akademiya Nauk SSSR, Institut Geografii, and Akademiya Nauk Kazakhskoi SSR, Kazakhskaya SSR: Ekonomiko-Geograficheskaya Kharakteristika (Moscow: Geografgiz, 1957), p. 116. This source listed the percentage of Kazakh grain moving to Central Asia in relation to the total Kazakh exports. Coal figures were based on D. T. Onika, Ugol'naya Promyshlennost' SSSR v Shestoi Pyatiletke (Moscow: Ugletekhizdat, 1956), p. 40.

Central Asia, however, seemed to be of secondary importance in the original decision to extend the branch line south from Karaganda in the late 1930's. The primary motive, then, was to facilitate the mining and smelting of copper in the area immediately north of Lake Balkhash and, also, to provide rail access to the copper-producing areas around Dzhezkazgan to the west. Construction of a 100,000-ton-capacity copper smelter in the town of Balkhash was completed in 1938; a year later this plant became the terminus of a rail line from Karaganda. The Balkhash smelter not only processes the low-grade copper ore of the Kounrad mines, linked to the plant by a 17-kilometer rail spur, but also processes some of the copper from the Dzhezkazgan mines, which contain the largest reserves of copper in the Soviet Union; equal to one-third the national total.[1]

An important industrial complex has evolved in the Dzhezkazgan area based upon the mining of copper at Dzhezkasgan and the smelting of part of this mineral at Karsakpai, as well as the mining of diversified minerals such as manganese. The construction of a 439-kilometer branch line to this region in 1940 removed one of the greatest impediments to the expansion of copper production. Prior to the coming of the railroad, the Karsakpai plant was linked to the outer world primarily by means of a primitive dirt highway, usable only eight months out of the year, to the desert village of Dzhusaly on the Kazalinsk route.[2] An unusual feature of the rail pattern of the Dzhezkazgan region is that the broad-gauge line from Zharyk to Dzhezkazgan is replaced by narrow-gauge track from the latter town to the smelter at Karsakpai.[3] Until recently, this narrow-gauge line also reached the brown coal mines around Baikonur. The depletion of these reserves, however, has resulted in the ripping up of the narrow-gauge track between Karsakpai and Baikonur and, also, has indirectly increased the movement of Karaganda coal to the Dzhezkazgan region.[4]

By 1960, an additional source of traffic generation using the branch line from Zharyk should supplement the existing flow of black copper, destined for refining in the Urals. According to present plans, the iron ores of the Ata-Su deposits are scheduled

---

[1] Ibid., p. 215.

[2] K. A. Ballod, "Na Putyakh k Osvoyeniyu Krupneishey Mednoi Bazy SSSR," Sotsialisticheskiy Transport, No. 11 (November, 1934), pp. 77-78.

[3] Kazakhskaya SSR, p. 215. [4] Ibid., p. 221.

to serve as the primary ores for the blast furnaces now being installed at Temir-Tau, just outside Karaganda. In 1956, the proven reserves of the sulfurous, hematite ores of the Ata-Su group were estimated at 116 million tons, with an average iron content of 55 per cent.[1] In 1960, the yearly production of ore in this region is scheduled to reach 2.5 million tons. By 1965, the maximum yearly production of 4.7 tons will be attained if present estimates are achieved.[2] However, after 1970, it is anticipated that the production of ore in this region will drop off sharply. At present, a 70-kilometer broad-gauge rail line is being laid from the iron ore mines to the Dzhezkazgan branch.[3]

The long rail branch to the Dzhezkazgan area has thus re-oriented the direction of interregional trade and allowed the large-scale interchange of commodities to take place. This, in turn, has had a decisive effect upon the expansion of production at existing mines as well as the opening up of additional mineral-producing regions.

The Trans-Kazakhstan and the Turk-Sib magistrals have not only played a key role in the interregional trade of the Central Asian republics, but have also contributed to the development of mineral resources in the Kazakh Republic. Even ignoring their effect on mineral sites now in the initial stages of exploitation, the importance of this function can be evidenced by the fact that in 1956, Kazakhstan accounted for more than three-fourths of the lead, 40 per cent of the black copper, and 40 per cent of the zinc produced in the Soviet Union.[4]

Other Lines on the Approaches to Central Asia

During the Soviet era the Kazalinsk route has retained its position as the most direct rail route between Central Asia and the European portions of the Soviet Union. As mentioned above, this single-track route has persistently handled a heavy traffic burden in relation to its limited technical capabilities. Although the section of the Kazalinsk route between Arys' and Dzhusaly was barely able to cope with a 1932 traffic density of 1.25 million

---

[1] _Zhelezorudnaya Baza Chernoi Metallurgii SSSR_, IX, _Zhelezorudnyye Mestorozhdeniya SSSR_, ed. I. P. Bardin (Moscow: Izdatel'stvo Akademii Nauk SSSR, 1957), p. 367.

[2] _Ibid._, p. 540.

[3] _Ibid._, p. 319.

[4] _Yezhegodnik Bol'shoi Sovetskoi Entsiklopedii: 1957_, p. 133.

ton-kilometers per kilometer of track, the planned 1937 freight movement on this section was scheduled to reach 3.4 million ton-kilometers per kilometer of track, or more than double the 1932 density.[1] Writing in 1934, a Soviet authority, M. I. Fedorov, stated: "The Kazalinsk Direction up to the present time is still one of the worst bottlenecks on the entire railroad network."[2] Similar complaints are still being echoed in Soviet journals.[3]

Since the section of the Kazalinsk route north of Orenburg (Chkalov) had the densest freight flow, plans were revived in the early 1930's to lay a bridge line from Sol'-Iletsk, south of Orenburg, westward to Ural'sk--a railroad on a spur from Saratov. This 275-kilometer line was designed primarily to relieve the traffic congestion of the Kazalinsk route north of Orenburg by creating another rail outlet to the European portions of the Soviet Union. Construction of this route was initially undertaken in 1913 and continued until 1917, at which time the project was placed in "conservation."[4] In 1924, plans to continue construction were abandoned and the tracks already laid were ripped up and shipped to other portions of the country. Only eight years later, however, this project was renewed, and was finally completed in 1939. The success of this line in reducing the traffic burden of the northern portion of the Kazalinsk seems rather limited in the light of the continued criticism up to the present day of the extreme overcrowding of this route.

In order to facilitate the flow of petroleum from the Caucasus to the Urals, the Soviets developed a rail line from the port of Gur'yev on the Caspian Sea to the city of Orsk in the southern Urals in 1944. The initial phase of construction of this line, entailing the replacement of narrow-gauge track from Gur'yev to Makat by broad-gauge track, began in 1936.[5] This line at present

---

[1]M. I. Fedorov, "Puti Rekonstruktsii Zheleznodorozhnykh Vykhodov iz Srednei Azii," Sotialisticheskiy Transport, No. 1 (January, 1934), p. 57.

[2]Ibid., p. 61.

[3]Tulyaganov, Zheleznodorozhnyy Transport, XXXVIII (September, 1957), 6.

[4]Gel'fman, Sotsialisticheskiy Transport, No. 11 (November, 1934), pp. 48-49.

[5]K. A. Ballod, "Perspektivy Razvitiya Seti Zheleznykh Dorog v Kazakhskoi SSR," Sotsialisticheskiy Transport, No. 7 (July, 1937), p. 75.

does not handle a large volume of transit traffic. In the year 1955, the total maritime trade of Kazkhstan (primarily Gur'yev) was only 711,000 tons, of which 590,000 tons, or 83 per cent of the total consisted of petroleum imports.[1] There are, however, several sources of local freight originations. One of these is petroleum; in crude form from the Emba oil fields served by the branch line to Koschagyl, and in refined form from the Gur'yev and Orsk refineries. But this also is evidently not a large-scale movement because the total petroleum production of Kazakhstan in 1955 was only 1.5 million tons and, also, because the Gur'yev-Orsk rail line is paralleled by a 12-inch pipeline with a yearly capacity of 1.2 million tons.[2] Other local centers of traffic generation are the extremely important chromite mines at Khrom-Tau, which ship ore to Aktyubinsk for processing, and the fishing industries along the Caspian. Although the Gur'yev-Orsk line at present evidently handles a relatively small volume of freight, construction of the long-delayed rail line from Gur'yev to Astrakhan could transform the Gur'yev-Orsk route into an important component of a Caucasus-Urals magistral.

Competition from the Caspian-Volga Route

At the time of the October Revolution, Central Asia had efficient rail communication only with European Russia. Although the Caspian Sea and Volga River offered an alternative route, the all-rail route was considerably more important. In 1914, the rail route via Kazalinsk handled 76 per cent of the grain, and 69 per cent of the lumber imported by Central Asia, as well as 61 per cent of the cotton-fiber exports of this region. The Caspian route, however, handled 90 per cent of the petroleum imported by Central Asia.[3] The relative significance of the Caspian-Volga route in the interregional trade of Central Asia has declined considerably during the Soviet era. In 1950, for example, the Turkmen Republic handled a total of 2.7 million tons of maritime commerce, as compared with an estimated 11.4 million tons of interregional trade moving by rail between Central Asia and other parts of the Soviet Union.[4] When petroleum exports and imports are excluded, the total

---

[1]Transport i Svyaz' SSSR, pp. 106-107.

[2]Shimkin, p. 214.

[3]Arkhipov, p. 132.

[4]Maritime traffic data taken from Transport i Svyaz' SSSR,

volume of Turkmen maritime freight in 1950 was only 810,000 tons. In 1955, the sea-borne commerce of this republic reached 4.4 million tons, while the volume of non-petroleum freight was only 1.6 million tons.[1] By contrast, during 1955, an estimated 18.5 million tons of rail-borne freight were exchanged between the Central Asian republics and other regions of the Soviet Union.

The Caspian-Volga route has many drawbacks which have contributed to its declining relative importance in the movement of diversified commodities to and from the Central Asian republics. The northern part of the Caspian is frozen from two to three months during the year, while the navigation season on the Volga decreases from seven to eight months in the Lower Volga to an average of only 6.5 months in the middle and upper courses of the river.[2] An even greater deterrent to movement on this route is the high cost of transshipment, particularly at the open roadstead port of Astrakhan (Fig. 16).

Goods moving on sea-going vessels from Krasnovodsk, for example, have to be transshipped at the 14-foot roadstead of the delta port of Astrakhan into shallow-draft vessels which traverse the 200 kilometers separating the river port from the roadstead. In Astrakhan, the goods are transshipped again; only this time, into river barges.[3] The problems of the port of Astrakhan have been intensified in the postwar era by the accelerated decline in the level of the Caspian Sea, caused primarily by the increased diversion of Volga water for other purposes, such as the formation of a huge reservoir in back of the dam now being completed at Kuybyshev. In 1956, the average level of the Caspian dropped to 27.9 meters below sea level--the lowest level in the last 300 years.[4] Unless some of the extremely ambitious plans to increase the level of the Caspian by the damming and drainage of large portions of this sea, or by diverting water from rivers in the northern portions of European Russia, are implemented, the declining

---

p. 106. For a detailed discussion of method used to estimate interregional freight volume handled by rail, see chap. v of this study.

[1] Transport i Svyaz' SSSR, p. 107.

[2] G. N. Cherdantsev, N. P. Nikitin, and B. A. Tutykhin, p. 218.

[3] A. S. Shaposhnikov, Astrakhan': Geograficheskiy Ocherk (Moscow: Geografgiz, 1956), pp. 33-34.

[4] Z. G. Freikin, p. 53.

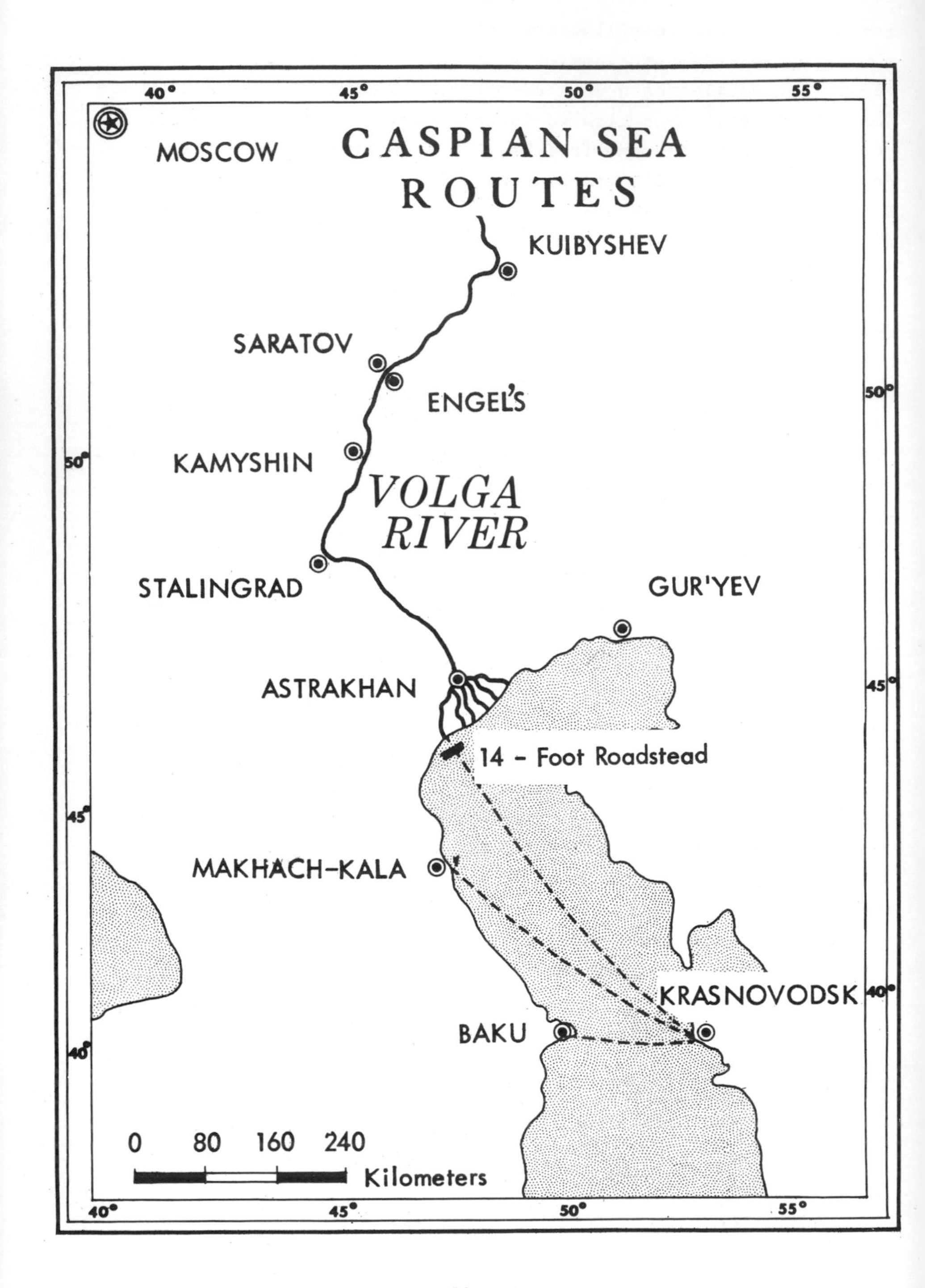
CASPIAN SEA
ROUTES
MOSCOW
KUIBYSHEV
SARATOV
ENGEL'S
KAMYSHIN
VOLGA
RIVER
STALINGRAD
GUR'YEV
ASTRAKHAN
14 - Foot Roadstead
MAKHACH-KALA
KRASNOVODSK
BAKU
0 80 160 240
Kilometers
40°
45°
50°
55°

Fig. 16

level of the Caspian will become an even more critical transportation problem after the completion of the huge Stalingrad Dam and the projected diversion of considerable quantities of Volga water for irrigation.[1] The high costs and delays of transshipment also greatly restrict the possibility of using a rail-water-rail route from Central Asia, with transshipments at Krasnovodsk and either Makhach-Kala or Baku in the Caucasus.

Still another problem limiting the growth of diversified movement on the Caspian-Volga route is that the economic center of gravity in Central Asia, in terms of both agricultural and industrial production, is located in the eastern portions of Uzbekistan--approximately 1,600 to 1,800 kilometers from the port of Krasnovodsk. For example, the rail transport inputs that would be incurred in the movement of ginned cotton from the Tashkent Oasis or the Fergana Basin to Krasnovodsk would almost be equal to those required to ship this commodity from the above-mentioned centers by railroad directly to the eastern rail approaches of the Volga. The restricted hinterland of the port of Krasnovodsk is also reflected in the fact that even the major cotton-growing region in the southern portions of the Turkmen Republic is located 900 kilometers from the port. However, Krasnovodsk is linked with the primary petroleum-producing center of Central Asia, at Vyshka, by pipeline. The easy access of Turkmen oil to the port of Krasnovodsk has helped intensify the specialized role of the Caspian Sea as a petroleum route. Finally, the Caspian-Volga route will encounter even greater competition from the railroad, in the event present plans to extend the Kungrad rail line to Makat some time after 1960 are materialized.

It seems surprising therefore that the Soviet Union has recently undertaken the development of enormous cotton-textile combines at the Volga cities of Kamyshin (approximately half-way between Saratov and Stalingrad) and Engel's (just outside Saratov). These plants evidently are going to receive substantial quantities of ginned cotton by water from Central Asia and Azerbaidzhan, but this by no means indicates that the Caspian Sea will regain its pre-eminence in the movement of ginned cotton from Central Asia. In fact, the rail lines will presumably handle a considerable

---

[1]The falling level of the Caspian has already greatly increased the cost of dredging the antiquated Volga-Caspian Canal, which links the city of Astrakhan with the Caspian Sea. Chances are, however, the worst is yet to come (Shaposhnikov, p. 16).

share of the ginned-cotton shipments to these plants. In this connection, the recently published economic geography of the Trans-Volga region, which was written at the Academy of Sciences of the USSR, states: "The selection of these points (Kamyshin and Engel's) for the creation of cotton-textile enterprises, to a large extent, was determined by the fact that the routes of existing rail lines and the rail lines under construction from the Lower Trans-Volga to the cotton regions of Central Asia are shorter than the old route by way of Chkalov-Kinel' (Kuybyshev)."[1]

Several methods have been proposed to increase the competitiveness of the Caspian-Volga route and thus relieve the traffic pressure on the Kazalinsk route. One of these was advanced in 1940 by K. Romanovskiy.[2] After citing the slowness and prohibitive expense of this route, he suggested that a train ferry service be instituted between Krasnovodsk and Baku in order to decrease the time and cost of transshipment, the major deterrent to movement on the Caspian. His proposal, however, has never been accepted. Soviet planners, at present, are attempting to develop relatively shallow-draft vessels which can travel from Krasnovodsk to Moscow without having to transship their cargo. This is the primary method now being adopted to overcome the imposing time-cost barrier to movement at the port of Astrakhan.[3] A third method designed to increase the utilization of the Caspian-Volga route is more of a punitive than a remedial nature. Under the general tariff reform of 1949, an exceptional tariff was levied on the movement of ginned cotton to the Industrial Center. From May 1 to September 30, the ginned cotton originating on the Ashkhabad and Tashkent Railroads (this includes all of Central Asia except northern Kirghiziya) for destinations in the Industrial Center via an all-rail route have to pay tariff rates 50 per cent greater than the general tariff for this movement.[4] However, as is usually the case with Soviet efforts to increase the relative importance of

---

[1]Akademiya Nauk Soyuza SSR, Institut Geografii, Povolzh'ye: Ekonomiko-Geograficheskaya Kharakteristika (Moscow: Geografgiz, 1957), p. 157. Cited hereafter as Povolzh'ye.

[2]Romanovskiy, "Paromnyye Perepravy," Zheleznodorozhnyy Transport, XXI (October, 1940), 52-53.

[3]Povolzh'ye, p. 433.

[4]D. I. Chernomordik, Zheleznodorozhnyye Gruzovyye Tarify SSSR (Moscow: Izdatel'stvo Akademii Nauk SSSR, 1953), p. 138.

mixed rail-water shipments, neither tariff inducements nor penalties have been able to compensate for the competitive debilities of the Caspian-Volga route. It might also be mentioned that highway movement between Central Asia and European Russia is virtually non-existent.

The Projected Interregional Rail Pattern

Since many of the freight-generating centers in western Central Asia now use a circuitous all-rail route by way of Kazalinsk to avoid using the Caspian route, the long-planned continuation of the Chardzhou-Kungrad line to Makat and Alexandrov-Gai would greatly increase the efficiency of the Central Asian interregional pattern (Fig. 17). The transformation of the Kungrad line into a transit route would shift the freight divide of the Kazalinsk route to an area just west of Ursat'yevskaya. This means that on the basis of distance alone it would be more efficient for areas located to the west of the above-mentioned point to use the Kungrad rather than the Kazalinsk route for trade with the European portions of the Soviet Union. A large portion of Uzbekistan, southern Tadzhikstan, and the entire Turkmen Republic would be in the zone of transit dominance of the Kungrad line. The following table shows some of the savings in distance:

TABLE 7

DISTANCES TO MOSCOW BY SELECTED ROUTES
(Kilometers)

Route	Kazalinsk Route	Kungrad Route
Moscow-Stalinabad	4,639	3,731
Moscow-Ashkhabad	4,640	3,494

Although the abandonment of the ambitious Main Turkmen Canal project and the emergence of higher-priority rail projects have evidently made the extension of a Chardzhou-Kungrad line to the northwest seem less urgent in the eyes of Soviet planners, as mentioned earlier, this line is still scheduled to be extended to Makat some time after 1960.[1]

The only portion of an interregional trunk-line in Central Asia scheduled for completion before 1960 is an important 312-

---

[1]V. I. Petrov and S. S. Tsenin, "Razvitiye Ekonomiki Vostochnykh Raionov i ikh Transportnoye Osvoyeniye," Zheleznodorozhnyy Transport, XXXVII (October, 1956), 45.

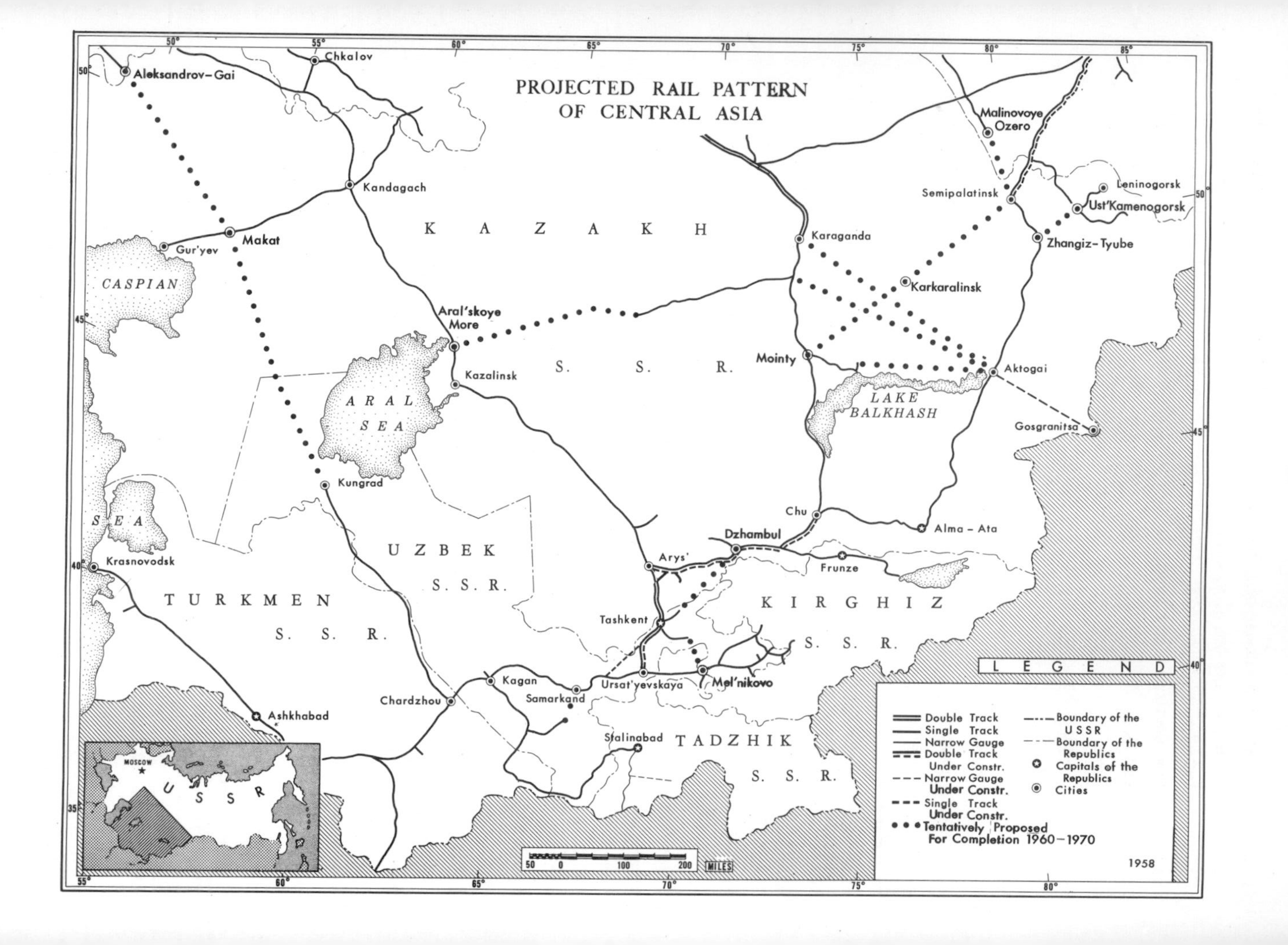
PROJECTED RAIL PATTERN
OF CENTRAL ASIA
Aleksandrov-Gai
Chkalov
Kandagach
Makat
Gur'yev
CASPIAN
SEA
K A Z A K H
S. S. R.
Aral'skoye
More
Kazalinsk
ARAL
SEA
Kungrad
UZBEK
S. S. R.
TURKMEN
S. S. R.
Krasnovodsk
Ashkhabad
Chardzhou
Kagan
Samarkand
Ursat'yevskaya
Mel'nikovo
Tashkent
Arys'
Dzhambul
Chu
Frunze
Alma - Ata
KIRGHIZ
S. S. R.
Stalinabad
TADZHIK
S. S. R.
Karaganda
Mointy
Karkaralinsk
Semipalatinsk
Malinovoye
Ozero
Leninogorsk
Ust'Kamenogorsk
Zhangiz-Tyube
Aktogai
LAKE
BALKHASH
Gosgranitsa
MOSCOW
U S S R
50 0 100 200 MILES
LEGEND
Double Track
Single Track
Narrow Gauge
Double Track
Under Constr.
Narrow Gauge
Under Constr.
Single Track
Under Constr.
Tentatively Proposed
For Completion 1960–1970
Boundary of the
USSR
Boundary of the
Republics
Capitals of the
Republics
Cities
1958

kilometer line from Aktogai, a village on the Turk-Sib, to the border station of Gosgranitsa in the Dzhungarian Gate (Fig. 17). At the Soviet-Chinese border this line is scheduled to meet the rail line now under construction from Lanchou to form another rail route between the Soviet Union and China. The original variant called for the construction of this line to Alma-Ata rather than the remote settlement of Aktogai, but it was rejected because of the high costs that would be entailed in crossing the difficult terrain on the approaches to the Kazakh capital.[1] If no connecting rail lines are laid in Kazakhstan, commodities using this route will have to follow a circuitous Turk-Sib-Kazalinsk or Turk-Sib-Trans-Siberian route in order to reach the European portions of the Soviet Union. One of the suggested alternatives proposes the construction of a short bridge line from Semipalatinsk to the railhead of Malinovoye Ozyero in order to provide Turk-Sib freight with a more direct route to the west. This line is now scheduled to be completed sometime between 1961 and 1970,[2] although it was originally planned to be finished between 1946 and 1950.[3]

The necessity of developing a more direct route between the Lanchou rail line and the European portions of the Soviet Union has resulted in ambitious plans to construct rail lines in Central Kazakhstan. One of the proposed variants calls for the extension of the Aktogai line to the branch line connecting Balkhash to the Trans-Kazakhstan magistral.[4] A different variant envisages the laying of a rail line from Aktogai to Zharyk, at the junction of the long feeder line to the copper-producing areas around Dzhezkazgan. The Dzhezkazgan branch line would be converted into a through route by construction of a frequently-proposed line to the Kazalinsk route.[5] A third proposal calls for the construction of a direct line from Aktogai to Karaganda.[6]

---

[1] N. G. Bochkarev, "Novoye Zheleznodorozhnoye Stroitel'stvo i Razvitiye Transportnykh Svyazyei," Zheleznodorozhnyy Transport, XXXVII (February, 1956), 34.

[2] Petrov and Tsenin, Zheleznodorozhnyy Transport, XXXVII (October, 1956), 45.

[3] I. V. Kovalyev, Zheleznodorozhnyy Transport v Novoi Stalinskoi Pyatiletke (Moscow: Transzheldorizdat, 1946), p. 18.

[4] Gudok, September 30, 1956. [5] Ibid.

[6] F. P. Mulyukin, "Neotlozhnyye Voprosy Povysheniya Effektivnosti Kapitalovlozheniy," Zheleznodorozhnyy Transport, XXXVIII (July, 1957), 10.

Regardless of which, if any, of the above variants is selected, construction will not begin until sometime after 1960.

Another rail line in the tentative planning stages would run from Semipalatinsk to Mointy by way of the small desert mining center of Karkaralinsk. This line would provide a shorter route for commodities interchanges between Central Asia and Western Siberia, and would also provide rail access to the iron ore reserves of Karkaralinsk.[1]

Thus, despite the construction of two long north-south trunk lines in the eastern half of Kazakhstan, a great deal of new construction needs to be undertaken in this region, not only to facilitate the interregional trade of Central Asia with Kazakhstan and Siberia, but also to cope with an anticipated, large-scale, east-west transit movement.

Summary

By far, the largest share of capital allocated for rail construction on the approaches to Central Asia has been devoted to the laying of interregional trunk-lines between Central Asia, on the one hand, and Northern Kazakhstan and Western Siberia, on the other, in order to re-orient the raw material supply base of Central Asian consumers. The most widely publicized of these lines, the Turk-Sib, was placed in permanent operation in 1930. Despite a slow start, the Turk-Sib has become an indispensable link between Central Asia and the lumber and grain regions of Siberia. The Trans-Kazakhstan magistral grew by accretion, with long intervals separating the different phases of construction, and was not placed in operation until 1953. Just as the Turk-Sib eventually re-oriented the economy of Central Asia to new regional bases of grain, coal, and lumber supply, the Trans-Kazakhstan trunk-line has effected an increase in the role of Northern Kazakhstan as a supplier of the first two of these commodities to Central Asian markets. Both of these lines have thus remedied the previous inflexibility in the interregional trade orientation of this region.

Some of the important transit characteristics of the three trunk-lines on the approaches to Central Asia are revealed by Fig. 18, which shows the freight divides of these lines. For example,

---

[1] Gudok, April 27, 1957.

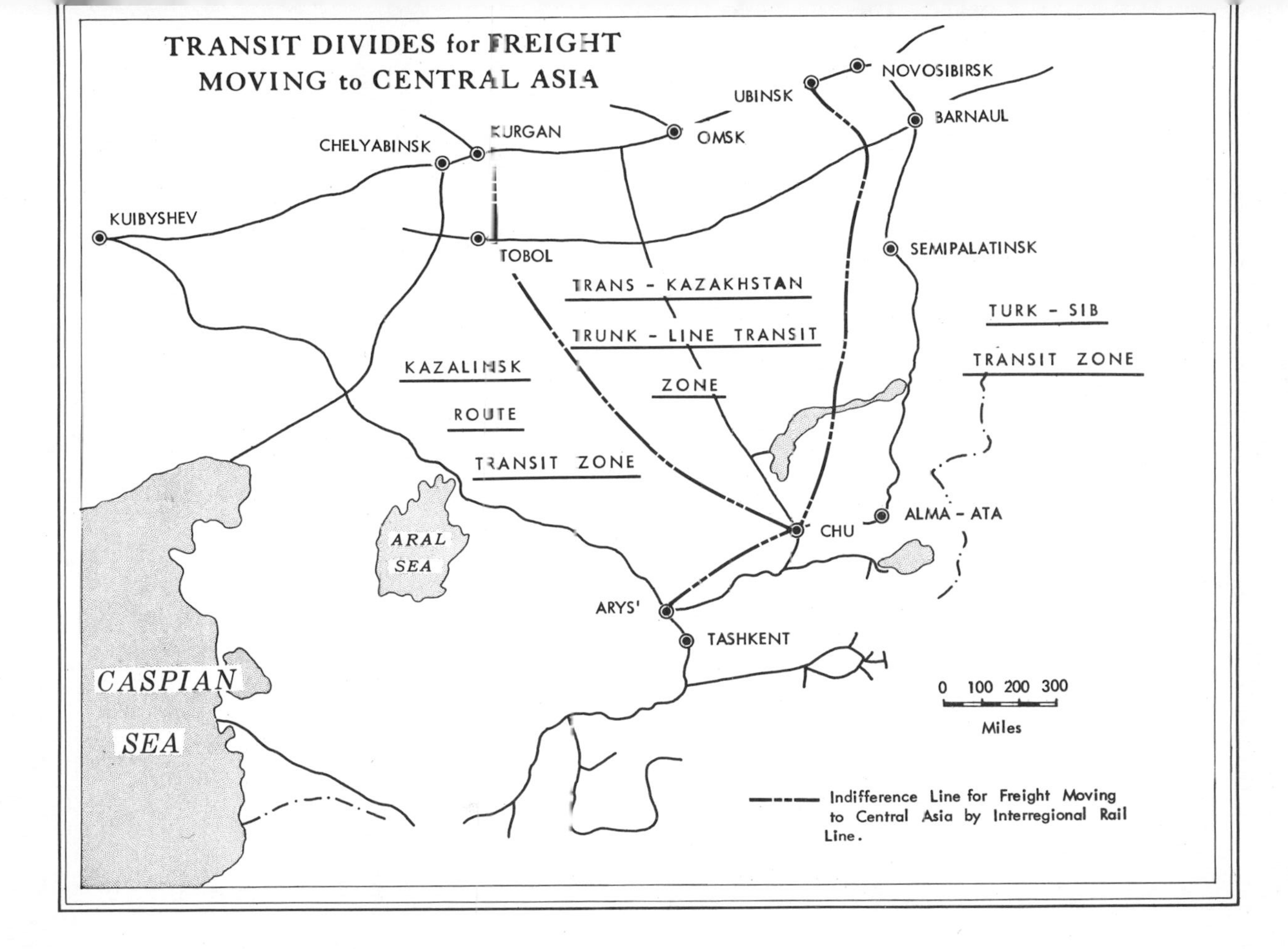
TRANSIT DIVIDES for FREIGHT
MOVING to CENTRAL ASIA
NOVOSIBIRSK
UBINSK
BARNAUL
KURGAN
OMSK
CHELYABINSK
KUIBYSHEV
TOBOL
SEMIPALATINSK
TRANS - KAZAKHSTAN
TRUNK - LINE TRANSIT
ZONE
TURK - SIB
TRANSIT ZONE
KAZALINSK
ROUTE
TRANSIT ZONE
ALMA - ATA
CHU
ARAL
SEA
ARYS'
TASHKENT
CASPIAN
SEA
0 100 200 300
Miles
Indifference Line for Freight Moving to Central Asia by Interregional Rail Line.

Fig. 18

freight divides of the Trans-Kazakhstan route were computed by determining the area within which the rail distance to Tashkent is less by use of this line than by the other two interregional routes.[1] Although Tashkent was used as the measuring point, the freight divides are applicable to all of Central Asia, except Northern Kirghiziya, because transit freight on the interregional lines must converge at the vital junction of Arys'. On the basis of this map the following conclusions can be reached:

1. The construction of the Mointy-Chu bridge line in 1953 to form the Trans-Kazakhstan Magistral has, in effect, created a wedge between the indifference lines separating the Turk-Sib line and the Kazalinsk route. This line has thus surmounted the imposing distance barriers in the form of circuitous rail routings which formerly impeded the establishment of effective interregional ties between Central Asia and the coal and grain producing regions of Northern Kazakhstan.

2. The Turk-Sib is still the most effective route for all transit freight moving to Central Asia from the Kuznetsk Basin and all the areas to the east of the basin.

3. According to distance indifference lines, the Kazalinsk direction would be the shortest all-rail route for all the freight interchanged between Central Asia and the Urals, as well as the area west of the Urals; that is, the entire European part of the Soviet Union. Movement from the Urals to the areas in Southern Kazakhstan east of the junction of Chu is shorter by way of the Trans-Kazakhstan line. However, when time and cost characteristics are taken into consideration, it quite probably would be cheaper and faster to ship commodities from the Urals into Central Asia by the Trans-Kazakhstan route.

The inefficiency of the shipment of commodities by way of the Caspian Sea, due in large part to the high costs of transshipment, and the high density of movement on the Kazalinsk route provide compelling reasons for the continuation of the long rail branch stretching from Chardzhou to Kungrad to the rail pattern of European Russia. However, the desire of the Soviet Union to another rail link to China seems to have given higher priority to the construction of rail lines designed to handle the anticipated, east-west international rail trade.

---

[1]All distances taken from the official passenger train schedule for the summer of 1957 (Ofitsial'nyy Ukazatel' Passazhirshikh Soobshcheniy: Leto 1957 Goda).

CHAPTER IV

THE TECHNICAL RENOVATION OF THE RAIL PATTERN OF SOVIET CENTRAL ASIA

The bulk of investment in the Soviet railroad system has been allocated for the improvement of the existing rail pattern rather than for the construction of new rail lines. A major result of the policy of emphasizing renovation rather than new construction has been a persistent increase in the average freight density per kilometer of route. At present, the Soviet rail system has by far the highest average density of movement per kilometer of route in the world.

TABLE 8

FREIGHT DENSITY OF THE SOVIET RAIL NET[a]
(Thousands of Ton-Kilometers per Kilometer of Route)

Year	Density
1913	1.1
1928	1.2
1932	2.1
1937	4.2
1950	5.2
1955	8.1
1956	9.0

[a]Transport i Svyaz' SSSR, p. 43

The methods adopted to achieve these high densities of movement were lucidly outlined by Tigran Khachaturov, the leading Soviet rail planner, in 1946:

> It is possible to recognize two main technical types of railway transport in economically developed countries: the American and European types. The American railways use heavy trains with a low density of movement. European railways use light trains with a high density of movement. . . .
> The railways of old Russia used light trains similar to those employed in Europe, but with a low density of traffic as in America. The railways of the USSR use heavyweight trains that approximate American weights. At the same time, they have

> a high density of traffic, as do European railways. Indeed, a new type of railway transport has been created, combining the best features of the American and European types of transport and ensuring a high level of efficiency in operation.[1]

The frequency of train movement in the Soviet Union has increased considerably since 1928 and is presently at a level equal to European standards. However, despite a rapid growth in train weights since the First Five-Year Plan, according to data compiled by Holland Hunter, the average gross train weights in the Soviet Union for the period 1951-1955, inclusive, were only 1,760 tons, or 61 per cent of the comparable American figure of 2,879 tons.[2] The Soviet Union is resolved to close this gap. The ambitious programs of rail electrification and dieselization now being carried out will undoubtedly increase average train weights considerably and should bring the Soviet Union closer to its goal of combining the "best" aspects of European and American operating methods.

In Central Asia and its approaches through Kazakhstan, there has been a great deal of rail construction since the October Revolution. However, as in other sections of the country, the growth of the demand for transportation has far outstripped the addition of new lines to this region (Table 9). The Soviets have been able to cope with the increasing volume of traffic by improving the technical characteristics of the pattern. Nonetheless, the rail lines serving Central Asia conform more closely to the European system of train operations in terms of train frequency and weight than the Soviet rail pattern as a whole. The congested, single-track lines of Central Asia handle a heavy volume of light-weight train movement.

Rather than attempt to present a comprehensive survey of the technical evolution of these lines, this section will deal with some of the recent efforts to expand the capacity of the rail pattern of Central Asia and its approaches in order to handle the enormous increments of traffic on the rail lines of this region since 1950. Most of the technical changes can be grouped into two categories: measures designed primarily to increase train speed and frequency; and measures which will increase train weight, as well as speed and frequency.

---

[1] Tigran S. Khachaturov, "The Organisation and Development of Railway Transport in the U.S.S.R.," International Affairs, XXI (April, 1945), 223. For an interesting comparison of Soviet and American rail operations see: Holland Hunter, Soviet Transportation Policy (Cambridge: Harvard University Press, 1957), pp. 126-44.

[2] Hunter, p. 140.

TABLE 9

THE GROWTH OF CENTRAL ASIAN RAIL FREIGHT, 1913-1956[a]
(Millions of Tons)

Year	Originations	Terminations
1913	2.7	2.2
1928	3.1	3.6
1940	12.9	13.8
1950	17.7	20.9
1955	25.8	31.3
1956	26.5	36.1

[a]Transport i Svyaz' SSSR, p. 67

Measures to Increase Train Speed and Frequency

Double-tracking.--Until recently, one of the most striking features of the development of the rail pattern of Soviet Central Asia and the approaches to this region was the complete absence of double-tracked lines. The rapid growth of freight movement in recent years, however, has led to the laying of second rails on those portions of line handling the heaviest volume of traffic (Fig. 19). At present, the double-tracking of the most important section of track in Central Asia, which is found between Arys' and Ursat'yeskaya, is almost completed.[1] All freight moving by rail between Central Asia (with the exception of northern Kirghiziya) and the rest of the country has to be funneled through this line. Traffic from the three interregional trunk-lines converges at Arys', while the junction of Ursat'yevskaya in the south is the focal point for rail lines serving the Fergana Basin and the western portions of Central Asia. In 1955, an estimated 18.5 million tons of rail freight in Central Asia was interregional and all but a small portion of this traffic had to be channeled through the section of track north and south of Tashkent. In addition, this section handles a great deal of local freight movement and through passenger traffic (see Fig. 20). In 1957, for example, a surprisingly high total of ten passenger trains daily in each direction traveled on the line between Tashkent and Arys'.[2] Thus, in the light

[1]Gudok, July 19, 1956. More precisely, double-tracking has taken place from Ursat'yevskaya to the junction of Shagir, approximately 30 kilometers south of Arys'.

[2]Ofitsial'nyy Ukazatel' Passazhirskikh Soobshcheniy: Leto 1957 Goda, pp. 483-91.

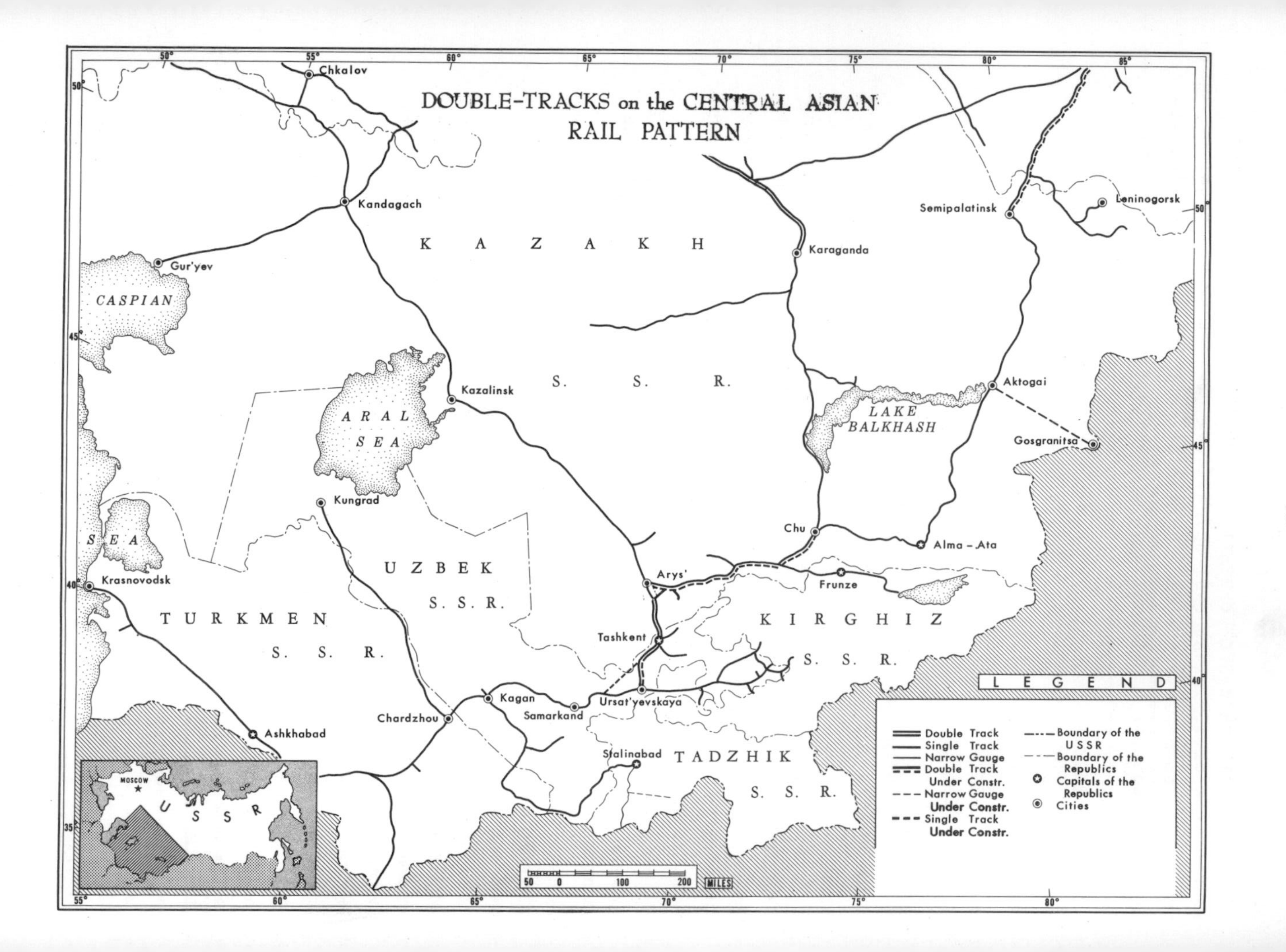
DOUBLE-TRACKS on the CENTRAL ASIAN RAIL PATTERN
K A Z A K H S. S. R.
U Z B E K S. S. R.
T U R K M E N S. S. R.
K I R G H I Z S. S. R.
T A D Z H I K S. S. R.
CASPIAN SEA
A R A L S E A
LAKE BALKHASH
Chkalov
Kandagach
Gur'yev
Kazalinsk
Karaganda
Semipalatinsk
Leninogorsk
Aktogai
Gosgranitsa
Alma - Ata
Frunze
Chu
Arys'
Tashkent
Ursat'yevskaya
Stalinabad
Samarkand
Kagan
Chardzhou
Kungrad
Ashkhabad
Krasnovodsk
L E G E N D
Double Track
Single Track
Narrow Gauge
Double Track Under Constr.
Narrow Gauge Under Constr.
Single Track Under Constr.
Boundary of the USSR
Boundary of the Republics
Capitals of the Republics
Cities
50 0 100 200 MILES
MOSCOW
U S S R

of the heavy traffic movement on the line between Arys' and Ursat'yevskaya, the laying of a second track is essential to the maintenance of efficient rail operations. Two other measures undertaken to relieve traffic congestion on this route, incidentally, have been the construction of a 36-kilometer bridge-line from the station of Badam, just west of Chimkent, to the station of Shagir in 1954 in order to by-pass the overcrowded Arys' junction, and the construction of the Dzhizak-Syr-Dar'inskiy line, which, among other things, will by-pass Ursat'yevskaya and shorten the transit distance on the Trans-Caspian by 50 kilometers.[1] The persistent failure of railroad administrations to divert sorting work from the large Arys' yards to other classification yards, however, has led to the use of the Badam-Shagir by-pass only by empty freight cars and direct-consignment petroleum shipments.[2] In the south, the construction of the Dzhizak-Syr-Dar'inskiy line is commencing at the same time the double-tracking of the parallel Syr-Dar'inskiy-Ursat'yevskaya route is being completed. Writing in Gudok, a Central Asian engineer, P. Chernov, estimates that after the completion of the Dzhizak by-pass the newly laid double tracks will be used to only 10-15 per cent of their capacity.[3]

Another section of intensively utilized route scheduled to receive a second track before 1960 runs from Chu, at the junction of the Turk-Sib and Trans-Kazakhstan routes, to the junction of Arys'.[4] The northern part of the Turk-Sib from Semipalatinsk to Aleisk has already been double-tracked, while a second track is now being laid from Aleisk to Barnaul through the fertile black earth lands of the Altai Krai in the Southern portion of Western Siberia.[5] However, from Chu to Semipalatinsk on the Turk-Sib there are no plans to lay another track on this line in the near future. Evidently Soviet planners feel that the single-track section of the Turk-Sib will be able to cope with the volume of traffic anticipated in the near future. The Chu-Arys' section evidently requires a second track to handle the interregional trade of Central Asia moving on the Trans-Kazakhstan and Turk-Sib trunk-lines, while the section of the Turk-Sib north of Semipalatinsk needs

---

[1]Gudok, July 19, 1956. [2]Ibid. [3]Ibid.

[4]V. S. Kulak, "Turkestano-Sibirskaya Zheleznaya Doroga-Pervenets Pyatiletok," Zheleznodorozhnyy Transport, XXXIX (October, 1957), 79.

[5]Gudok, March 31, 1956.

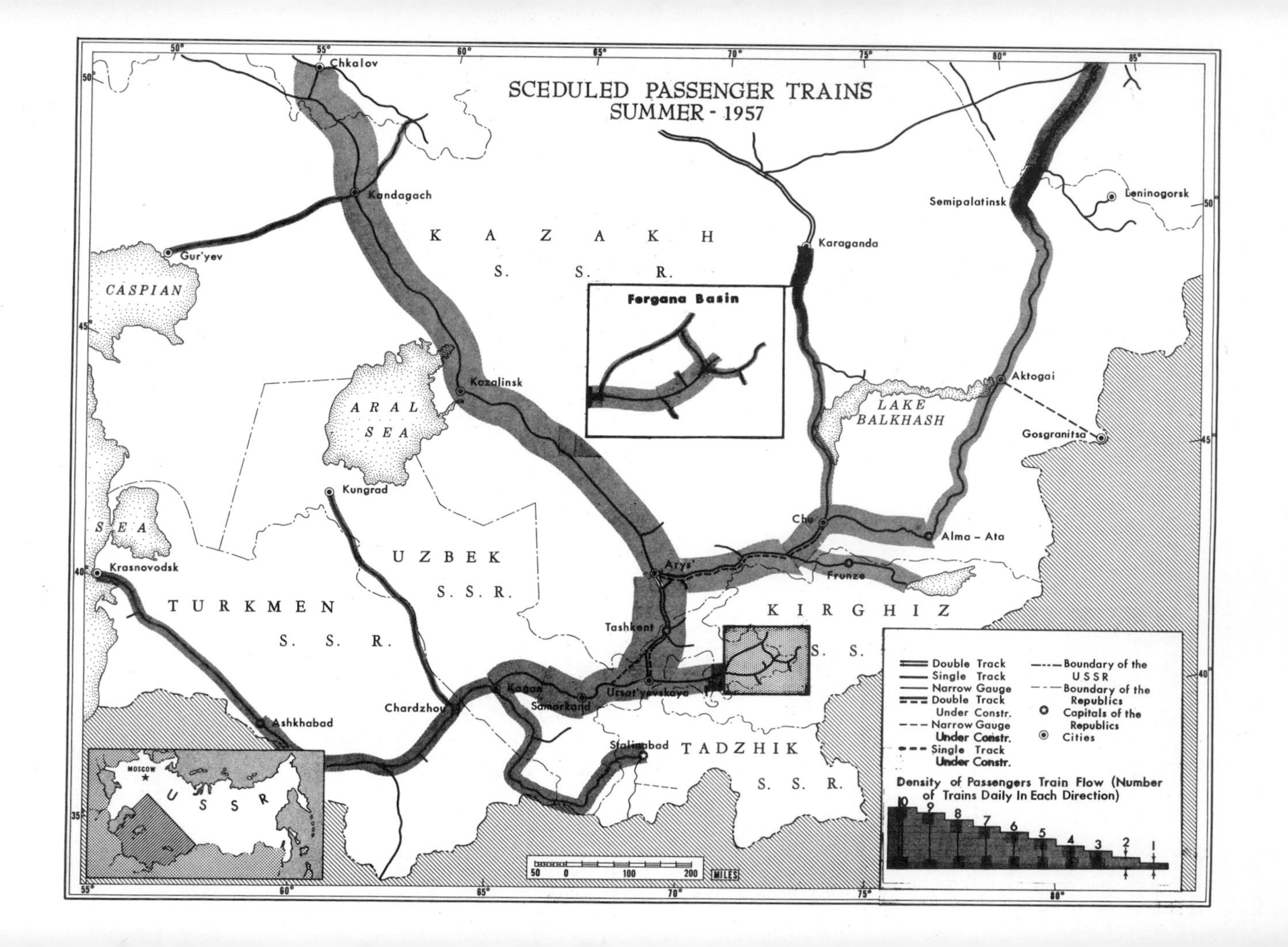

SCEDULED PASSENGER TRAINS
SUMMER - 1957
Fergana Basin
KAZAKH
S. S. R.
UZBEK
S. S. R.
TURKMEN
S. S. R.
KIRGHIZ
S. S.
TADZHIK
S. S. R.
CASPIAN
SEA
ARAL
SEA
LAKE
BALKHASH
Chkalov
Kandagach
Gur'yev
Kazalinsk
Karaganda
Semipalatinsk
Leninogorsk
Aktogai
Gosgranitsa
Kungrad
Krasnovodsk
Ashkhabad
Chardzhou
Kagan
Samarkand
Ursat'yevskaya
Tashkent
Arys'
Chu
Frunze
Alma - Ata
Stalinabad
MOSCOW
USSR
Double Track
Single Track
Narrow Gauge
Double Track Under Constr.
Narrow Gauge Under Constr.
Single Track Under Constr.
Boundary of the USSR
Boundary of the Republics
Capitals of the Republics
Cities
Density of Passengers Train Flow (Number of Trains Daily In Each Direction)
10 9 8 7 6 5 4 3 2 1
50 0 100 200 MILES

another track in order to cope with the increments of freight traffic generated by the opening of the virgin lands of the Altai Kray to cultivation.

One of the main reasons for the lack of double tracks on such lines as the Kazalinsk route is that, generally speaking, the laying of double tracks in the Soviet Union costs approximately 60-70 per cent as much as the construction of a new line.[1] Other less expensive methods have been more widely adopted to increase the freight capacity of the rail lines serving Central Asia. As a result, the lack of second tracks on the interregional magistrals remains one of the major technical limitations of the rail pattern of Central Asia and its approaches.

Signaling.--One of the most important developments in the technology of Central Asian and Kazakhstan railroads has been the intensified installation of advanced methods of signaling on the interregional trunk-lines since 1950 (Fig. 21). Prior to this year, the standard type of signaling on virtually all the rail lines of Soviet Central Asia was the antiquated electric-staff system under which trains relayed a metal rod which gave them the exclusive right to traverse the track between stations as long as the rod was in their possession. Thus, if a train immediately preceded another train in the same direction, it had to wait until a train in the other direction returned the rod.[2] Although electric-staff signaling evidently still predominates on most of the rail pattern within the four Central Asian republics, many changes have recently taken place on the interregional trunk-lines. One of the most important changes in signaling has been the introduction of automatic block signaling, with colored lights, on the double-track section of track from Tashkent to Arys' and the single-track line from Dzhusaly to Kandagach on the Kazalinsk route.[3] In addition, the Turk-Sib north of Aleisk is now being installed with automatic-block signaling.[4]

The installation of automatic block signals, which are set

---

[1]T. S. Khachaturov, Zheleznodorzhnyy Transport SSSR (Moscow: Transzheldorizdat, 1952), p. 137.

[2]Ibid., pp. 227-28.

[3]G. D. Orobinskiy, "Vazhnyye Voprosy Povysheniya Effektivnosti Ekspluatatsii Teplovozov," Zheleznodorozhnyy Transport, XXXVII (September, 1956), 18.

[4]Kulak, Zheleznodorozhnyy Transport, XXXVIII (October, 1957), 78.

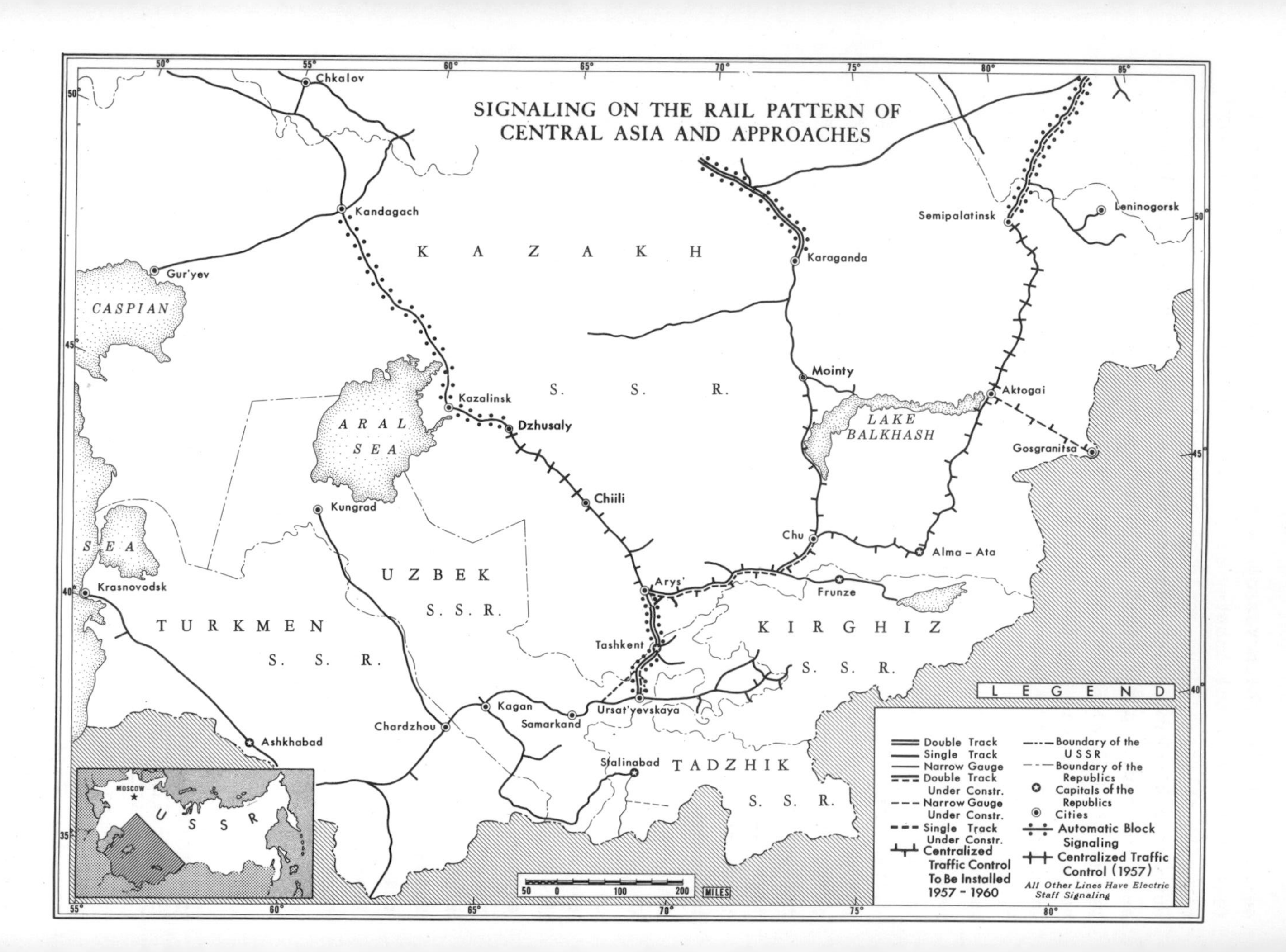
SIGNALING ON THE RAIL PATTERN OF
CENTRAL ASIA AND APPROACHES
Chkalov
Kandagach
Gur'yev
CASPIAN
SEA
Krasnovodsk
Ashkhabad
Kazalinsk
Dzhusaly
ARAL SEA
Kungrad
Chiili
Karaganda
Mointy
Semipalatinsk
Leninogorsk
Aktogai
Gosgranitsa
LAKE BALKHASH
Chu
Alma - Ata
Frunze
Arys'
Tashkent
Ursat'yevskaya
Samarkand
Kagan
Chardzhou
Stalinabad
KAZAKH S. S. R.
UZBEK S. S. R.
TURKMEN S. S. R.
KIRGHIZ S. S. R.
TADZHIK S. S. R.
MOSCOW
USSR
50 0 100 200 MILES
LEGEND
Double Track
Single Track
Narrow Gauge
Double Track Under Constr.
Narrow Gauge Under Constr.
Single Track Under Constr.
Centralized Traffic Control To Be Installed 1957 - 1960
Boundary of the USSR
Boundary of the Republics
Capitals of the Republics
Cities
Automatic Block Signaling
Centralized Traffic Control (1957)
All Other Lines Have Electric Staff Signaling

automatically by the movement of trains, is particularly effective on double-track lines. According to Soviet estimates, freight capacity on these lines could be doubled with the installation of automatic blocking at an average cost of 100,000 rubles per kilometer of route, as compared to an estimated cost of 480,000-750,000 rubles per kilometer for the laying of a double track in areas with level terrain (excluding the large-scale reconstruction of stations).[1] Automatic blocking is much less effective when applied to single-track lines, such as the line between Dzhusaly and Kandagach, because, on the basis of Soviet engineering data, the installation of automatic block signals on a single-track route will increase train capacity by only 7 to 10 per cent, on the average, in comparison with the electric-staff system although train safety is enhanced considerably.[2] However, the use of partial-packet movement, which consists of the allocation of time blocks for the movement of groups of trains in one direction, could increase possible train frequency by as much as 40 per cent.[3] One of the problems which has thus far hampered the effectiveness of automatic-block signaling on the Kazalinsk route is that on the section from Kandagach to Dzhusaly the only station with electric centralization of switches and signals is the junction of Kandagach.[4]

Another type of signaling receiving a great deal of emphasis on the approaches to Central Asia is centralized traffic control (hereafter referred to as CTC), by which colored-light signals on a 150-200 kilometer stretch of track are operated from a single control center. In 1936, the Soviet Union had 67 kilometers of track operated by CTC, and by 1954 this figure had been raised only to a little more than 300 kilometers,[5] as compared to a total of 19,572 miles of CTC route in the United States in the same year.[6] However, in the last few years CTC has become more

---

[1] A. E. Gibshman et al., Osnovy Proyektirovaniya Zheleznykh Dorog (Moscow: Transzheldorizdat, 1954), p. 318.

[2] Khachaturov, p. 228.

[3] B. M. Maksimovich and E. D. Fel'dman, "Effektivnoye Ispol'zovaniye Sredstv Uvelicheniya Propusknoi Sposobnosti," Zheleznodorozhnyy Transport, XXXVII (January, 1956), 13.

[4] Orobinskiy, Zheleznodorozhnyy Transport, XXXVII (September, 1956), 15.

[5] Naporko, p. 172.

[6] U.S., Interstate Commerce Commission, Sixty-Eighth Annual Report on Transport Statistics in the United States for the Year

popular with Soviet rail planners. Nearly all the sections of track in the Soviet Union with CTC are found on the approaches to Central Asia and, in particular, on the 275-kilometer stretch of track between Dzhusaly and Chiili on the Kazalinsk route,[1] and a 470-kilometer section on the Turk-Sib from Semipalatinsk to Aktogai.[2] The Director of the Turk-Sib recently reported that before 1960 the CTC system of signaling will be in operation from Semipalatinsk to the key junction of Arys'.[3] Finally, the portion of the Trans-Kazakhstan magistral from Mointy to Chu and, also, the rail line now under construction from Aktogai to the Chinese border are scheduled to be installed with CTC before 1960.[4] The primary motivation for the installation of CTC on these routes seems to be to allow the relatively freight-dense sections of track found in the desert and semi-desert regions of southern and central Kazakhstan to expand the frequency of train movement and at the same time reduce the number of signaling posts, which are expensive to maintain in these regions.

Soviet engineering data state that the installation of CTC on single-track lines should increase train capacity by only 14 per cent in comparison with electric-staff signaling. However, if the number of passings on the route is increased simultaneously, single-track train capacity should increase by 40 per cent on the average.[5] Thus far, the experience of the sections of the Turk-Sib and Kazalinsk routes equipped with CTC has fallen far short of the latter goal. After one year of operation, the train capacity of the sections of the Kazalinsk equipped with CTC increased by 20 per cent, while a comparable figure for the Turk-Sib was a disappointing 14 per cent.[6] After the installation of CTC, the average commercial speed (speed between classification yards including intermediate stops) on the Kazalinsk route increased only from 23.3

Ended December 31, 1954 (Washington: Government Printing Office, 1955), p. 9.

[1]G. I. Kolyada, "Ob Effektivnosti Primeneniya i Tempakh Stroitel'stva Avtomatiki i Telemekhaniki," Zheleznodorozhnyy Transport, XXXVII (September, 1956), 73.

[2]Kulak, Zheleznodorozhnyy Transport, XXXVIII (October, 1957), 78.

[3]Ibid., p. 79.

[4]Gudok, September 30, 1956.

[5]Maksimovich and Fel'dman, Zheleznodorozhnyy Transport, XXXVII (January, 1956), 13.

[6]Kolyada, Zheleznodorozhnyy Transport, XXXVII (September, 1956), 73.

kilometers per hour to 27.0 kilometers per hour, while commercial speeds on the Turk-Sib were raised from 25.3 kilometers per hour to 30.7 kilometers per hour.[1] Although these figures compare favorably with the 1956 netwide average commercial speed of 24.8 kilometers per hour, it should be remembered that the Kazakh lines quite probably have a considerably lower density of intermediate stops than the national average. Average speeds on the Turk-Sib route, incidentally, are scheduled to be increased substantially by 1960, when the electric centralization of switches and signals on the major freight stations of the system, including Semipalatinsk, Alma-Ata, and Chu is completed.[2]

Another characteristic of train frequency and signaling which deserves mention is the high density of train movement which the Soviets have been able to obtain by the more intensive use of such relatively outmoded measures of signaling as the electric-staff system. For example, in 1956, the section of the Ashkhabad Railroad between Ziadin and Kagan, which is equipped with electric-staff signaling, handled roughly 16 trains daily in each direction, including 11 freight trains, while sections of the Turk-Sib with CTC handled an estimated 15 trains daily, of which 12 were freight trains, and the CTC-equipped portions of the Kazalinsk route handled an estimated 24 trains daily in each direction.[3]

---

[1] Ibid.

[2] Kulak, Zheleznodorozhnyy Transport, XXXVIII (October, 1957), 78.

[3] The number of trains moving on the Ashkhabad Railroad is taken from a graphic schedule appearing in V. N. Osyannikov and V. N. Larin, "Vysokoproisvoditel'noye Ispol'zovaniye Teplovozov," Zheleznodorozhnyy Transport, XXXVIII (July, 1957), 67. Since trains not shown on this schedule also might have moved on this section of track, it seems likely the above figure of 16 trains daily in each direction is on the conservative side.

The density of train movement on the Kazalinsk route and the Turk-Sib was computed from data in: Kolyada, Zheleznodorozhnyy Transport, XXXVII (September, 1956), 73 and N. G. Kosorotov, "Tekhniko-Ekonomicheskaya Effektivnost' Vnedreniya Dispetcherskoi Tsentralizatsii," Zheleznodorozhnyy Transport, XXXIX (April, 1958), p. 67. In 1956, after the installation of CTC on a 275-kilometer stretch of the Kazalinsk route, for example, 58.9 freight train hours per day were saved. The average commercial speed of trains on this section (including intermediate stops) before the installation of CTC was 23.3 kilometers per hour, while after CTC was installed, this figure rose to 27.0 kilometers per hour. The time consumed by a train in traveling the 275 kilometers on this stretch at the post-CTC speed of 27.0 kilometers was subtracted from the time required by trains at the pre-CTC average speed of 23.3 kilometers per hour to arrive at the savings in hours and minutes of

Thus in an effort to move a greater number of trains at higher speeds, Soviet planners have accelerated the laying of double tracks and the installation of advanced methods of signaling in the period after 1950. Most of this investment has been channeled into the interregional trunk-lines converging upon Tashkent--the major gateway to Central Asia. Although these technical changes have increased the ability of the interregional lines to cope with the rapidly expanding demand for transportation, the existing high density of train movement, such as the estimated average of 48 trains daily on the sections of the Kazalinsk route with CTC (combined north-south movement), renders measures designed to increase train capacity, short of double-tracking, less effective than increasing average train weights.

Measures Designed to Increase Train Weight As Well As Speed and Frequency

Ruling grades.--One of the technical features limiting the weight and speed of trains is the ruling grade. In the Technical Rules of Rail Construction of the Soviet Union the maximum ruling grade of main lines is set at 1.2 per cent, while the maximum grade of branch lines is set at 2 per cent.[1] However, in several instances these figures have been exceeded. The ruling grade on most Soviet railways today varies from 0.35 to 1.5 per cent, with the heaviest concentration of ruling gradients falling within the category of 0.7 to 1.0 per cent.[2]

After the October Revolution, the Kazalinsk route was handicapped by the maximum grade north of Kazalinsk, a relatively high 1.1 per cent.[3] One of the goals of the first two Five-Year Plans was to reduce the maximum gradient to a more respectable 0.8 or 0.6 per cent. But apparently the grades on this route are still at least as great as 0.9 per cent. This is only slightly more than

---

an individual freight time after CTC was installed. This figure was then divided into the total freight-train hours per day saved by the installation of CTC to arrive at the number of freight trains daily traversing this section of the Kazalinsk route. The same procedure was used in estimating train density on the Turk-Sib. Incidentally, the figure of 24 freight and passenger trains daily in each direction on the Kazalinsk route is rarely exceeded on a single track line in the Soviet Union according to Tigran Khachaturov (Khachaturov, p. 150).

[1] A. E. Gibshman *et al.*, pp. 343-44. [2] *Ibid.*

[3] *Problemy Turkmenii*, pp. 335-36.

the ruling grade of 0.8 per cent on the Turk-Sib in the freight direction[1] and 0.7 per cent on the line from Mointy to Chu.[2] Although these ruling grades are not particularly high, Central Asian rail planners feel that double traction will be required on the most difficult portions of the Turk-Sib and the Kazalinsk route in order to handle trains weighing over 3,000 tons at reasonably fast speeds.[3]

One of the highest ruling grades on a main line in Central Asia is the 1.1 per cent grade encountered by the Trans-Caspian route as it crosses the Turkestan range just east of Samarkand.[4] But this figure seems quite low by comparison with the 2.7 per cent grade surmounted by the extremely expensive line from Stalinabad to Kurgan-Tyube.[5] This is just another of the numerous contrasts between the technical conditions on the interregional trunk-lines and the local rail lines within the Central Asian republics.

Rails.--Another factor influencing train weight is the weight of rails. The light weight of rails has been a major obstacle to the introduction of heavy locomotives. In 1925, for example, the heaviest rail in use on the Soviet rail net (Type I-A) weighed only 88 pounds per yard, while 89 per cent of the rail pattern had rails weighing less than 78 pounds per yard.[6] However, by 1939, 56 per cent of the rail pattern fell into the latter category.[7] In the postwar Five-Year Plans, the Soviets intensified their efforts to increase average rail weight. In the Fourth Five-Year Plan (1946-1950) two new types of rails, the R-43, weighing 88 pounds per yard, and the R-50, weighing 101 pounds per yard, were scheduled to replace 50,000 kilometers of lighter rail.[8] However, it seems likely that this program fell short of the

---

[1]Gel'fman, Sotialisticheskiy Transport (November, 1934), p. 53.

[2]B. I. Levin, "Stroitel'stvo Zheleznykh Dorog i Vtorykh Putey," Osnovnyye Voprosy Pyatiletnego Plana Vosstanovleniya i Razvitiya Zheleznodorozhnogo Transporta na 1946-1950 gg.: Sbornik Statey, ed. B. I. Levin (Moscow: Transzheldorizdat, 1947), p. 297.

[3]I. G. Beskrovnyy and M. N. Belen'kiy, "Effektivnost' Primeneniya Teplovoznoi Tyagi na Dorogakh Sredney Azii i Kazakhstana," Zheleznodorozhnyy Transport, XXXVII (November, 1956), 19.

[4]Uzkekskaya SSR, p. 248.

[5]Gel'fman, Sotialisticheskiy Transport (November, 1934), p. 53.

[6]Khachaturov, p. 159. [7]Ibid. [8]Ibid.

planned goals since type R-43 and R-50 rails were not produced on a large scale until 1947 and 1949, respectively.[1] In the Fifth Five-Year Plan, the policy of laying R-43 and R-50 rails was intensified, while a few short stretches of track with an extremely heavy freight density, such as the line from Novosibirsk to the Kuznetsk Basin, were equipped with a type R-65 rail, which weighs 131 pounds per yard.[2] As of January 1, 1955, slightly more than 41 per cent of the main lines of the Soviet Union were equipped with rails weighing more than 88 pounds per yard, most of which consisted of type R-43.[3] By contrast in the United States, 75 per cent of the rail net is equipped with rails weighing 89 pounds per yard or more.[4] Another difference is that in the Soviet Union, as of January 1, 1956, 18 per cent of the rail pattern had rails weighing 101 pounds per yard or more, most of which consisted of type R-50 rails, which weighed exactly 101 pounds per yard,[5] while approximately 60 per cent of the rail pattern of the United States was equipped with rails weighing 100 pounds per yard or more. Approximately 20 per cent of the United States pattern in 1954 had rails weighing more than 130 pounds per yard.[6] By 1960, the Soviet Union hopes to remedy some of the inadequacies in the weight of rails by converting an additional 58,000 kilometers of track to heavier rails.[7]

One of the goals of the Second Five-Year Plan (1933-1937) was to lay heavier rails on the entire Kazalinsk route and the entire Trans-Caspian line. However, rail weight on these routes was scheduled to increase to only 78 pounds per yard.[8] This means

---

[1]A. G. Naporko, Ocherki Razvitiya Zheleznodorozhnogo Transporta SSSR (Moscow: Transzheldorizdat, 1954), p. 229.

[2]Ibid.

[3]A. N. Naumov, "Perspektivy Usileniya Puti i Mekhanizatsii Putevykh Rabot," Zheleznodorozhnyy Transport, XXXVII (February, 1956), 9.

[4]ICC, Sixty-Eighth Annual Report on Transport Statistics in the United States, p. 9.

[5]Naumov, Zheleznodorozhnyy Transport, XXXVII (February, 1956), 9.

[6]ICC, Sixty-Eighth Annual Report on Transport Statistics in the United States, p. 9.

[7]Naumov, Zheleznodorozhnyy Transport, XXXVII (February, 1956), 9.

[8]U.S.S.R. Gosplan pri Sovete Narodnykh Komissarov Soyuza

that the weight of rails on the Kazalinsk route during the early 1930's when it experienced great difficulty in coping with the freight demands imposed upon it were of the type III-a, weighing only 68 pounds per yard. During the postwar era, particularly after 1950, heavier rails have been laid on the main interregional trunk-lines serving Central Asia. It seems reasonable to infer that these rails, for the most part, are type R-43 (88 pounds per yard), although the sections of track with the greatest freight density are probably receiving R-50 rails. At present, the R-43 rails are just barely able to cope with the 21-ton axle loadings of the recently introduced TE-2 and TE-3 Diesel-electric road locomotives, but if the planned train weights of 4,000 to 5,000 tons by 1965 or 1970 are to be achieved, a considerable investment will be required to replace the existing rails with still heavier ones.

Dieselization.--The most significant change in the technology of rail transportation in Soviet Central Asia and its approaches has been the widespread introduction of powerful Diesel-electric road locomotives since 1950 (Fig. 22). Although the locomotives on the Trans-Caspian route in the pre-revolutionary era burned petroleum in their boilers, coal became the primary fuel of the railroads of Central Asia shortly after the October Revolution. In the prewar Five-Year Plans, steam-condensing locomotives, the SO^{k} type, were introduced on sections of the rail lines of Central Asia and Kazakhstan experiencing great difficulty in water supply. In addition, low-power Diesel-electric locomotives were introduced on the Ashkhabad railway (the western part of the Trans-Caspian route) in the pre-war Five-Year Plans. However, Soviet efforts to increase the importance of Diesel traction did not begin in earnest until the first postwar Five-Year Plan.

By 1947, the Soviet Union had produced a total of only 48 low-power, Diesel-electric locomotives, although the first Diesel-electric locomotive was produced in the Soviet Union in the year 1931.[1] From 1947 to 1955, however, 873 Diesel-electric locomotives were constructed,[2] while from 1955 to 1960, 2,250 Diesel-electric

---

SSR, Proyekt Vtorogo Pyatiletnego Plana Razvitiya Narodnogo Khozyaistva SSSR: (1933-1937 gg.), I (Moscow: Partizdat, 1934), 238.

[1]Promyshlennost' SSSR, p. 220. [2]Ibid.

DIESEL TRACTION ON THE RAIL PATTERN
OF CENTRAL ASIA AND APPROACHES
Chkalov
Kandagach
Gur'yev
CASPIAN
SEA
Krasnovodsk
K A Z A K H
S. S. R.
Karaganda
Dar'ya
Semipalatinsk
Leninogorsk
Aktogai
Gosgranitsa
LAKE
BALKHASH
Kazalinsk
ARAL
SEA
Chiili
Kungrad
Chu
Alma - Ata
Lugovaya
Frunze
Arys'
U Z B E K
S. S. R.
T U R K M E N
S. S. R.
Tashkent
Angren
K I R G H I Z
S. S. R.
Ziadin
Kagan
Samarkand
Ursat'yevskaya
Chardzhou
Ashkhabad
Karshi
Stalinabad
T A D Z H I K
S. S. R.
MOSCOW
U S S R
L E G E N D
Double Track
Single Track
Narrow Gauge
Double Track Under Constr.
Narrow Gauge Under Constr.
Single Track Under Constr.
Rail Lines To Be Dieselized By 1960
Boundary of the USSR
Boundary of the Republics
Capitals of the Republics
Cities
Dieselized Rail Line
1958
50 0 100 200 MILES

road locomotives are scheduled to be placed in operation.[1] The three major types of Diesel-electric freight locomotive now in use in the Soviet Union are the 1,000 horsepower TE-1, the 2,000 horsepower TE-2, and the recently introduced 4,000 horsepower, two-section TE-3, which is scheduled to become the primary type of Diesel locomotive in use by 1960 (Fig. 23). The latter two types have axle loadings slightly over 21 tons.[2]

By 1960, slightly less than 25,000 kilometers of route in the Soviet Union were scheduled to be served by Diesel traction.[3] If implemented this would represent a significant achievement, since only 7,000 kilometers were Dieselized by 1955.[4] In 1955, Diesel traction handled only 5.7 per cent of the total rail traffic of the Soviet Union, but by 1960, the freight share of Diesel traction was scheduled to rise to 24 per cent; and by 1965, 42 per cent.[5]

At present (1956), 80 per cent of all the Dieselized rail lines in the Soviet Union are found in Kazakhstan and Central Asia. However, out of the total 14,700 kilometers of rail route in these republics, only 5,400 kilometers, or 36 per cent of the total, are Dieselized.[6] The use of Diesel-electric locomotives on the railroads of Central Asia and its rail approaches has many advantages over the use of coal-burning locomotives. Some of these are as follows:

1. The lower water consumption of Diesel traction. This, of course, is particularly important in Central Asia because all the major routes pass through desert or semi-desert regions.

2. The lower operating and repair costs of Diesel-electric locomotives.

3. The increase in both train weight and speed Diesel traction makes possible.

4. The more efficient use of fuel associated not only with the inherent characteristics of petroleum and Diesel traction, but also by the replacement of bulky, long-haul coals, or low-grade local coals, by petroleum from the Turkmen Republic, the Fergana

---

[1] B. P. Beshchev, Zheleznodorozhnyy Transport SSSR v Shestoi Pyatiletke (Moscow: Transzheldorizdat, 1957), p. 61.

[2] Beshchev, p. 61.

[3] Gudok, November 14, 1956.

[4] Hunter, p. 125.

[5] Gudok, November 14, 1956.

[6] Beskrovnyy and Belen'kiy, Zheleznodorozhnyy Transport, XXXVII (November, 1956), 19.

Basin, or the southern portions of the "Second Baku." The increased use of petroleum in the Soviet Union since 1955 represents a sharp reversal of the previous Soviet policy of conserving petroleum at almost any cost.

Since 1950, the introduction of Diesel-electric traction on the interregional trunk-lines on the approaches to Central Asia has proceeded at a rapid rate (Fig. 22). Diesel-electric locomotives are presently in operation on the Kazalinsk route from Kandagach to Chiili, as the first stage in the installation of Diesel traction on the section between Kandagach and Arys' by 1960.[1] The Mointy-Chu line, which has been Dieselized since its construction in 1953, now serves as the core for the spread of Dieselization to the north and west. By 1960, Diesel-electric locomotives will serve the sections of the Trans-Kazakhstan trunk-line from Mointy to Karaganda and, also, the long branch to the Dzhezkazgan copper mines.[2] By the same year, Diesel-electric locomotives will have replaced steam locomotives on the freight dense section of track between Chu and Arys' on the Turk-Sib.[3] North of Chu, however, the Turk-Sib will still rely upon coal-burning locomotives. Another line now served by Diesel traction is the trunk-line between Arys' and Ursat'yevskaya.

The primary type of Diesel-electric locomotive now in use on the Ashkhabad Railroad is the 1,000 horsepower TE-1, which is usually operated as a single unit. The low power of this form of traction is reflected in the low average gross train weight of this rail system, which equalled 1,370 tons in 1956,[4] as compared with the national average of 1,831 tons and the national average for Diesel traction of 1,939 tons.[5] In describing the TE-1 locomotive, Khachaturov states: "The 1,000 horsepower TE-1 Diesel series is designed for slow speeds. It is ineffective, and cannot

---

[1]D. P. Zaglyadimov, A. P. Petrov, and E. S. Sergeyev, Organizatsiya Gruzovogo Dvizheniya (3d ed. rev.; Moscow: Transzheldorizdat, 1956) (inset map); "Rabota Zheleznodorozhnogo Transporta v 1957 g.," Zheleznodorozhnyy Transport, XXXIX (February, 1958), 26.

[2]Zaglyadimov, Petrov, and Sergeyev (map).

[3]Kulak, Zheleznodorozhnyy Transport, XXXVIII (October, 1957), 79.

[4]Osyannikov and Larin, Zheleznodorozhnyy Transport, XXXVIII (July, 1957), 66.

[5]Transport i Svyaz', p. 61.

cope with any large-scale freight flow."[1] Central Asian rail planners have called for the replacement of TE-1 locomotives on the main line of the Ashkhabad Railroad by TE-2 type locomotives.[2]

The 2,000 horsepower TE-2 locomotive presently in use on the Kazalinsk route and the line from Arys' to Ursat'yevskaya has allowed train weight norms on these routes to be increased significantly. After Dieselization, train weight norms on the Kazalinsk route increased from 1,600 to 2,000 tons.[3] On the Tashkent Railroad (Fig. 24) prior to the introduction of Diesel traction, train weight norms were a very low 1,500 tons. After Dieselization, gross train weight norms in the "freight direction" (toward Tashkent) were increased to 2,300 tons, while trains weighing up to 1,800 tons were formed in the "empty" direction (away from Tashkent).[4] More recently (1956) trains weighing up to 2,700 tons in the "freight" direction and 2,300 tons in the "empty" direction have been operating between Tashkent and Syr-Dar'inskiy, to the south.[5] On the Turk-Sib route, large increases in train weight norms have been made possible by the use of double traction, consisting primarily of coupled SO^k steam locomotives.[6]

By 1960, the recently introduced, two-section TE-3 Diesel-electric locomotive, which has a power rating of 4,000 horsepower, is expected to become the standard type of Diesel-electric road locomotive on the rail pattern of Central Asia and approaches (Fig. 23). Only the Ashkhabad Railroad and the section of the Kazalinsk route between Kazalinsk and Arys', which has a relatively flat profile, can achieve high train weight norms with TE-2 type Diesel traction.[7] By the same year, Central Asian planners envisage train weight norms of 3,200 tons in the "freight" direction and 2,800 tons in the "empty" direction on the interregional trunk-

---

[1]Khachaturov, p. 201.

[2]Beskrovnyy and Belen'kiy, Zheleznodorozhnyy Transport, XXXVII (November, 1956), 19.

[3]Beshchev, p. 51.

[4]A. P. Troitskiy, "Opyt Vnedreniya Teplovoznoi Tyagi na Tashkentskoi Doroge," Zheleznodorozhnyy Transport, XXXVII (May, 1956), 33.

[5]*Ibid.*

[6]Kulak, Zheleznodorozhnyy Transport, XXXVIII (October, 1957), 79.

[7]Beskrovnyy and Belen'kiy, Zheleznodorozhnyy Transport, XXXVII (November, 1956), 19.

RAILROAD SYSTEMS IN CENTRAL ASIA
AND APPROACHES - 1957
Chkalov
Kandagach
Gur'yev
CASPIAN
SEA
KAZAKH
S. S. R.
ORENBURG
RAILROAD
Kazalinsk
Dzhusaly
ARAL
SEA
Kungrad
TASHKENT
RAILROAD
UZBEK
S. S. R.
TURKMEN
S. S. R.
ASHKHABAD
RAILROAD
Krasnovodsk
Ashkhabad
Chardzhou
Kagan
Ziadin
Samarkand
Ursat'yevskaya
Tashkent
Arys'
Tyul'kubas
Stalinabad
TADZHIK
S. S. R.
KIRGHIZ
S. S. R.
Frunze
Chu
Alma - Ata
TURK-SIB
RAILROAD
LAKE
BALKHASH
Mointy
Karaganda
KARAGANDA
RAILROAD
Aktogai
Gosgranitsa
Semipalatinsk
Leninogorsk
Aleiskaya
MOSCOW
USSR
50 0 100 200 MILES
LEGEND
Double Track
Single Track
Narrow Gauge
Double Track Under Constr.
Narrow Gauge Under Constr.
Single Track Under Constr.
Boundary of the USSR
Boundary of the Republics
Capitals of the Republics
Cities
Boundary Between Railroad Systems
Division Points Between Railroad Systems Are Underlined
1958
55°
60°
65°
70°
75°
80°
35°
40°
45°
50°

Fig. 24

lines serving Central Asia. The use of trains weighing 3,200 tons would actually decrease traffic capacity, however, on the portions of the Turk-Sib and Kazalinsk route with difficult profiles.[1] In addition to increasing train weights, rail planners believe that the use of Diesel traction will allow technical speeds (speed between classification yards excluding intermediate stops) to increase from 20 to 40 per cent from 1956 to 1960.[2] In this connection, however, it should be pointed out that in 1956 the net-wide average technical speed of steam locomotives was 37.2 kilometers per hour, which was almost as high as the 37.5 average technical speed of Diesel traction in the Soviet Union.[3] However, the more extensive use of relatively powerful types of Diesel-electric locomotives quite probably will increase the difference in the technical speed of steam and Diesel traction to the advantage of the latter form of traction.

Although the introduction of large Diesel-electric locomotives is an effective means of coping with the existing and anticipated levels of Central Asian freight traffic, many weaknesses are apparent in the present stage in the installation of this type traction on the railroads of Central Asia and Kazakhstan. Three of the problems which can be cited are: the lack of Diesel traction on many rail lines in this region; the extreme shortage of Diesel switching locomotives for yard switching work; and the widespread use of the relatively inefficient TE-1 Diesel-electric locomotive. The last of these problems has been described above. At present, the main lines of Central Asia are hampered by the lack of a uniform form of traction. The continuity of Diesel traction on the Trans-Caspian route from Krasnovodsk to Tashkent is interrupted by the freight-dense section from the junction of Ziadin to Ursat'yevskaya, which relies on coal-burning steam locomotives. As of early 1958, the section of the Kazalinsk route from Chiili to Arys' used steam locomotives, as well as the section of track northwest of Kandagach (Fig. 22). By 1960, however, Diesel-traction is scheduled to be extended southward to Arys'.[4] The entire main line of the Turk-Sib at present relies upon coal-burning locomotives with the exception of a small stretch of Dieselized route

---

[1] Ibid. [2] Ibid. [3] Transport i Svyaz', p. 54.

[4] Beshchev, p. 60.

between Chu and Lugovaya.[1] Even by 1960, only the portion of the Turk-Sib between Chu and Arys' will handle freight movement by use of Diesel traction.

Another type of line frequently lacking Diesel traction in Central Asia is the branch line. Diesel-electric road locomotives handle freight moving on the lightly loaded Chardzhou-Kungrad line, which, incidentally, uses TE-1 type locomotives, the freight-dense Tashkent-Angren branch, and a recently Dieselized 157-kilometer section from Kagan to Karshi.[2] But, for the most part, branch line traffic in Central Asia must still rely upon steam traction. Among the routes using steam traction are the rail lines of the Fergana Basin, the Stalinabad route from Karshi to the Tadzhik capital, and the branch line through northern Kirghiziya. By 1965, however, Central Asian rail planners hope that all the freight work performed by the rail lines of Central Asia and Kazakhstan will be handled by Diesel-electric locomotives.

Perhaps the most glaring defect in the Dieselization of the rail pattern of Central Asia and its approaches is the performance of nearly all the switching work in the classification yards of Central Asia and approaches by old, inefficient coal-burning locomotives, rather than by quick-starting, direct-transmission, Diesel-switching locomotives. Antiquated light-weight steam locomotives of the "Shch" series as well as other types of coal-burning locomotives handle most of the yard-switching work on routes even where the main lines are serviced by Diesel-electric locomotives. The contrast between the large, new TE-3 locomotives and the quaint steam locomotives standing side by side in a Central Asian freight yard is quite striking. In addition to being slow-starting and generally inefficient, the switching steam locomotives also make it impossible for stations on Dieselized routes to get rid of space-consuming installations associated with coal-burning locomotives, such as coal storage bins. The continued use of inefficient steam switching locomotives in Central Asia, as well as the rest of the country, is a problem recognized by Soviet planners. B. P. Beshchev, the Soviet Minister of the Means of Communication, writing in 1957, stated: "Regardless of the great effectiveness of the application of Diesel locomotives to

---

[1]"Rabota Zheleznodorozhnogo Transporta v 1957 g.," _Zheleznodorozhnyy Transporta_, XXXIX (February, 1958), 26.

[2]Osyannikov and Larin, _Zheleznodorozhnyy Transport_, XXXVIII (July, 1957), 67.

switching work, rail transport, at present, does not possess Diesel-switching locomotives, excluding the small quantity of low-power Diesel-motor locomotives now in use. In the 5th Five-Year Plan (1956-1960) a certain number of Diesel-switchers with different power capacities should be delivered to the railroads. For work at hump yards and large classification yards, a 1,100-1,200 horsepower Diesel and the TE-1 series of Diesel locomotive should be used."[1] Recently, Diesel-switching locomotives were introduced at the extremely large hump-type classification yard at Arys', evidently with good results.[2] TE-1 locomotives are also being used for yard-switching work at several Central Asian freight yards.[3]

Length of classification tracks.--A characteristic of the Central Asian rail pattern limiting the weight of trains which can be formed is the length of classification tracks in freight stations and also the length of route passings. The maximum length of classification tracks in the freight stations of this region, until recently, was 720 meters, which means that the longest trains that could be formed with 4-axle, 50-ton capacity boxcars with the standard length (including couples) of 14.73 meters could consist of only 49 freight cars.[4] At present, however, most of the large

---

[1]Beshchev, p. 62.

[2]Beskrovnyy and Belen'kiy, Zheleznodorozhnyy Transport, XXXVIII (November, 1956), 22.

[3]Osyannikov, Zheleznodorozhnyy Transport, XXXVIII (July, 1957), 67.

[4]At present, two standardized lengths of classification tracks predominate on the Soviet rail system--720 meters and 850 meters. However, before 1960, the Soviet Union hopes to lengthen the classification tracks on the Trans-Siberian between the Urals and the Kuznetsk Basin to 1,050 meters, according to N. P. Belen'kiy and N. P. Vasil'yev ("Udlineniye Priyemo-Otpravochnykh Putey-Vazhneisheye Zveno Rekonstruktsii Stantsii," Zheleznodorozhnyy Transport, XXXVII [August, 1956], 38-40). To compute the number of freight cars that can be grouped into trains on these short tracks, the length of coupled four-axle boxcars, taken from Khachaturov, p. 206, is divided into the length of the classification track. By contrast, in the Proviso yards of the Chicago and Northwestern Railway, the average length of the 59 classification tracks in use is 927 meters. However, trains of great length can be formed by the use of two or more departure tracks. (Interview with Harold Lenske, Director of Public Relations, Chicago and Northwestern Railway, June 7, 1958.) In the Soviet Union, because of the limited number of tracks in classification yards, the relatively short length of sidings, passings, and other reasons, maximum train lengths are usually computed on the basis of individual classification tracks.

classification yards on the interregional trunk-lines are extending the maximum length of their classification tracks to 850 meters,[1] which would allow trains consisting of 57 four-axle boxcars to be formed. Usually, however, trains longer than this latter figure travel on Central Asian rail lines by mixing boxcars with coal hoppers, which have a length of 10.03 meters, and also by continuing to use two-axle freight cars. The 850-meter length will be adequate to handle the anticipated train weights of 3,200 tons by 1960, but the planned train weights of 4,000 to 5,000 tons scheduled for the period between 1960 and 1970 would require the additional lengthening of classification tracks to 1,050 meters.[2]

Conclusions

The following conclusions emerge from the preceding discussion of the technical characteristics of the rail lines of Central Asia and Kazakhstan:

1. The primary method of coping with the rapid growth of freight movement on the rail lines of Central Asia and Kazakhstan since the early 1930's has been technical renovation rather than the construction of additional rail lines. Most of the technical improvements have been concentrated on the interregional magistrals and, also, the vital route between Arys' and Ursat'yevskaya via Tashkent, which forms the only rail link between the interregional trunk-lines and the internal pattern of the Central Asia (excluding northern Kirghiziya).

2. The less-expensive installation of advanced methods of signaling has had precedence over double-tracking as a means for increasing the train capacity of the interregional trunk-lines. Double-track lines are found on only the relatively short sections of track with the highest density of freight movement, and in particular, on sections of track where interregional traffic converges. On all the interregional rail lines, the installation of centralized traffic control, or automatic block signals, has proceeded at a rapid rate, particularly since 1950. However, most of the rail mileage within Central Asia still relies upon the relatively antiquated electric-staff method of signaling, but yet maintains rela-

---

[1]Beskrovnyy and Velen'kiy, Zheleznodorozhnyy Transport, XXXVIII (November, 1956), 2.

[2]Ibid.

tively high frequencies of train movement. The prospects of increasing the density of train movement on the single-track interregional trunk-lines beyond 1960, without the laying of a second track, seem rather limited because of the existing high density of train movement.

3. The most important method of increasing the capacity of the rail lines of Central Asia and Kazakhstan to handle the anticipated 35 to 45 per cent growth in traffic from 1955 to 1960 will be to raise the average weight of trains. This will be achieved primarily by the widespread introduction of relatively powerful Diesel-electric locomotives. By 1965, Soviet rail planners hope to eliminate two of the major weaknesses in the present stage of Dieselization in Central Asia and Kazakhstan: the lack of uniform Diesel service on main lines and branch lines; and, the use of coal-burning steam locomotives to handle yard-switching work. Increasing the weight of trains to handle the expected volume of traffic after 1960, however, is going to require large-scale additional investment for projects such as the laying of heavier rails and the lengthening of classification tracks in Central Asian freight stations.

4. Soviet transportation policy in Central Asia and Kazakhstan, until recently, has been characterized by persistent delays in the installation of technical improvements, such as second tracks and advanced methods of signaling. Most of the traffic growth of this region was handled by means of the more intensive utilization of existing plant and equipment. To a certain extent, this policy has now been reversed because of the unprecedented absolute growth of traffic since 1950; the apparent inability of "reserve" capacity to cope with the existing and anticipated demand for transportation; and the increased ability of the industrial sector of the Soviet economy to respond to the demands of the Soviet rail system for additional plant and equipment.

CHAPTER V

THE INTERREGIONAL TRADE OF SELECTED COMMODITIES

The rapid economic growth of Soviet Central Asia and Kazakhstan during the Five-Year Plans has not only been accompanied by the construction of many rail lines and technical renovation, but also by an enormous increase in the volume of rail freight originated and terminated in this region. Table 10 lists the changes in rail originations and terminations of the four Central Asian republics.

TABLE 10

CENTRAL ASIAN ORIGINATIONS AND TERMINATIONS BY RAIL[a]
(Millions of Tons)

Republic	1913		1928		1940		1950		1955		1956	
	Originations	Terminations	Originations	Terminations	Originations	Terminations	Originations	Terminations	Originations	Terminations	Originations	Terminations
Uzbek	1.1	1.7	1.6	2.4	5.4	8.7	8.8	12.0	13.1	18.4	13.3	21.4
Tadzhik[b]	0.1	..	0.1	0.1	1.8	0.9	1.8	1.9	2.6	3.3	2.7	4.0
Kirghiz	..	..	0.1	0.1	2.0	1.3	2.4	2.0	3.3	3.2	3.6	3.7
Turkmen[c]	0.5	0.5	1.3	1.0	3.7	2.9	4.7	5.0	6.8	6.4	6.9	7.0
Total	2.7	2.2	3.1	3.6	12.9	13.8	17.7	20.9	25.8	31.3	26.5	36.1
Difference between Orig. and Term.	0.5		-0.5		-0.9		-2.2		-5.5		-9.6	

[a] Transport i Svyaz' SSSR, p. 67.

[b] Tadzhik originations include a double-counting of coal mined at Shurab.

[c] Originations for Turkmen Republic include freight transshipped from the Caspian Sea to rail, while Turkmen terminations include rail-borne commerce transshipped to Caspian vessels.

From 1928 to 1956, the volume of freight originated by the Central Asian republics increased 8.8 times, while in the same period terminations increased ten times. Despite the enormous absolute increases in freight traffic, the share of Central Asian rail freight in the national total has remained remarkably stable since 1928. In that year, Central Asian rail originations accounted for 2.0 per cent of the national figure and terminations amounted to 2.4 per cent of all-union terminations, while in 1956 these figures were 2.0 and 2.7 respectively. Thus the growth of Central Asian rail traffic has proceeded at a rate similar to the national average. Another important characteristic of the rail freight of Central Asia is the dominance of the Uzbek Republic in the freight originations and terminations of this region. In 1956, for example, Uzbekistan originated 50 per cent of Central Asian rail originations, while terminating 59 per cent of the total volume of rail terminations in this region.

The detailed discussion of the evolution of individual commodity flows which will follow should first be placed in broader perspective by examining a set of maps depicting the changing role of four commodity groups--grain, forest products, coal (including lignite), and petroleum--in the rail freight of the Central Asian republics from 1940 to 1956, a period which is of particular interest to this study (see Figs. 25 to 28). Unfortunately detailed information about the movement of other important commodities, such as ginned cotton, is unavailable. Another qualification to these maps is that the four commodities listed above were depicted only if they accounted for 5 per cent or more of the freight of a particular union republic on the individual origination and termination maps.

In examining the maps showing the freight originations of Central Asia in 1940 and 1956 (Figs. 25 and 26), one of the conclusions which emerges is that only coal and petroleum, of the commodity groups mentioned above, accounted for sizable percentages of the rail originations of any of the Central Asian republics in either year. The most striking features of these maps are the dominance of coal in the freight originations of the Kirghiz and Tadzhik republics and the importance of petroleum in the rail originations of the Turkmen Republic. Part of the petroleum originations in this republic, however, actually consists of imports of Caucasian oil via the Caspian Sea which are transshipped at Krasnovodsk. The most significant change from 1940 to 1956 shown on these maps is

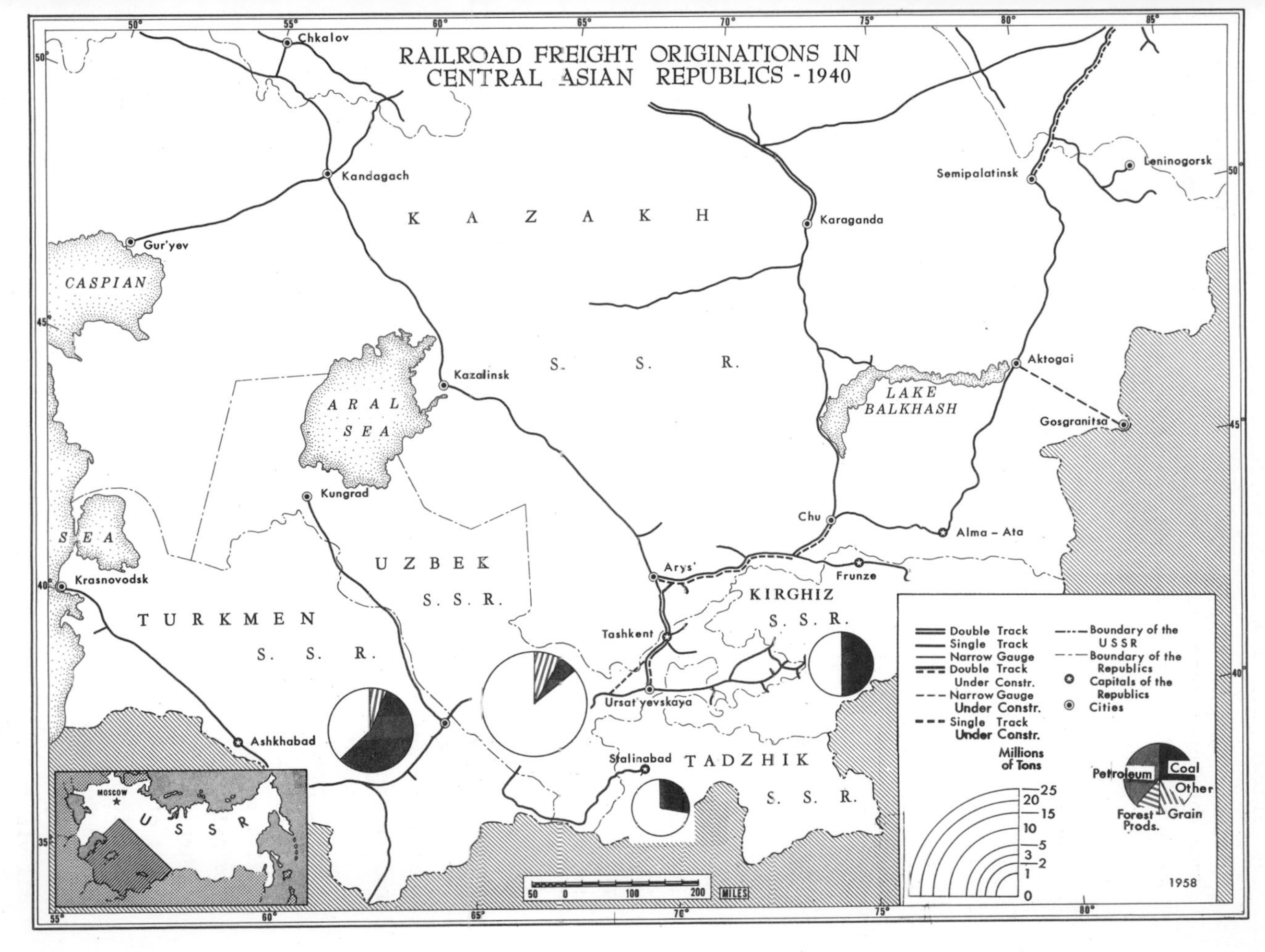
RAILROAD FREIGHT ORIGINATIONS IN CENTRAL ASIAN REPUBLICS - 1940
Chkalov
Kandagach
Gur'yev
CASPIAN SEA
Krasnovodsk
Ashkhabad
ARAL SEA
Kungrad
Kazalinsk
Karaganda
Semipalatinsk
Leninogorsk
Aktogai
Gosgranitsa
LAKE BALKHASH
Chu
Alma - Ata
Frunze
Arys'
Tashkent
Ursat'yevskaya
Stalinabad
K A Z A K H S. S. R.
T U R K M E N S. S. R.
U Z B E K S. S. R.
KIRGHIZ S. S. R.
T A D Z H I K S. S. R.
U S S R
MOSCOW
Double Track
Single Track
Narrow Gauge
Double Track Under Constr.
Narrow Gauge Under Constr.
Single Track Under Constr.
Boundary of the U S S R
Boundary of the Republics
Capitals of the Republics
Cities
Millions of Tons
25
20
15
10
5
3
2
1
0
Coal
Petroleum
Other
Forest Prods.
Grain
1958
50 0 100 200 MILES

Fig. 25

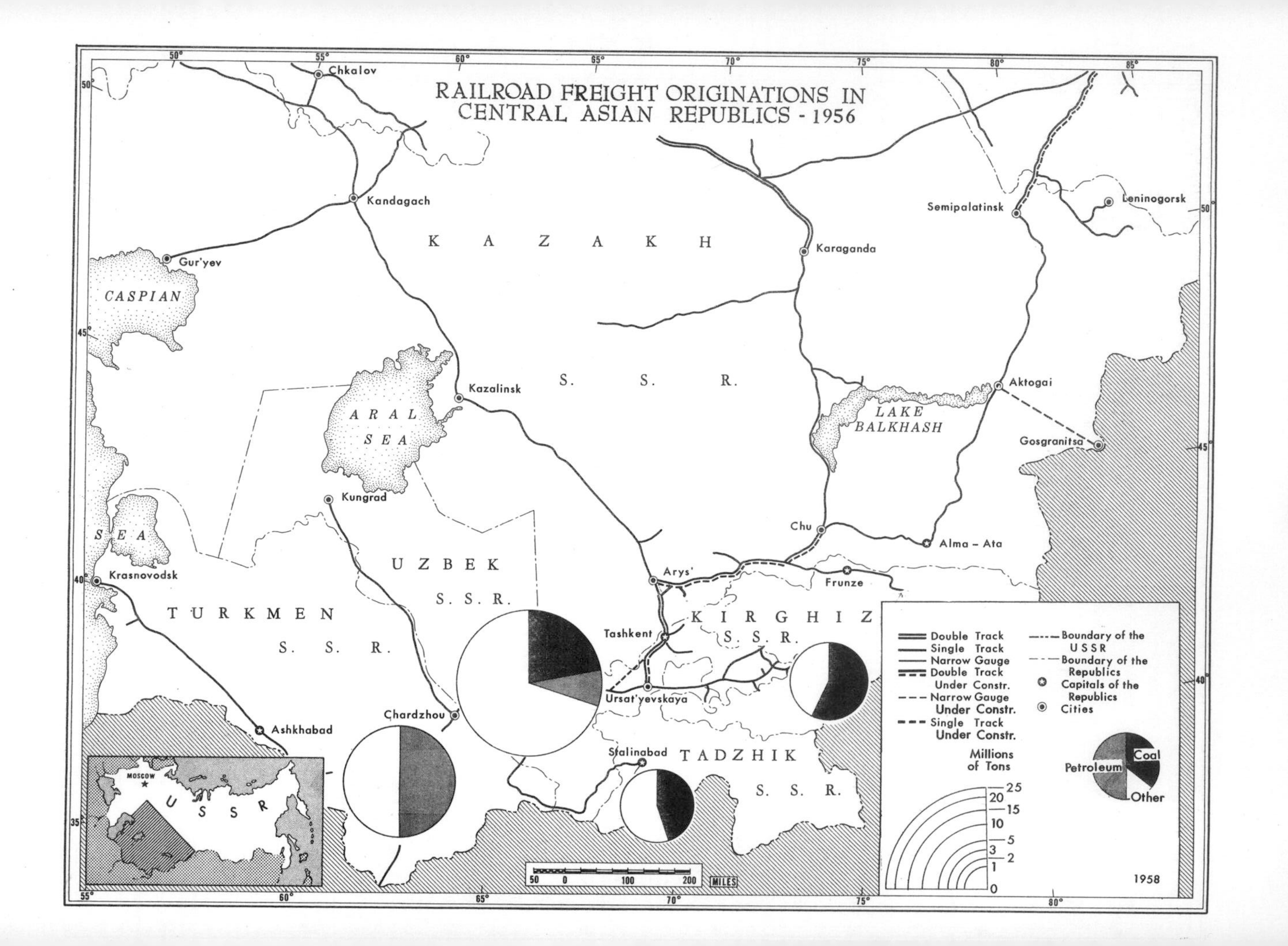

RAILROAD FREIGHT ORIGINATIONS IN
CENTRAL ASIAN REPUBLICS - 1956
KAZAKH
S. S. R.
UZBEK
S. S. R.
TURKMEN
S. S. R.
KIRGHIZ
S. S. R.
TADZHIK
S. S. R.
CASPIAN
SEA
ARAL
SEA
LAKE
BALKHASH
Chkalov
Kandagach
Gur'yev
Kazalinsk
Kungrad
Krasnovodsk
Ashkhabad
Chardzhou
Karaganda
Semipalatinsk
Leninogorsk
Aktogai
Gosgranitsa
Chu
Alma - Ata
Arys'
Frunze
Tashkent
Ursat'yevskaya
Stalinabad
MOSCOW
USSR
50
0
100
200
MILES
Double Track
Single Track
Narrow Gauge
Double Track
Under Constr.
Narrow Gauge
Under Constr.
Single Track
Under Constr.
Boundary of the
USSR
Boundary of the
Republics
Capitals of the
Republics
Cities
Millions
of Tons
25
20
15
10
5
3
2
1
0
Coal
Petroleum
Other
1958

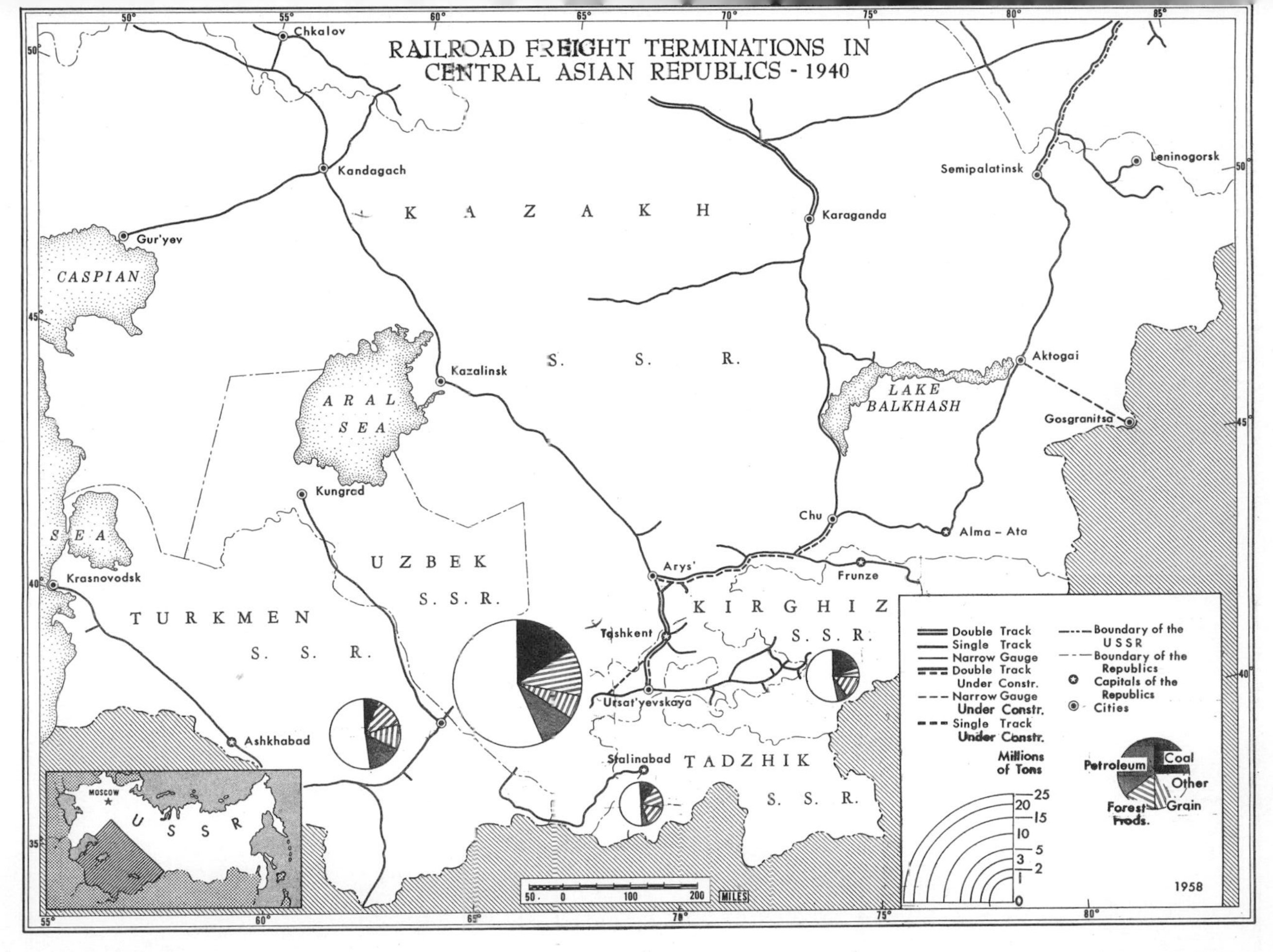
RAILROAD FREIGHT TERMINATIONS IN
CENTRAL ASIAN REPUBLICS - 1940
Chkalov
Kandagach
Gur'yev
CASPIAN
SEA
Krasnovodsk
Ashkhabad
K A Z A K H
S. S. R.
Karaganda
Semipalatinsk
Leninogorsk
Aktogai
Gosgranitsa
LAKE
BALKHASH
Chu
Alma - Ata
Frunze
Arys'
Tashkent
Utsat'yevskaya
Stalinabad
Kazalinsk
ARAL
SEA
Kungrad
UZBEK
S. S. R.
TURKMEN
S. S. R.
KIRGHIZ
S. S. R.
TADZHIK
S. S. R.
USSR
MOSCOW
Double Track
Single Track
Narrow Gauge
Double Track Under Constr.
Narrow Gauge Under Constr.
Single Track Under Constr.
Boundary of the USSR
Boundary of the Republics
Capitals of the Republics
Cities
Millions of Tons
25
20
15
10
5
3
2
1
0
Petroleum
Coal
Other
Grain
Forest Prods.
1958
50 0 100 200 MILES

Fig. 27

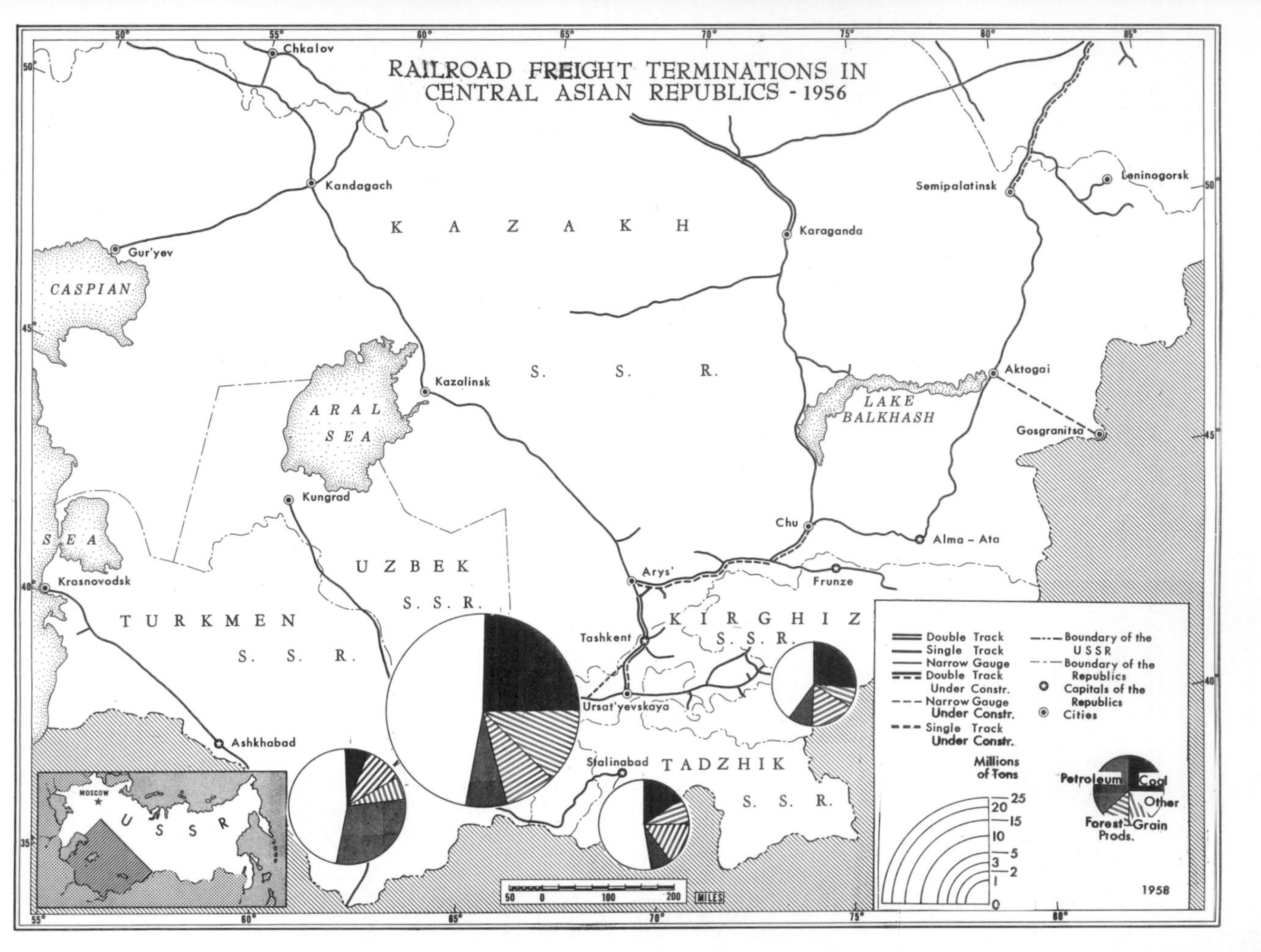
RAILROAD FREIGHT TERMINATIONS IN
CENTRAL ASIAN REPUBLICS - 1956
KAZAKH
S. S. R.
UZBEK
S. S. R.
TURKMEN
S. S. R.
KIRGHIZ
S. S. R.
TADZHIK
S. S. R.
CASPIAN
SEA
ARAL
SEA
LAKE
BALKHASH
Chkalov
Kandagach
Gur'yev
Kazalinsk
Kungrad
Krasnovodsk
Ashkhabad
Karaganda
Semipalatinsk
Leninogorsk
Aktogai
Gosgranitsa
Chu
Alma - Ata
Frunze
Arys'
Tashkent
Ursat'yevskaya
Stalinabad
MOSCOW
U S S R
Double Track
Single Track
Narrow Gauge
Double Track Under Constr.
Narrow Gauge Under Constr.
Single Track Under Constr.
Boundary of the USSR
Boundary of the Republics
Capitals of the Republics
Cities
Millions of Tons
25
20
15
10
5
3
2
1
0
Petroleum
Coal
Other
Forest Prods.
Grain
1958
50 0 100 200 MILES

Fig. 28

the growth of coal originations in the Uzbek Republic, primarily as a result of the intensified exploitation of Angren lignites.

The combined tonnage of grain, forest products, coal, and petroleum terminating in Central Asia is considerably greater than the volume of rail freight resulting from the origination of these commodities in this region. As Figures 27 and 28 reveal, the rapidly expanded volume of Central Asian rail terminations between 1940 and 1956 has been accompanied by a sizable increase in the relative share of these four commodities, taken as a whole, in the rail freight of Central Asia. In 1956, these commodities accounted for 49 per cent of total Central Asian rail terminations and 54 per cent of the terminated freight of the Uzbek Republic. Although coal was the single most important commodity, in terms of tonnage, on all the origination and termination maps, an important difference between these two sets of maps is the sharp contrast between the volume of grain and lumber originations and terminations. This reflects the large-scale interregional flow of these commodities to the Central Asian market. Thus, a study of the rail originations and terminations of grain, lumber, coal, and petroleum, together with an examination of ginned cotton freight movement based on less detailed statistical evidence, should provide valuable insights into Central Asian interregional trade and economic development in relation to the development of interregional rail lines.

Cotton

The primary interregional export of Central Asia is pressed, ginned cotton. Although the estimated volume of ginned cotton exports from this region in 1955 was only an estimated 1,114,000 tons, as compared to an estimated 656,800 tons in 1940, the extremely long hauls involved in the shipment of most of these exports to the major center of consumption, the Moscow region, have resulted in a large volume of rail ton-kilometer work. The greatest share of this freight burden has fallen on the Kazalinsk route.[1] It should be mentioned, however, that under the Five-Year Plans, cot-

---

[1]From data in Promyshlennost' SSSR, pp. 324-25, it was determined that Central Asia produced 3.9 per cent and 2.4 per cent of the spun cotton produced in the Soviet Union during 1955 and 1940, respectively. The volume of ginned cotton production in Central Asia in those years was then multiplied by the above percentages to arrive at an estimate of the amount of ginned cotton consumed within Central Asia. The resulting figures were then subtracted from total Central Asian ginned cotton production to arrive at the estimated volume of interregional exports.

ton textile combines constructed at Barnaul and Novosibirsk in Western Siberia, and Kansk in Eastern Siberia, utilize ginned cotton imported from Central Asia via the Turk-Sib. The enormous cotton textile combines at Kamyshin and Engel's on the Volga will import substantial quantities of Central Asian cotton by way of the Sol'-Iletsk-Saratov by-pass route, rather than by the main line of the Kazalinsk route through Chkalov. Despite the rapid growth of cotton-textile production in different regions of the Soviet Union, including Central Asia, since the October Revolution, the relative percentage of the Center, that is, the Moscow area, in the national production of cotton textiles only declined from 91 per cent in 1913 to 81 per cent in 1955.[1] As a result, the dominant flow pattern of ginned cotton still remains the movement from Central Asia to the Moscow region by way of the Kazalinsk route.

The development of rail access to the cotton-growing oases of Central Asia prior to the revolution made possible the transformation of this region into a highly specialized zone of commercial agriculture. The replacement of primitive modes of overland communication by relatively inexpensive and efficient rail transportation opened up the markets of European Russia for the cotton of Central Asia. This, in turn, contributed to the expansion of cotton acreage and the introduction of more efficient American types of cotton to replace the coarse, short-fiber indigenous types.

On the eve of the First Five-Year Plan rail transportation was called upon again to help intensify the specialization of the agricultural economy of Central Asia. During the Bashmakh Insurrection in the early 1920's, most of the cotton-growing areas of Central Asia were decimated. The harvest of raw cotton in Uzbekistan declined from 516,000 tons in 1913 to only 14,000 tons in 1921.[2] As late as 1928, the production of ginned cotton in Central Asia was below the 1913 level. The net result was that prior to the First Five-Year Plan, the Soviet Union was forced to import a large percentage of the ginned cotton consumed by her textile mills (Table 11). An effective method for achieving national self-sufficiency in the shortest possible time was to increase cotton acreage. As mentioned in an earlier chapter, one of the methods undertaken was to increase cotton sowings on the unirrigated lands of the Ukraine and North Caucasus. By far the most important

---

[1] Promyshlennost' SSSR, p. 332.

[2] Uzbekskaya SSR, p. 224.

TABLE 11

RELATIVE SHARE OF DOMESTIC GINNED COTTON IN TOTAL CONSUMPTION[a]

Years[b]	Per Cent
1907-1914	57.2
1924-25	42.3
1926-27	54.9
1927-28	59.0
1931	86.4
1933	97.4

[a]Uzbekskaya SSR, p. 225.

[b]The data from 1924 to 1928 are shown for years beginning on July 1 and terminating June 30.

methods of expanding cotton production, however, were to increase the amount of irrigated cotton acreage through the irrigation of new lands in Central Asia and, also, by the planting of cotton on large amounts of irrigated acreage in this region formerly devoted to the production of wheat (Table 12).

TABLE 12

IRRIGATED ACREAGE OF SELECTED CROPS IN CENTRAL ASIA[a]
(Thousands of Hectares)

Crop	1928	1931[b]-1932	Difference
Cotton	749	1,368	619
Wheat	844	305	-539
Rice	134	96	- 38
Vegetables and Melons	82	196	114

[a]Gaister, pp. 9-10.

[b]Data for cotton acreage are for the year 1931, while the remaining data in this column are for the year 1932.

A large percentage of the vast increases in the irrigated cotton acreage of Central Asia from 1928 to 1931 was achieved by a concomitant decrease in irrigated wheat acreage. Although the displacement of wheat to the lower-yield, dry-farming lands in the loessial foothills--fringing the mountainous regions of Central Asia--has increased considerably since 1928, the total Central Asian wheat acreage in 1956 of 1,517,000 hectares was still below the 1913 acreage of 1,769,000 hectares.[1] As a result of the increased irrigated acreage devoted to the production of cotton, Central Asia was able to increase its production of ginned cotton from 184,000 tons in 1928 to 321,000 tons in 1932[2] and, thus, help achieve national autarky. These increases occurred despite a drop in the average yield of raw cotton from 9.4 centners per hectare to 8.2 centners per hectare in the major cotton producing region--the Uzbek Republic.[3]

By 1955, primarily because of an increase in average yields to over 20 centners per hectare, but also because of an increase in irrigated cotton acreage to 1,741,200 hectares,[4] as compared to 1,368,000 hectares in 1931,[5] the Central Asian republics were able to produce 1,263,900 tons of ginned cotton--almost four times as much as was produced in 1932.[6] The continued intensification of the specialization of the irrigated lands of Central Asia on the production of cotton since 1928 is reflected in the fact that 56 per cent of the irrigated land of the Uzbek Republic in 1956 was occupied by cotton,[7] as compared to 33 per cent in the former year.[8]

The enormous increments in the production of cotton fiber in the Central Asian republics under the Five-Year Plans has far-reaching transport implications. One of these is that the growth in the interregional movement of ginned cotton from this region to European Russia has added considerably to the freight burden of the Kazalinsk route. Efforts to expand the relative share of the eastern regions of the Soviet Union in the production of cotton cloth, which would increase the relative importance of the Turk-Sib in the handling of Central Asian ginned cotton exports, have met with

---

[1] Narodnoye Khozyaistvo SSSR v 1956 Godu, p. 119.

[2] Promyshlennost' SSSR, p. 324. [3] Uzbekskaya SSR, p. 26.

[4] Narodnoye Khozyaistvo SSSR v 1956 Godu, p. 121.

[5] Gaister, p. 10. [6] Promyshlennost' SSSR, p. 324.

[7] D. Erlikh, "Ekonomicheskiye Problemy Razvitiya Sistemy Mashin v Khlopkovodstve," Voprosy Ekonomiki, XI (January, 1958), 47; B. Firsov, "Za Novyy Pod'yem Sovetskogo Khlopkovodstva," Planovoye Khozyaistvo, No. 3 (March, 1958), p. 57.

[8] Gaister, p. 9.

only modest success. The concentration of cotton-textile production in the Moscow area reflects the market orientation of this industry. Moscow is well-located to serve the densely-settled European part of the Soviet Union and industrial consumers, such as the nearby automobile tire factories.

Of greater significance than the increase in regional exports, however, has been the rapid growth of regional imports, particularly grain and lumber, accompanying the expansion of the cotton-based economy of Central Asia.

Grain and Lumber

The Turk-Sib was constructed specifically for the purpose of helping Central Asia to expand cotton production, which in turn would help attain national autarky in cotton fiber by making possible the large-scale import of grain from Western Siberia to fill the gap created by the anticipated decline of Central Asian grain production after 1928. At the same time, it was believed this line would relieve the overstrained Kazalinsk route from the task of meeting the lumber, as well as the grain, requirements of the Central Asian republics. The actual contribution of the Turk-Sib to the achievement of these goals, however, fell far short of the planner's expectations during the early 1930's. In the first place, the "cotton crisis" associated with the dependence of the Soviet Union on foreign supplies of cotton fiber had been resolved by 1931, the year the Turk-Sib was placed in permanent operation. The major criticism of this railroad after 1931 was that it failed to supply Central Asian consumers with the needed amounts of grain and lumber and, also, failed to divert a significant volume of traffic from the Kazalinsk route. The widespread disappointment in the Turk-Sib during this period was reflected in a talk given by the Central Asian delegate to the Conference on the Distribution of the Productive Forces of the Soviet Union in 1932, when he stated:

> The Turk-Sib was constructed to bring grain and lumber from Siberia. We are forced to admit that grain and lumber have not been shipped into Central Asia via the Turk-Sib by the end of the First Five-Year Plan. . . . In the First Five-Year Plan, we vigorously squeezed out grain cultivation, knowing that as a specialized sub-tropical region, we should develop cotton production for the entire nation. But we should receive grain and lumber from Siberia. Central Asia itself does not have an adequate supply of lumber, and, as for grain, generally speaking, Central Asia could produce sufficient quantities,

even more than it consumes, but this could be done only to the detriment of cotton.[1]

The primary reason for the failure of the Turk-Sib to meet its commitments in the early 1930's seems to have been a lack of coordination between the planning of the railroad and the Siberian economy. At the same time Siberia was called upon to supply Central Asia with grain and lumber, the Siberian grain and forest lands were just barely able to meet the needs of their local market, and hardly in a position to produce a surplus for Central Asian consumption. An official decree issued in May, 1932, called for the diversion to the Turk-Sib of all grain and flour moving to Central Asia by way of the Kazalinsk route and, also, directed that lumber production be expanded in Siberia to supply Central Asian needs.[2] Although the Turk-Sib had not lived up to expectations in reorienting the grain and lumber supply base of Central Asia, Soviet planners did not abandon their hopes of transforming this rail line into the fundamental route for the movement of these two commodities into Central Asia. A study of the evolving flow patterns of grain and lumber terminating in Central Asian markets since the early 1930's will provide a clearer insight into the interaction of the rail pattern and the interregional trade ties of the Central Asian republics.

Grain.--The grain traffic data shown in Table 13 indicate the significant increase in the minimum grain deficit (the difference between originations and terminations) of Central Asia during the prewar Five-Year Plans.[3] The increase in the minimum grain

---

[1]Ibid., p. 22. [2]Ibid., pp. 179-80.

[3]Determining the difference between the originations and terminations of particular commodities within the four Central Asian republics provides an estimate of the minimum amount of interregional rail trade in these commodities. This, in turn, provides an estimate of the minimum amount of trade because subtracting originations from terminations assumes that all originations of a particular commodity terminate locally. However, a certain amount of the originations of commodities that are relatively scarce in Central Asia, such as lumber, undoubtedly move beyond the boundaries of these region to nearby areas such as the southern portions of Kazakhstan. Even more important are qualitative differences obscured by the broad commodity groupings, such as in the case of ferrous metals, which also generate interregional exports of ostensibly deficit commodities.

The possible distorting effects of double-counting associated with interregional maritime trade on the minimum deficit or surplus of rail-borne commodities seem to be of negligible importance for every commodity except petroleum for two reasons: (1) Slightly less than two-thirds of the modest maritime trade of Cen-

TABLE 13

RAIL ORIGINATIONS AND TERMINATIONS OF GRAIN IN CENTRAL ASIA[a]
(Thousands of Tons)

Region	1928[b]	1940	1950	1955	1956
Uzbek SSR					
Originations	238	433	313	640	372
Terminations	613[c]	1,158	1,040	1,166	2,782
Difference	-375	- 725	- 727	- 526	-2,410
Turkmen SSR					
Originations	63	188	72	189	301
Terminations	148	314	196	590	924
Difference	- 85	- 126	- 124	- 401	- 623
Tadzhik SSR					
Originations	3	44	25	31	32
Terminations	0	140	113	185	408
Difference	- 3	- 96	- 88	- 154	- 376
Kirghiz SSR					
Originations	28	151	213	176	107
Terminations	10	98	72	187	223
Difference	18	53	141	- 11	- 116
Central Asia (total)					
Originations	332	816	623	1,036	812
Terminations	771	1,710	1,421	2,128	4,337
Difference......	-439	- 894	- 798	-1,092	-3,525

[a]Transport i Svyaz' SSR, p. 74; Mezhraionniy Gruzooborot, pp. 170-71.

[b]Data for the year 1928-29.

[c]Estimated from 1927-28 freight data from Mezhraionniy Gruzooborot.

deficit between 1928 and 1940 was caused primarily by increased terminations rather than decreased originations of grain by rail, despite the fact that grain crops occupied only 12 per cent of the total irrigated acreage of Uzbekistan in the latter year,[1] as compared to 52 per cent in 1928.[2] A major increase in the grain

tral Asia consists of the movement of petroleum, while only minor quantities of other commodities move by sea; (2) although commodities imported by sea and then transshipped to rail are listed as Central Asian rail originations, most of these commodities also terminate within the Central Asian republics and, thus, do not affect the minimum interregional trade estimates.

[1]G. N. Cherdantsev, N. P. Nikitin, and B. A. Tutykhin, p. 289.

[2]Gaister, p. 9.

deficit of Central Asia has occurred since 1950, particularly since 1955, because of increased terminations of grain.

The increasing grain deficits of Central Asia, associated with low, relatively stable production and rapidly expanding consumption, emphasize the importance of the interregional rail routes in the supply of this commodity to the highly specialized cotton-growing oases of Central Asia. Despite official decrees issued in the early 1930's calling for the Turk-Sib to handle all the grain imports of Central Asia, this goal was far from being achieved in 1937. In that year Central Asia imported grain from the following regions:

TABLE 14

CENTRAL ASIAN GRAIN IMPORTS BY RAIL, 1937[a]
(Millions of Tons)

Region	Imports
Trans-Volga	0.1
Northern Caucasus and Trans-Caucasus.	0.3
Urals	0.3
Ukraine	0.1
Western Siberia	0.1
Total	0.9

[a]A. E. Galitskiy, <u>Planirovoniye Perevozok</u> (Moscow: Gosplanizdat, 1939), p. 37.

Out of the total 0.9 million tons imported by the Central Asian Republics in 1937, it can be inferred that the Turk-Sib handled only the grain imports from Western Siberia, which totaled 0.1 million tons, while the Kazalinsk route handled the remaining 0.8 million tons. However, by 1940, the Turk-Sib finally became the main route for the flow of grain to Central Asian markets, when it handled 0.6 million tons of West Siberian grain imports, as compared to 0.4 million tons moving by the Kazalinsk route.

The most significant changes in the interregional grain trade of Central Asia has occurred since the opening of the virgin and idle lands of Western Siberia and Kazakhstan in 1954. The jump in the minimum grain deficit of Central Asia from 1.1 million tons in 1955 to 3.5 million tons in 1956, to a considerable extent, can be associated with the bumper harvest of grain in the virgin lands in the latter year. The vast increment in the grain terminations of Central Asia in 1956 indicates that quite probably Central Asia stored a large quantity of these imports for future consumption.

If so, these reserves would have played a vital role in meeting Central Asian needs during the 1957 drought which decimated the wheat crop in the virgin and idle lands.

Although the grain acreage of Western Siberia has increased considerably as a result of the virgin and idle lands program, the relative importance of West Siberian grain seems to have declined as a result of increased competition from Kazakhstan associated with the completion of the Trans-Kazakhstan trunk-line in 1953, and the expansion of the acreage under wheat in the Kazakh Republic from 4.0 million hectares in 1953 to 18.3 million hectares in 1956 as part of the virgin and idle lands program.[1] Kazakh grain enjoys a certain competitive advantage in the Central Asian market since the major zone of grain cultivation on the Trans-Kazakhstan magistral begins around Karaganda, 1,485 kilometers from Tashkent, while the closest area of intensive grain cultivation in Western Siberia is found in the black-earth Altai Krai, which is over 2,000 kilometers from Tashkent. The grain of the Altai region, which moves on the Turk-Sib, must traverse longer distances than Kazakh grain shipped on the Trans-Kazakhstan line to reach Central Asian and Southern Kazakhstan markets located to the west of a point which is 47 kilometers west of Alma-Ata. Despite the advantage of proximity to the Central Asian market, in 1955, a year of drought in the virgin lands, Kazakhstan supplied only about 142,000 tons of grain to Central Asia, which filled 13 per cent of the minimum deficit in that year.[2] The remainder of this deficit was filled by imports from Western Siberia, which also was hit by the drought, and from the Urals, the Trans-Volga region, and European Russia. However, even in years when the Kazakh lands produce a bumper grain harvest, substantial quantities of West Siberian grain are consumed in the Central Asian market.

The Turk-Sib, aided by the recently completed Trans-Kazakhstan trunk-line, has effected a somewhat belated re-orientation in the grain supply base of Central Asia to Western Siberia and Kazakhstan, which, in turn, has promoted the further specialization of the Central Asian economy. The strength of these interregional trade ties to a considerable extent, however, is related to the climatic uncertainties affecting wheat production in the virgin lands; although the stockpiling of grain in either the cen-

---

[1] Narodnoye Khozyaistvo SSSR v 1956 Godu, p. 119.

[2] Derived from Kazakhskaya SSSR, p. 116.

ters of consumption or production could help insure the dominance of Kazakh and Siberian grain in Central Asian consumption.

Lumber.--The movement of lumber to Central Asia via the Turk-Sib presents a picture quite different from grain flow on this route. Although the role of the Turk-Sib as the major route for the flow of lumber to Central Asia was also handicapped by a slow start, by 1937 Central Asia received most of its lumber from areas in Siberia tributary to the Turk-Sib, as Table 15 reveals.

TABLE 15

CENTRAL ASIAN LUMBER IMPORTS BY RAIL, 1937[a]
(Millions of Tons)

Region	Imports
Upper Volga	0.1
Lower Volga	0.1
Urals	0.1
West Siberia	0.6
East Siberia	0.5
Total	1.4

[a]Galitskiy, p. 35

In appraising the role of the interregional routes in the supplying of grain and lumber to Central Asia, a distinction should be made between the two commodities since the role of the Turk-Sib as a lumber supplier to the deficit regions of Central Asia at present encounters little competition from the other interregional rail lines, or the Caspian route. The growing importance of this function of the Turk-Sib can best be seen by examining Table 16. From 1928 to 1956, the total volume of rail-originated forest products in the Central Asian republics declined from 182,000 tons to 124,000 tons, while in the same period, the volume of forest products (primarily lumber) terminating on the rail lines of this region increased from 420,000 tons to 3,743,000 tons. Thus, the minimum deficit of Central Asia in forest products during the period from 1928 to 1956 rose from a mere 238,000 tons to 3,619,000 tons. The importance of lumber and grain in the interregional trade of Central Asia is reflected in the fact that the combined minimum deficits of these commodities in the latter year amounted to 7,144,000 tons, or an estimated 40 per cent of the total interregional terminations of the Central Asian republics. This means that if the Central Asian republics themselves consumed all the grain and lumber they produced, they still would have to import 7,144,000 tons in order to meet their consumption needs, assuming that the volume of rail freight originated and terminated in Central Asia is equal to the production and consumption, respectively, of these commodities.

TABLE 16

RAIL ORIGINATIONS AND TERMINATIONS OF FOREST PRODUCTS IN CENTRAL ASIA[a]
(Thousands of Tons)

Region	1928	1940	1950	1955	1956
Uzbek SSR					
Originations	97	34	34	40	44
Terminations	297	532	1,046	1,874	1,981
Difference	-200	- 498	-1,012	-1,834	-1,947
Turkmen SSR					
Originations	78	24	44	65	59
Terminations	96	317	407	448	444
Difference	- 18	- 293	- 363	- 383	- 385
Tadzhik SSR					
Originations	4	2	14	4	8
Terminations	10	146	360	565	644
Difference	- 6	- 142	- 346	- 561	- 636
Kirghiz SSR					
Originations	3	2	7	8	13
Terminations	17	191	343	625	674
Difference	- 14	- 189	- 336	- 617	- 661
Central Asia (total)					
Originations	182	62	99	117	124
Terminations	420	1,186	2,156	3,512	3,743
Difference	-238	-1,124	-2,057	-3,395	-3,619

[a]*Transport i Svyaz' SSSR*, p. 73

The rapidly widening gap between the production and consumption of grain and lumber in Central Asia, coupled with the expansion of the production of grain in Western Siberia and Kazakhstan and the vast increases in the production of Siberian lumber, has given the two interregional trunk-lines linking these regions a vital role, which has more than compensated for the earlier disappointments with the Turk-Sib.

TABLE 17

RAIL ORIGINATIONS OF COAL AND COKE IN CENTRAL ASIA[a]
(Thousands of Tons)

Region	1928	1940	1950	1955	1956
Uzbek SSR					
Originations	126	10	1,392	2,440	2,667
Terminations	172	1,408	3,239	4,617	5,105
Difference	- 46	-1,398	-1,847	-2,177	-2,438
Turkmen SSR					
Originations	3	2	7	8	8
Terminations	15	152	289	361	388
Difference	- 12	- 150	- 282	- 353	- 380
Tadzhik SSR[b]					
Originations	93	519	723	1,071	1,216
Adjusted	(13)	(204)	(449)	(578)	(657)
Terminations	2	107	385	608	681
Difference	91	412	338	463	535
Adjusted	(11)	(98)	(64)	(- 30)	(- 24)
Kirghiz SSR					
Originations	6	967	1,352	1,857	2,106
Terminations	3	236	500	784	1,009
Difference	3	731	852	1,073	1,097
Central Asia (total)[c]					
Originations	228	1,538	3,474	5,376	5,997
Terminations	192	1,903	4,413	6,370	7,183
Difference	36	- 365	- 939	- 994	-1,186
Adjusted	(- 44)	(- 680)	(-1,213)	(-1,487)	(-1,749)

[a]Transport i Svyaz', p. 70.

[b]Data include lignites and brown coal.

[c]The originations of coal in the Tadzhik Republic are from two to seven times greater than the volume of coal production in this republic because of a discrepancy of data in Transport i Svyaz' SSSR which is of undetermined origin. Since these differences are not compensated for by increased terminations of coal in this republic, an adjusted figure for coal originations which is equal to coal production in Tadzhikstan is used to compute the minimum coal deficit of Central Asia. The estimated minimum deficit of coal in Central Asia based on the adjusted data in 1955 was 1,487,000 tons. This seems to be a more accurate estimate since the Uzbek Republic, which terminated 72 per cent of Central Asian coal, imported a little more than 1.5 million tons of coal from Karaganda and the Kuzbass in that year.

Coal

One of the most important features of the policy of increasing the degree of regional autarky enunciated in the late 1930's was the intensified development of local supplies of fuel. In Central Asia, the increased utilization of local, low-grade bituminous coal and lignite was designed to free this region from the necessity of long-haul coal imports, primarily from the Kuznetsk Basin. Table 17 indicates that the minimum coal deficit of Central Asia (adjusted) has continued to increase in volume, while coal imports have decreased when expressed as a percentage of total consumption. The adjusted minimum volume of Central Asian coal imports was equal to 35 per cent of total coal terminations in 1940 and 24 per cent of the total in 1956. During this period, local coal and lignite production jumped from 1,919,000 tons to 6,436,000 tons. In the latter year, as a result of rapidly expanded local production, the Central Asian minimum coal deficit was 1,749,000 tons as compared to minimum deficits of 3,619,000 tons of lumber and 3,525,000 tons of grain, despite the fact that total coal terminations were almost as large as the combined terminations of lumber and grain. The continued increase in the absolute volume of coal imports demonstrates that the industrialization of Central Asia has given rise to a demand for coal which local production is unable to satisfy completely either quantitatively or qualitatively.[1]

One of the purposes of the construction of the Mointy-Chu bridge line to form the Trans-Kazakhstan trunk-line can now be re-evaluated. From the initial proposals in the early 1930's to build a trunk-line to link northern and southern Kazakhstan with Central Asia until the actual completion of this line in 1953, one of the primary motives for its construction was to facilitate the movement of coal to Central Asia from Karaganda, which is located 1,485 kilometers from Tashkent, as a means of reducing long-haul imports of coal from the Kuznetsk Basin over distances averaging 2,700 kilometers. At the same time this line was being completed in the early 1950's, Soviet policy was ostensibly attempting to make Central Asia completely self-sufficient in terms of coal supply. An objection to the construction of the Trans-Kazakhstan magistral on these grounds had been forcibly expressed some twenty years earlier, in 1932, by the Central Asian delegate to the Conference on the Distribution of Productive Forces in the USSR, when he stated:

> Central Asia has adequate coal reserves to develop a fuel balance on the basis of local resources. Let us stop saying that there are no coal reserves in Central Asia, or that it is

---

[1] Promyshlennost' SSSR, p. 146; Narodnoye Khozyaistvo SSSR v 1956 Godu, p. 74.

> necessary to ship coal from Karaganda to Central Asia, and that, in order to do this, it will be necessary to construct new Trans-Kazakhstan magistrals. . . . We are against such a use for badly needed rails, which, first of all, are needed for the rail line from Chardzhou to Alexandrov-Gai. . . . We need this immediately, instead of a magistral for the shipment of coal into Central Asia from Kazakhstan. This is local separatism in the report of Kazakhstan, which wishes to supply Central Asia with everything except what is really useful.[1]

However, the coal-hauling motivation for the construction of the Mointy-Chu line seems considerably less inconsistent with the avowed goals of coal production in Central Asia in the light of the failure of rapidly expanded local production to keep pace with the growth of Central Asian coal consumption, and, also, the qualitative differences between Karaganda and Central Asian coals. Although Karaganda coals leave much to be desired in terms of quality because of their extremely high ash content of 22.1 per cent (1955),[2] they are still considerably higher in quality than the coals of Central Asia. In 1955, 84.5 per cent of the coals mined in Central Asia and the southern portions of Kazakhstan consisted of brown coals.[3] During the same year, as mentioned earlier, Central Asia and the portions of Kazakhstan south of Alma-Ata imported approximately 1.9 million tons of coal from Karaganda, most of which was consumed in the Central Asian republics. In turn, the higher quality of Kuznetsk Basin coal by comparison with Karaganda coal seems to be one of the major reasons for the flow of approximately 440,000 tons of long-haul Kuzbass coals in 1955 into Central Asia and the portions of Kazakhstan south of Alma-Ata.[4]

Petroleum

In contrast to the origination-termination tables for lumber, grain, and coal, the differences between the originations and terminations of petroleum in Central Asia as a whole cast little light on the dynamic flow patterns of this commodity, primarily, be cause of the importance of maritime movement in the interregional

---

[1]Gaister, p. 22.

[2]Ugol'naya Promyshlennost' SSSR, p. 84.

[3]Ibid., pp. 48-49.

[4]Onika, p. 40.

petroleum trade of this region. For this reason, there exists a sharp distinction between the petroleum trade of the Turkmen Republic, on the one hand, and petroleum shipments in the remaining republics of Central Asia, which lack access to the Caspian Sea, on the other.

TABLE 18

RAIL ORIGINATIONS AND TERMINATIONS OF PETROLEUM AND PETROLEUM PRODUCTS IN CENTRAL ASIA[a]
(Thousands of Tons)

Region	1928	1940	1950	1955	1956
Uzbek SSR					
Originations	45	331	1,402	1,116	1,057
Terminations	225	801	805	1,556	1,705
Difference	-180	- 470	597	- 440	- 648
Turkmen SSR[b]					
Originations	491	1,971	2,546	3,650	3,462
Terminations	131	572	1,534	1,992	2,016
Difference	360	1,399	1,012	1,658	1,446
Tadzhik SSR					
Originations	6	20	8	6	21
Terminations	4	57	108	213	271
Difference	2	- 37	- 100	- 207	- 251
Kirghiz SSR					
Originations	..	1	..	1	1
Terminations	14	91	125	298	333
Difference	- 14	- 90	- 125	- 297	- 332
Central Asia (total)					
Originations	542	2,323	3,956	4,773	4,541
Terminations	374	1,521	2,572	4,059	4,325
Difference	168	802	1,384	714	216

[a]Transport i Syvaz' SSSR, p. 71.

[b]Originations include petroleum imports by sea, while terminations include maritime exports of petroleum.

In 1956, each of the three Central Asian republics lacking maritime access terminated more petroleum freight than it originated, which resulted in a total minimum deficit of 1,231,000 tons. The creation of a large petroleum deficit in 1956 stands in sharp contrast to 1950, when these republics had a total surplus of 372,000 tons. The reason for the shift of the area in Central Asia outside the Turkmen Republic from a petroleum surplus to a petroleum deficit region can be seen in the petroleum freight data for the Uzbek Republic (Table 18). Because of a decline in the production of petroleum in this republic from 1,342,000 tons in 1950 to 1,029,000 tons in 1956,[1] Uzbek petroleum loadings dropped from 1,402,000 tons in the former year to 1,057,000 tons in the latter. Of much greater importance, however, has been the rapid expansion of petroleum terminations in the Uzbek Republic since 1950, apparently due, in large part, to the introduction of powerful Diesel-electric locomotives on the Tashkent Railroad. In 1950, Uzbekistan terminated 805,000 tons of petroleum, or only 4,000 tons more than in 1940. But by 1956, petroleum terminations reached 1,705,000 tons, or more than double the quantity terminated just six years earlier.

In the pre-war Five-Year Plans, the Turkmen Republic imported large quantities of petroleum products from the Caucasus through the port of Krasnovodsk. At Krasnovodsk, these products were transshipped to rail for destinations not only in Central Asia, but also in Kazakhstan and Siberia. In 1937, for example, the railroads of Central Asia shipped 300,000 tons of petroleum to Siberia.[2] In fact, even in the year 1955, the railroads of Central Asia and Kazakhstan supplied 19 per cent of total petroleum consumption in Western Siberia, and 25 per cent of East Siberian consumption.[3] However, the completion of the pipelines now under construction from the area of the Second Baku to Omsk, in Western Siberia, and Irkutsk, at the southeastern edge of Lake Baikal, will undoubtedly greatly diminish the transit functions of the Trans-Caspian line in the movement of petroleum products from the Caucasus to Siberia.[4]

The most important change in the petroleum trade of the Turkmen Republic since 1928 has been the transformation of this republic into an exporter of locally produced petroleum, rather than an exporter of petroleum imported by sea from the Caucasus. The growth of maritime exports of petroleum from the Turkmen Republic, as well as rail exports to the east, to a large extent is

---

[1] Narodnoye Khozyaistvo SSSR v 1956 Godu, p. 75.

[2] Galitskiy, p. 30.

[3] B. V. Krich, "Puti Ratsionalizatsii Perevozok Neftegruzov," Voprosy Ratsionalizatsii Perevozok Vazneishikh Gruzov, ed. V. P. Potapov and B. I. Shafirkin (Moscow: Transzheldorizdat, 1957), p. 74. The figure of 19 per cent for Western Siberian petroleum terminations appears as an obvious misprint of 69 per cent in a table on p. 74 of this text.

[4] Gudok, October 26, 1956.

based upon the expansion of crude oil production in this republic from a meager 8,000 tons in 1928 to 3,126,000 tons in 1955.[1] Thus, in the latter year, the volume of the petroleum products exported from the Turkmen Republic was equal to over half the volume of Turkmen crude oil production.

TABLE 19

MARITIME PETROLEUM TRADE OF THE TURKMEN REPUBLIC[a]
(Thousands of Tons)

Type of Movement	1930[b]	1950	1955
Exports	1	952	1,617
Imports	827	799	1,183
Difference	-826	153	434

[a]Transport i Svyaz' SSR, p. 107; Materialy po Statistike Putey Soobshcheniya, CXXXI, 227.

[b]1930 data based upon the volume of petroleum freight originating and terminating at Krasnovodsk by rail.

The most paradoxical feature of the interregional rail and maritime petroleum trade of the Central Asian republics is the large volume of apparent cross-hauling. However, most of the cross-hauls apparently taking place actually consist of the interchange of diversified petroleum products which are grouped into the single broad category used in Table 18. A large share of the interregional petroleum trade of Central Asia is induced by regional variations in the quality of crude petroleum and, even more important, in the development of refining facilities. For instance, Central Asia imports large quantities of sulfurous furnace fuel from the refineries at Gur'yev and Orsk. At the same time, the refinery at Vannovskaya, in the Fergana Basin, ships to the Urals and Kazakhstan a great deal of furnace fuel with a low sulfur content, which is more suited to the exacting demands of metallurgy.[2] In addition, Central Asian rail lines import large quantities of Diesel fuel from the Gur'yev and Orsk refineries, while

[1]Promyshlennost' SSSR, p. 155.

[2]B. V. Krich, Voprosy Ratsionalizatsii Perevozok Vazneishikh Gruzov, p. 85.

large amounts of highly specialized refined products such as illuminating kerosene are exported from the Central Asian republics.[1] Thus, a large volume of interregional petroleum traffic can be associated with the highly specialized nature of Central Asian petroleum refining.

Other Commodities

Rather than inventory the remaining commodities in the interregional trade balance of Central Asia, this discussion will focus on the relation between Central Asian production and consumption of two commodity groups--mineral fertilizers and ferrous metals.

Mineral fertilizers.--The development of a highly specialized, cotton-growing base in Central Asia and southern Kazakhstan has resulted in vast increases in the demand for mineral fertilizers and has also led to the rapid development of local production of these products. Central Asian and Kazakh production of mineral fertilizers increased from only 1,600 tons in 1940 to 979,000 tons in 1955.[2] However, even in the latter year these republics produced only 46.5 per cent of the artificial nitrogen fertilizers. They consumed only about 70 per cent of their total phosphate fertilizer consumption.[3] A reduction in the percentage of irrigated land devoted to alfalfa (in relation to irrigated cotton acreage) in recent years in order to expand the amount of irrigated land devoted to cotton has intensified Central Asian consumption of nitrogenous fertilizers.

Ferrous metals.--In contrast with the movement of mineral fertilizers to the cotton-growing areas of Central Asia, the vast increases in Central Asian imports of ferrous metals in recent years reflect the rapid expansion of consumption in the industrial sector of the Central Asian economy. In 1956, Central Asia terminated 1,247,000 tons of diversified ferrous metals, as compared to 156,000 tons in 1940.[4] In the latter year, locally originated ferrous metals were equal to 52 per cent of terminations, while in 1956 local originations were equal to 55 per cent of local

---

[1] Ibid., p. 83. [2] Promyshlennost' SSSR, p. 193.

[3] V. I. Cherkasova and A. A. Nikolayev, "Ratsionalizatsiya Perevozok Mineral'nykh i Khimicheskikh Udobreniy," Voprosy Ratsionalizatsii Perevozok Vazneishikh Gruzov, pp. 164-65.

[4] Transport i Svyaz' SSSR, p. 72.

terminations, despite the construction during World War II of the first and only steel plant in Central Asia at Begovat. A large volume of interregional trade has also been generated by the total absence of pig-iron production in Central Asia and the inadequate assortment of locally produced, rolled steel products. The Begovat plant imports large quantities of pig iron from the Kuznetsk Basin and, in turn, exports steel ingots to the steel plant just outside Karaganda, at Temir-Tau.[1] At the same time, Central Asian industries are forced to import considerable quantities of rolled steel products from different portions of the country.

Summary

The rapid expansion of agriculture and industry in the Central Asian republics under the Five-Year Plans has generated a persistently expanding volume of rail freight. One of the results of the increased specialization of Central Asian agriculture on the production of cotton has been the rapid growth of ginned cotton exports; particularly to the Moscow region. In addition to increasing the export of cotton and other agricultural products, such as wool and fruit, Central Asia has strengthened its export functions by intensifying the exploitation of the petroleum reserves of the Turkmen Republic and, to a lesser extent, the Uzbek Republic. Despite the growth of regional exports, the most significant transport effect of the rapid economic growth of Central Asia has been the vast increments of interregional imports, particularly grain, lumber, and coal from Kazakhstan and Siberia made possible by the construction of the Turk-Sib and Trans-Kazakhstan trunk-lines.

The changes in the interregional trade of Central Asia since 1940 can best be seen by studying Figures 29 and 30, which portray the minimum surpluses and deficits of the Central Asian republics in 1940 and 1956. One of the most striking changes brought out by these maps is the expansion of minimum commodity deficits, particularly in the Uzbek Republic. These maps also reveal important differences between commodity groups. Although Central Asian coal terminations in 1956 were almost twice as large as the combined terminations of lumber and grain in this region,

---

[1]I. I. Pomerantsev, "Voprosy Ratsionalizatsii Perevozok Chernykh Metallov," Voprosy Ratsionalizatsii Perevozok Vazneishikh Gruzov, p. 104.

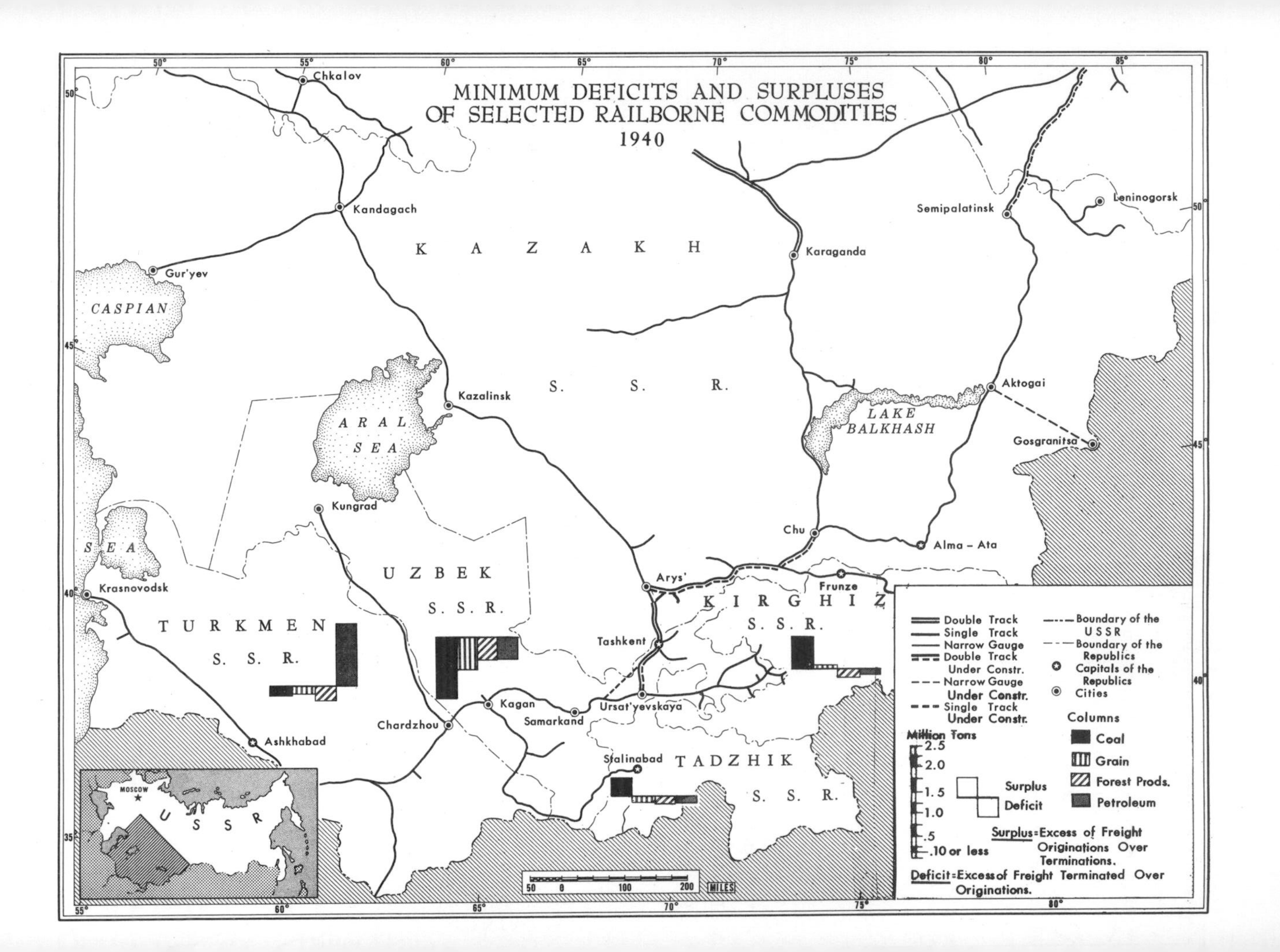
MINIMUM DEFICITS AND SURPLUSES
OF SELECTED RAILBORNE COMMODITIES
1940
K A Z A K H
S. S. R.
U Z B E K
S. S. R.
T U R K M E N
S. S. R.
K I R G H I Z
S. S. R.
T A D Z H I K
S. S. R.
ARAL SEA
CASPIAN
SEA
LAKE BALKHASH
Chkalov
Kandagach
Gur'yev
Krasnovodsk
Ashkhabad
Kungrad
Chardzhou
Kagan
Samarkand
Ursat'yevskaya
Tashkent
Stalinabad
Arys'
Kazalinsk
Karaganda
Chu
Frunze
Alma - Ata
Aktogai
Gosgranitsa
Semipalatinsk
Leninogorsk
Double Track
Single Track
Narrow Gauge
Double Track Under Constr.
Narrow Gauge Under Constr.
Single Track Under Constr.
Boundary of the USSR
Boundary of the Republics
Capitals of the Republics
Cities
Columns
Coal
Grain
Forest Prods.
Petroleum
Million Tons
2.5
2.0
1.5
1.0
.5
.10 or less
Surplus
Deficit
Surplus=Excess of Freight Originations Over Terminations.
Deficit=Excess of Freight Terminated Over Originations.
50 0 100 200 MILES
MOSCOW
U S S R

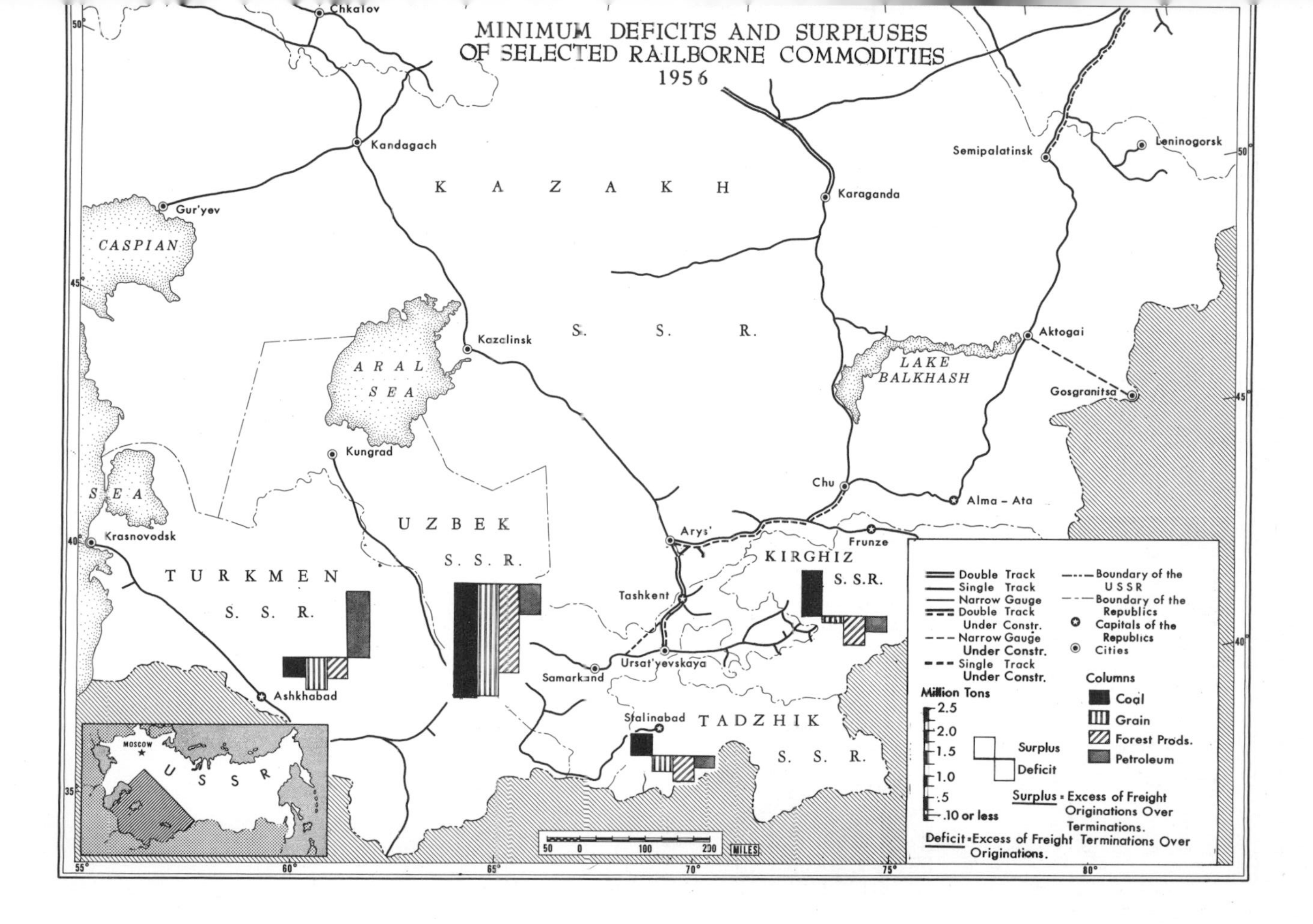

MINIMUM DEFICITS AND SURPLUSES
OF SELECTED RAILBORNE COMMODITIES
1956
K A Z A K H
S. S. R.
UZBEK
S. S. R.
TURKMEN
S. S. R.
KIRGHIZ
S. S. R.
TADZHIK
S. S. R.
ARAL SEA
LAKE BALKHASH
CASPIAN
SEA
Chkalov
Kandagach
Gur'yev
Kazalinsk
Karaganda
Semipalatinsk
Leninogorsk
Aktogai
Gosgranitsa
Alma - Ata
Chu
Frunze
Arys'
Tashkent
Ursat'yevskaya
Samarkand
Stalinabad
Kungrad
Ashkhabad
Krasnovodsk
Double Track
Single Track
Narrow Gauge
Double Track Under Constr.
Narrow Gauge Under Constr.
Single Track Under Constr.
Boundary of the USSR
Boundary of the Republics
Capitals of the Republics
Cities
Million Tons
2.5
2.0
1.5
1.0
.5
.10 or less
Surplus
Deficit
Columns
Coal
Grain
Forest Prods.
Petroleum
Surplus = Excess of Freight Originations Over Terminations.
Deficit = Excess of Freight Terminations Over Originations.
MILES
50 0 100 200
MOSCOW
U S S R
50°
45°
40°
35°
55°
60°
65°
70°
75°
80°

Fig. 30

the minimum coal deficit was only about half as large as the minimum deficit of either lumber or grain. As Figure 30 shows, the minimum coal deficit of the Uzbek Republic in 1956 was slightly larger than the minimum deficit of either grain or lumber in this republic, despite the rapid growth of lignite production at Angren. But, a large portion of the Uzbek coal deficit was filled by surplus coal production in the Kirghiz and Tadzhik republics (using unadjusted data for Tadzhik coal originations). By contrast, all the Central Asian republics were grain and lumber deficit regions in 1956, although the Kirghiz Republic had a modest grain surplus in 1940. The petroleum surplus of the Turkmen Republic, as shown in these maps, remained remarkably stable from 1940 to 1956. In the former year, however, most of the petroleum surplus of this republic consisted of oil imports from the Caucasus moving to other Central Asian republics and Siberia, while in 1956, the exportable surplus of petroleum from the Turkmen Republic derived primarily from expanded local production. This chapter has thus provided a substantive base for an investigation in the next chapter of the extremely long average distance of haul of Central Asian rail traffic as an extra cost of economic development in this region.

CHAPTER VI

THE EXTRA COSTS OF CENTRAL ASIAN INTERREGIONAL RAIL TRADE AND ATTEMPTS TO REDUCE THEM

A common thread running through the preceding discussion of individual commodity flow patterns was the persistent expansion of the long-haul, interregional trade of the Central Asian republics handled by rail. This chapter will attempt to shed some light on the extra costs associated with this movement. First, however, the sense in which the phrase extra cost is being used should be clarified. Chapters Two and Three have already sketched the extra transportation costs involved in the construction and renovation of the rail pattern of Central Asia and Kazakhstan that would probably not have been incurred had not this region undergone intensive economic development during the Soviet era. In another sense, however, this phrase can be used to refer to the longer distances involved in the interregional trade of emerging regional economies in the outlying areas of a country in comparison with the rest of the country. For the most part it is in this sense that the concept of extra transportation costs will be used in the remainder of this chapter. Another type of extra transportation cost to be examined in the following discussion is the large-scale movement of empty freight cars on the Central Asian interregional trunk-lines caused by a pronounced imbalance in the tonnage of Central Asian interregional freight originations and terminations.

The Extra Costs of Central Asian Interregional Trade

Extra Costs Associated with the Regional Average Distance of Haul

The separation of the major nodes of economic activity on the loessial piedmont plains of Central Asia and the relatively few lowland desert oases of this region from their primary interregional markets and sources of supply by a vast zone of barren desert has contributed greatly to the extremely long hauls involved in the origination and termination of commodities on the railroads of this region.

Interregional exports.--The largest share of the major export of Central Asia, ginned cotton, still moves to the textile mills of the Industrial Center (the Moscow region) over distances of approximately 3,500 kilometers, despite the diversion of a small portion of the ginned cotton exports of Central Asia to closer cotton-textile plants, such as the one at Barnaul in Western Siberia. The concentration of cotton-growing and ginning in Central Asia and the continued dominance of the Industrial Center in the manufacture of cotton textiles led to a national average length of haul for ginned cotton of 3,327 kilometers in 1954, which was one of the longest average hauls, if not the longest, of any broad commodity group in the Soviet Union.[1] This distance was also four times greater than the national average distance of haul for all commodities in that year. In comparison with 1940, the average distance of haul of ginned cotton in the Soviet Union in 1954 had increased by 127 kilometers, partially as a result of the rapid decline in cotton growing on the non-irrigated lands of European Russia and the concomitant intensification of cotton production in Central Asia.[2] Other major interregional exports of Central Asia, including cotton by-products, silk, wool, fruit and a wide variety of other products also must travel over enormous distances to reach their major markets in the European portions of the Soviet Union.

Interregional imports.--The effect of Central Asian imports on the extra traffic volume of the Soviet rail net will be examined in much greater detail than the interregional exports of this region because of the availability of regional average length of haul data for rail terminations and, also, because Central Asia imports a considerably larger volume of freight than it exports. In 1956, for example, the interregional imports of the Central Asian republics by rail were an estimated 18.1 million tons, as compared to an estimated 8.4 million tons of interregional exports (see Table 30, Appendix C).

The average distance of haul of terminated tonnage on the rail lines of this region, shown in Table 20, is almost twice as long as the national average. A breakdown of the aggregate data by commodity groupings is also illuminating. The only major com-

---

[1]Khanukov, p. 122. [2]Ibid.

TABLE 20

AVERAGE LENGTH OF HAUL OF GOODS TERMINATED ON CENTRAL ASIAN RAILROADS, 1952[a]
(Kilometers)

Railroad	Total	Coal	Petro- leum	Ferrous Products	Forest Products	Grain	Cement	Machin- ery	Mineral Fertilizers[b]
National average	749	655	1,233	1,253	1,172	836	723	1,756	1,422
Tashkent	1,410	960	1,055	2,350	3,525	1,970	515	2,575	1,360
Ashkhabad	1,460	1,420	540	3,040	3,950	2,075	1,280	2,900	2,750
Turk-Sib	1,450	1,430	2,610	2,295	2,300	1,065	2,270	3,000	1,135

[a]Khanukov, p. 237.
These data are based on the average haul information for four months in 1952 (one month from each quarter) which were adjusted into a yearly figure in the original source (Khanukov).

[b]The average haul for mineral fertilizers includes apatite concentrates.

modity group with an average distance of haul less than the national average on both the Ashkhabad and Tashkent railroads is petroleum. The only other commodities with an average length of haul less than the national figure are cement and mineral fertilizers on the Turk-Sib. Many of the major commodities terminating on the railroads of Central Asia, such as lumber and grain, have average hauls two to three times longer than the national average.

Despite considerable statistical difficulties, it seems feasible to attempt to estimate a regional average distance of haul of terminated commodities for Central Asia as a whole and also for the major bulk commodity imports for a number of reasons. For one thing, the differences between the average length of haul of total terminations, as well as the average hauls of certain commodities, on the railroads serving Central Asia are relatively slight. Even an unweighted mean figure could not deviate greatly from the actual average length of haul. However, to obtain greater accuracy the average haul data of individual railroads will be weighted by the estimated tonnage of their terminations. When more than one railroad serves a union republic (the only statistical unit in Central Asia for which freight tonnage data are available), the tonnage of terminations will be apportioned among the railroads serving the Republic on the basis of the share of the urban population of the oblasts served by individual railroads in the total urban population of a union republic (see Table 28, Appendix A). The resulting figures are shown in Table 21.

The extremely long hauls involved in the termination of commodities in Central Asia resulted in an estimated regional average length of haul of 1,431 kilometers in 1952, which was 91 per cent longer than the national average in that year--a clear reflection on the real, extra transportation costs of economic development in Central Asia associated with distance.

Another method of measuring these extra freight costs is by determining the difference between the actual volume of freight terminated in the Central Asian republics, expressed in ton-kilometers, and the ton-kilometer volume of Central Asian terminations if the average distance of rail haul had been the same as that of the rest of the country (Table 22). An estimated 17.6 billion ton-kilometers of rail freight work in 1952 would not have been incurred had the regional average distance of haul in Central Asia been equal to that of the rest of the Soviet Union; this amounted to 2.3 per cent of the total freight volume of the Soviet rail net

TABLE 21

CENTRAL ASIAN RAIL TERMINATIONS, BY RAILROAD ADMINISTRATION[a]

Railroad	Estimated Per Cent of Terminations, 1952[b]	Average Length of Haul, 1952[c] (Kilometers)
Central Asia	100	1,431
Tashkent Railroad ...	56	1,410
Ashkhabad Railroad ..	38	1,460
Turk-Sib Railroad[d] ..	6	1,450

[a]Derived from Khanukov, p. 237; Transport i Syvaz', p. 67.

[b]See Table 20, Appendix A, for method used in apportioning union republic terminations among railroads.

[c]The average length of haul for Central Asia as a whole represents the mean of the length of terminations on individual rail lines weighted by an average of the per cent of total Central Asian terminations these railroads handled in 1950 and 1955.

[d]Average distance of haul data on the Turk-Sib are applied only to the estimated tonnage of terminations in the northern oblasts of the Kirghiz SSR.

TABLE 22

TON-KILOMETER RAIL TERMINATIONS IN CENTRAL ASIA, 1952[a]
(Billions of Ton-Kilometers)

Region	1952
Central Asian freight (estimate of actual volume)[b]	35.7
Central Asian terminated ton-kilometers if the average length of haul for the rest of the Soviet Union had obtained[c]	18.1
Difference	17.6

[a]Derived from Khanukov, p. 237; Transport i Syvaz', p. 67.

[b]The estimated regional average length of haul was applied to the tonnage of Central Asian terminations to produce the estimated volume of ton-kilometer terminations in 1952.

[c]In 1952 the national average distance of haul was 749 kilometers. After deducting the tonnage and ton-kilometers of Central Asian terminations in that year from the comparable national figures, the national average length of haul was reduced to 726 kilometers. This latter figure was applied to the tonnage of Central Asian terminations to arrive at the ton-kilometer volume of freight if the national average length of haul (excluding Central Asia) has obtained.

in that year. Thus, even ignoring the high costs of the construction and technical renovation of the long interregional trunk-lines traversing the deserts of Central Asia and Kazakhstan, the transformation of Central Asia into a highly specialized center of economic activity has resulted in a volume of rail ton-kilometer work per unit of terminated tonnage that is almost twice as great as the amount of rail ton-kilometers generated by the termination of an equal tonnage of freight in the rest of the country as a whole. This has significantly increased the real costs of economic development in this region.

Inasmuch as important regional contrasts between the average length of haul of terminated commodities might be obscured by a comparison between Central Asian data and an average for the rest of the country, Table 23 relates the average distance of haul for the rail terminations of this region to comparable figures for the other basic economic regions of the Soviet Union. On the basis of the data in this table it can be seen that the extremely long average distance of the freight terminated in Central Asia not only exceeds the average length for the rest of the country as a whole but, also, is longer than the average length of haul in every enlarged economic region of the Soviet Union, with the exception of the remote Soviet Far East. When individual railroads are considered, the only railroads of the Soviet Union with an average distance of terminated freight movement greater than that of any of the Central Asian railroads were the three railroads located in the Soviet Far East and the eastern margins of East Siberia (Fig. 31).

One of the principal reasons for the extremely long average distance of haul for commodity terminations in Central Asia is the large volume of lumber imported by this region over distances exceeding 3,500 kilometers on the average. Although forest products accounted for 10.3 per cent of total Central Asian terminated tonnage in 1950, these commodities accounted for an estimated 25.4 per cent of the total ton-kilometers of freight work involved in the termination of rail-borne commerce in Central Asia in that year.[1] This is almost twice as great as a comparable figure for the next leading commodity--coal.

---

[1]To arrive at this estimate, the tonnage of forest products terminated in the union republics of Central Asia in 1950 was allocated among the three railroad systems of this region by use of the method outlined in Table 28, Appendix A. The resulting figures were then multiplied by the 1952 average distances of haul

TABLE 23

AVERAGE LENGTH OF HAUL OF TERMINATED COMMODITIES IN THE BASIC ECONOMIC REGIONS, 1952[a]
(Kilometers)

Region	Average Length of Haul[b]
Central Asia[c]	1,440
Northwest	1,020
West	615
Center	703
North	695
Ukraine	545
Caucasus	813
Trans-Volga	738
Urals	667
Kazakhstan[d]	830
Western Siberia	898
Eastern Siberia[e]	973
Soviet Far East	2,020

[a]Based on information in Khanukov, p. 237.

[b]Since freight data broken down by individual railroads are unavailable, the regional average lengths of haul shown above are unweighted means of the average length of haul on individual rail lines, either completely or predominately within specific enlarged economic regions. Since the railroads with the lowest average distance of haul within these regions are usually those terminating the largest volume of freight, the unweighted regional mean hauls presumably understate the actual regional average distance (see Table 29, Appendix B).

[c]Including the Turk-Sib.

[d]Excluding the Turk-Sib.

[e]This figure is based on the average haul data of the Krasnoyarsk and East Siberian railroads. The third East Siberian railroad, the Trans-Baikal Railroad, which runs from a point located approximately 300 kilometers east of Lake Baikal to the border of the Soviet Far East, is grouped with the two railroads of the Soviet Far East because of the sharp divide in the average length of haul to the east and west of Petrovskiy Zavod (see Table 29, Appendix B, and Fig. 31).

Extra Transportation Costs Associated with the Regional Imbalance in Movement

Another type of real transportation cost, which is considerably less important than those associated with the extremely long

---

for forest products terminated on these lines to arrive at the estimated volume of ton-kilometers involved in the termination of forest products in Central Asia.

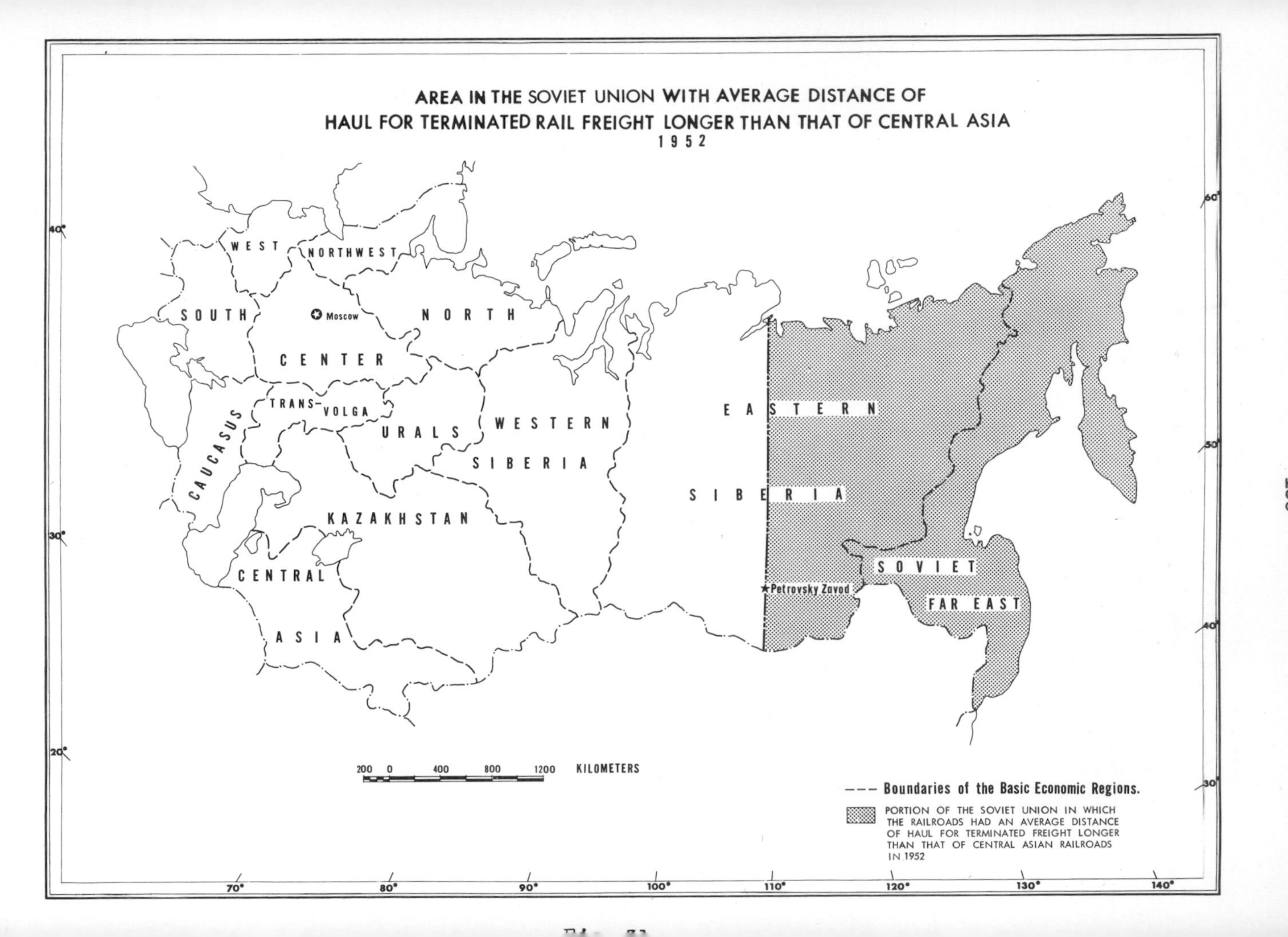
AREA IN THE SOVIET UNION WITH AVERAGE DISTANCE OF
HAUL FOR TERMINATED RAIL FREIGHT LONGER THAN THAT OF CENTRAL ASIA
1952
WEST
NORTHWEST
SOUTH
Moscow
NORTH
CENTER
TRANS-VOLGA
CAUCASUS
URALS
WESTERN SIBERIA
KAZAKHSTAN
CENTRAL ASIA
EASTERN SIBERIA
SOVIET FAR EAST
Petrovsky Zavod
200 0 400 800 1200 KILOMETERS
Boundaries of the Basic Economic Regions.
PORTION OF THE SOVIET UNION IN WHICH THE RAILROADS HAD AN AVERAGE DISTANCE OF HAUL FOR TERMINATED FREIGHT LONGER THAN THAT OF CENTRAL ASIAN RAILROADS IN 1952
40°
30°
20°
60°
50°
40°
30°
70°
80°
90°
100°
110°
120°
130°
140°

average distance of haul, is the large-scale movement of empty freight cars resulting from an imbalance in the volume of regional imports and exports. In terms of tonnage relationships, Central Asia is primarily an importing rather than an exporting region. In 1956, as mentioned above, Central Asian republics imported an estimated 18.1 billion tons by rail, while exporting an estimated 8.4 million tons. Because of the location of the primary market for Central Asian interregional exports in European Russia, export traffic--to a large extent--is concentrated on the Kazalinsk route; leaving a pronounced imbalance of movement on the Trans-Kazakhstan and Turk-Sib route. The resulting large-scale flow of empty freight cars on the Turk-Sib is shown in Table 24.

TABLE 24

DENSITY OF EMPTY FREIGHT CAR FLOW ON THE TURK-SIB, 1940 and 1953[a]
(Thousands)

Junction	Density of Empty Car Flow Toward Arys'		Density of Empty Car Flow Toward Semipalatinsk	
	1940	1953	1940	1953
Semipalatinsk ...	5	10	213	238
Alma-Ata	5	7	175	237
Arys'	3	15	167	186

[a]Khanukov, p. 319

The large volume of empty freight cars moving toward Semipalatinsk on the Turk-Sib reflects the inability of Central Asia or the southern portions of Kazakhstan to balance the bulky southbound flow of grain, lumber, coal, and other commodities with northbound tonnage. The contrast between the empty car flows in the different directions of the Turk-Sib is heightened by the intensive utilization of the "freight" direction of the Turk-Sib (toward Arys'). Although southbound freight flow on the Turk-Sib was several million tons in 1953, the daily average flow of only twenty empty freight cars was recorded at Alma-Ata, in contrast to the daily flow of 652 empty freight cars, on the average, moving toward the north. It should be mentioned that the completion of the Mointy-Chu bridge line in late 1953 has evidently diverted a large share of the empty freight car movement on the Turk-Sib to the Trans-Kazakhstan trunk-line, particularly the flow of empty coal hoppers and boxcars.

Thus, the existence of a pronounced freight imbalance in Central Asia is reflected in a large-scale, unproductive flow of empty freight cars to areas of bulky raw material supply in Kazakhstan and Siberia over extremely long distances. Although by 1953 the absolute volume of empty freight cars flowing to the north from Central Asia was only slightly greater than in 1940, the more rapid growth of Central Asian freight terminations than originations since 1953 has undoubtedly increased greatly the northbound empty-car movement. Another implication of the empty-car flow data is that internal reserves for the increase of traffic on the Turk-Sib and Trans-Kazakhstan lines without large-scale capital expenditures exist in the form of possible utilization of empty freight cars, but because of the directional orientation of Central Asian interregional trade, as well as the excess of imports over exports, these reserves cannot be utilized.

Attempts to Reduce the Average Distance of Haul of Rail Freight Terminated in Central Asia

The rapid growth of the volume of long-haul interregional rail trade carried on between Central Asia and her distant sources of supply, as well as the long-haul northbound flow of empty freight cars, provide compelling motivation for recent attempts to check the growth of ton-kilometer freight work associated with the termination of commodities in the Central Asian republics. Two methods for achieving this goal deserve closer attention: the establishment of closer trade ties with the contiguous Kazakh Republic through the construction of the Mointy Chu bridge line; and the attempt to increase the degree of self-sufficiency, or "comprehensive" development, in Central Asia.

Increasing the Trade Ties between Central Asia and Kazakhstan through the Construction of the Mointy-Chu Line

The most distinctive feature of the trade pattern of Central Asian rail terminations in comparison with the other enlarged economic regions of the Soviet Union is the inverse distance relationships between the areas serving as supply regions for Central Asian consumers, as Table 25 and Figure 37 reveals.

Although the 63 per cent of Central Asian terminations which originated locally in 1952 corresponded rather closely to

TABLE 25

PER CENT OF TOTAL TERMINATIONS BY REGION OF ORIGIN, 1952[a]

Region	Originating Within Region	Originating in Contiguous Region	Originating in Non-Contiguous Region
National average[b]	67.9	21.9	10.3
Central Asia[c] ...	63.0	6.5	30.5
North	79.5	16.2	4.3
Northwest	48.0	31.0	21.0
West	64.3	29.3	6.4
Center	59.3	27.0	13.6
South	85.3	9.1	5.1
Caucasus	66.9	20.4	12.7
Trans-Volga	39.6	57.2	3.2
Urals	66.9	25.7	7.4
Kazakh SSR	53.6	36.5	9.9
West Siberia	68.3	25.0	6.7
East Siberia	76.4	7.3	16.3
Far East	78.2	6.1	15.7

[a]Khanukov, p. 233.

[b]National averages represent mean figures weighted by the tonnage of terminations within individual economic regions, rather than an unweighted mean of the averages listed in the columns of this table.

[c]Kazakhstan is the only contiguous region of Central Asia since maritime imports via the Caspian Sea are regarded as locally originated freight.

the weighted national mean of 67.9 per cent, sharp contrasts exist between the per cent of Central Asian rail terminations originating in contiguous and non-contiguous regions and comparable data for the other enlarged economic regions of the Soviet Union. In 1952, the republics of Central Asia received only 6.5 per cent of their rail-borne freight from the contiguous republic of Kazkhstan, while terminating 30.5 per cent of their total rail termination from non-contiguous, or "distant," regions. These data can be placed in broader perspective by glancing at Table 25. Weaker trade links than those between Central Asia and its contiguous interregional supply area in 1952 were found only in the trade relations between the Soviet Far East and Eastern Siberia. However, Central Asia is unique among the enlarged economic regions of the Soviet Union in terms of the percentage of rail terminations coming from non-contiguous regions. The closest competitor to Central Asia in this respect was the Northwest (around Leningrad), which terminated 21.0 per cent of its freight from "distant" regions in 1952. Even the remote Soviet Far East, which is also a border region, received 15.7 of its rail terminations from non-contiguous regions, or slightly more than one-half the comparable percentage for the Central Asian republics.

One of the reasons for the inverse distance relationships between the tonnage of freight terminated in Central Asia from contiguous and non-contiguous regions in 1952 was the lack of direct rail communication from the primary centers of traffic generation in Kazakhstan, which are located in the central and northern portions of the republic. In effect, many of the major commodities produced in Kazakhstan, including coal from the Karaganda Basin and wheat from the virgin lands, were excluded from the Central Asian market by a formidable time-cost barrier to movement in the form of extreme route circuity. The construction in 1953 of a bridge-line from Mointy to Chu to form a direct rail link between Central and Northern Kazakhstan, on the one hand, and Central Asia, on the other, was designed to strengthen the trade ties between these regions.

Although flow data for the Trans-Kazakhstan trunk-line, which came into being with the completion of the Mointy-Chu line in 1953, are unavailable, information is available about the export rail trade of the Kazakh Republic before and after the completion of the Mointy-Chu line. Although it is impossible to determine exactly what percentage of the trade increments between these regions was handled by the Trans-Kazkhstan trunk-line, certain inferences can be drawn by examining Figures 32 and 33. These maps depict the per cent of Kazakh rail exports flowing to neighboring regions in 1952, on the eve of the completion of the Mointy-Chu bridge line, and in 1955, two years after this line was initially placed in operation (also see Table 31, Appendix D). Figure 32 reveals that in the former year the Central Asian market absorbed only 7.0 per cent of the total rail exports of the Kazakh Republic. By 1955, as Figure 33 points out, the flow of commodities to Central Asia constituted 10.6 per cent of total Kazakh rail exports. In absolute terms, Kazakhstan exported approximately 4.5 million tons of freight to Central Asia in 1955, as compared to approximately 1.7 million tons in 1952. By contrast, the Urals received over 14 million tons of Kazakh-originated freight in 1955. However, by 1955, the share of Kazakh originated freight in total Central Asian terminations increased from 6.5 per cent to

THE RELATIVE SHARE OF NEIGBORING REGIONS IN THE RAIL EXPORTS OF KAZAKHSTAN - 1952

Fig. 32

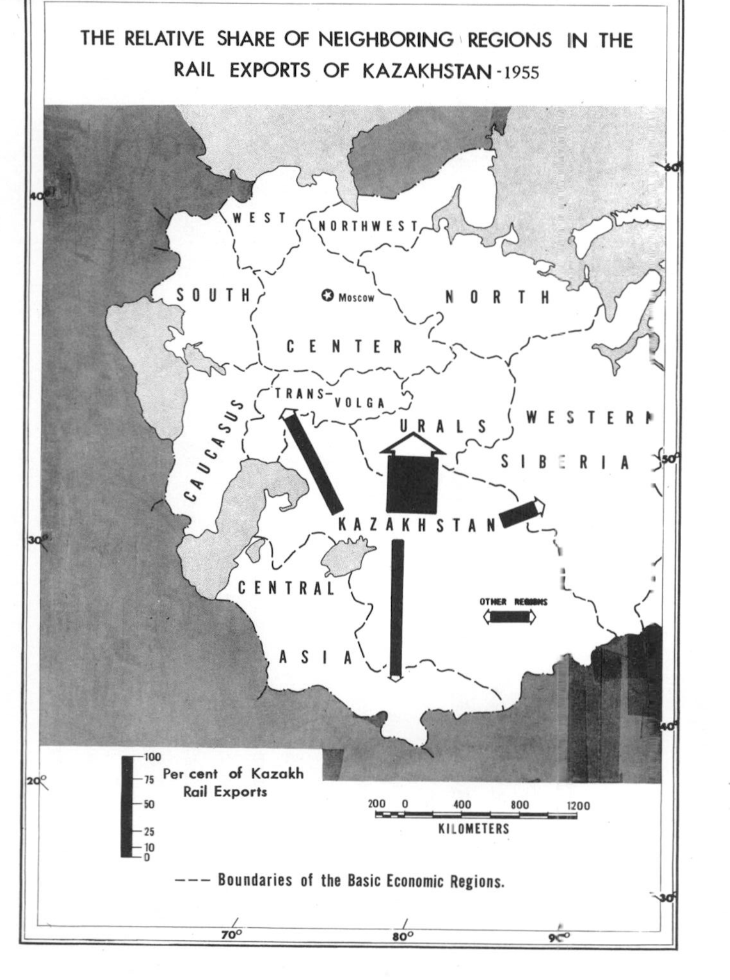

Fig. 33

an estimated 14.3 per cent in 1955, or more than double the 1952 percentage. Although the exact contribution of the Trans-Kazakhstan trunk-line to the increased traffic flow from Kazakhstan to Central Asia cannot be ascertained, it seems reasonable to infer that the completion of this line played an important role in the strengthening of the weak trade links between these areas which existed prior to its construction.

Nonetheless, the role of this route in re-orienting the interregional supply base of Central Asia, as of 1955 at least, was not as important as might be assumed from the preceding discussion. For one thing, the increase in the relative share of Kazakh originated freight in Central Asian terminations from 6.5 per cent to an estimated 14.3 per cent in 1955 would still leave 22.5 per cent of Central Asian terminations to originate in "distant" regions, assuming that Central Asia continued to receive the same percentage of terminations from areas beyond her boundaries in 1955 as it received in 1955. As will be pointed out in a latter section of this chapter, since 1952 Central Asia has evidently become increasingly less self-sufficient and, as a result, the increased trade ties with Kazakhstan have, in part, at least, filled a gap created by a decline in the per cent of locally originated terminations. This, in turn, has lessened the role of the Trans-Kazakhstan route in reducing the dependence of Central Asia on long-haul imports from non-contiguous regions, and in decreasing the Central Asian average distance of haul. Another qualification essential to an appraisal of the effect of the Trans-Kazakhstan trunk-line on the trade ties between Central Asia and Kazakhstan is that a considerable share of the increased traffic between these regions has evidently occurred as a result of the growth of freight movement from the areas in Southern Kazakhstan located on the main line of the Turk-Sib to the Central Asian republics. For example, most of the rapidly expanded production of phosphate fertilizers in the huge combine at Dzhambul is shipped to Central Asia. In addition, there is evidently a large-scale flow of diversified building materials from Southern Kazakhstan to consumers in Central Asia.

Some of the factors tending to impede the effectiveness of the Trans-Kazakhstan trunk-line in creating stronger trade ties between Central Asia and Kazakhstan may be seen by examining the flow patterns of the two commodities dominating the southbound flow on this route--coal from the Karaganda Basin and from the virgin lands of Kazakhstan.

Prior to the completion of the Trans-Kazakhstan trunkline, Central Asia and the portions of southern Kazakhstan south of Alma-Ata received nearly all their coal imports from the Kuznetsk Basin as can be seen in Table 26:

TABLE 26

COAL IMPORTS OF CENTRAL ASIA AND SOUTHERN KAZAKHSTAN SOUTH OF ALMA-ATA--1940-1955[a]

Originating Region	1940	1950	1952[b]	1955[c]
Kuznetsk Basin				
Per cent of total production	4.27	5.19	5.03	0.77
Millions of tons[d]	0.90	1.91	2.13	0.44
Karaganda Basin				
Per cent of total production	....	0.46	1.58	7.06
Millions of tons[d]	....	0.08	0.30	1.90

[a]Onika, p. 40; Ugol'naya Promyshlennost' SSSR, pp. 32-33.

[b]The 1952 flow data for the Karaganda Basin might include movement on the Mointy-Chu before it was placed in permanent operation in 1953.

[c]Although the volume of coal imported by Central Asia and the portion of southern Kazakhstan south of Alma-Ata seems to have been stabilized from 1952, as pointed out earlier, the minimum coal deficit of Central Asia increased in the periods from 1950 to 1955 and from 1955 to 1956.

[d]Percentage data from Onika were converted into absolute figures by use of production data from Ugol'naya Promyshlennost' SSSR.

As this table points out, the Karaganda Basin replaced the Kuznetsk Basin as the primary supplier of bituminous coal to Central Asia and the area in southern Kazakhstan south of Alma-Ata. Thus, a significant change in the interregional supply orientation of the Central Asian republics can be directly attributed to the creation of a direct rail link to the Karaganda coal basin. The substitution of Karaganda coal for Kuznetsk coal in Central Asia not only tends to reduce the average length of haul for the coal imports of Central Asia, but also tends to have the same effect on the overall movement of coal on the Soviet rail net as is demonstrated in Table 27:

TABLE 27

SAVINGS IN DISTANCE BY USE OF KARAGANDA COAL IN CENTRAL ASIA[a]
(Kilometers)

Points	Distance
Kuznetsk Basin (Novokuznetsk)--Tashkent	2,751
Karaganda--Tashkent	1,485
Savings in distance by use of Karaganda coal	1,266
Kuznetsk Basin (Novokuznetsk)--Magnitogorsk via South Siberian railroad	2,173
Karaganda--Magnitogorsk	1,173
Savings in distance by use of Karaganda coal	1,000
Savings in distance by replacement of Kuznetsk coal in Central Asia by Karaganda coal and Karaganda coal in the Urals by Kuznetsk coal	266

[a]All distances taken from Ofitial'nyy Ukazatel': Leto 1957 Goda.

The substitution of one ton of Kuznetsk coal by a ton of Karaganda coal in Central Asia and the reverse substitution in the Urals would thus save 266 ton-kilometers of rail freight work. An even greater justification for the use of Karaganda coal in Central Asia to divert more Kuznetsk coal to the Urals is the higher quality of the latter coal. In the blast furnaces of Magnitogorsk, for example, Karaganda coal can form no more than 40 per cent of the coke mix.[1]

However, the replacement of the Kuznetsk Basin by the Karaganda Basin as the major source of Central Asian coal imports has not had a great impact on the relative share of Kazakh-originated freight in total Central Asian terminations. As mentioned earlier, the rapid growth of coal production (including brown coals) in Central Asia has greatly reduced the relative dependence of this region on coal imports, while the absolute volume of imported coal has increased slowly. Although most of the 1.9 million tons of southbound Karaganda coal in 1955 was consumed in the Central Asian republics, as opposed to southern Kazakhstan, this volume of freight only amounted to a relatively small percentage of total Central Asian rail imports. The potential volume of Karaganda coal flowing toward the south has also been reduced by the continued movement of Kuznetsk coal into Central Asia and the portions of southern Kazakhstan located south of Alma-Ata. The shipment of roughly 440,000

[1]M. Gardner Clark, The Economics of Soviet Steel (Cambridge: Harvard University Press, 1956), p. 134.

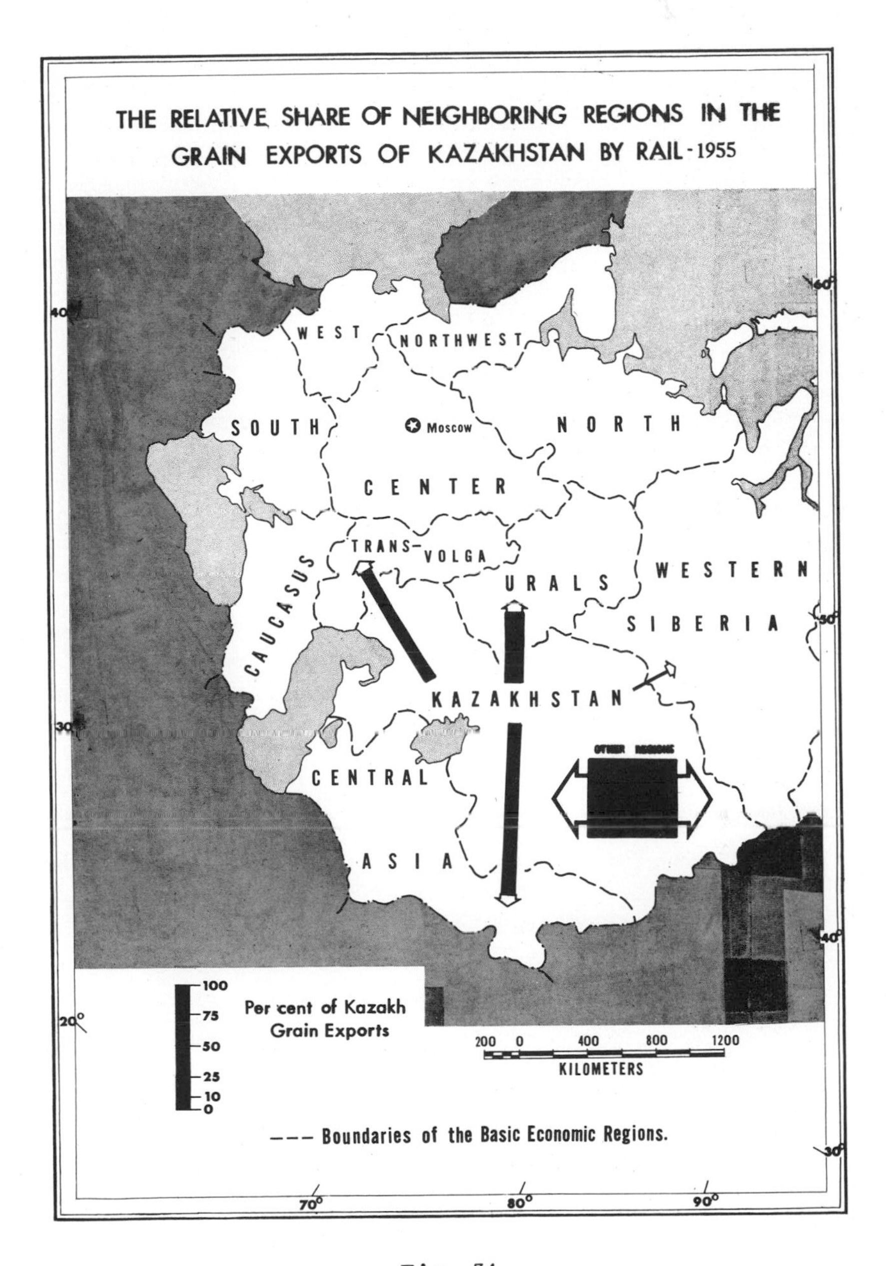
THE RELATIVE SHARE OF NEIGHBORING REGIONS IN THE GRAIN EXPORTS OF KAZAKHSTAN BY RAIL - 1955
WEST
NORTHWEST
SOUTH
Moscow
NORTH
CENTER
TRANS-VOLGA
CAUCASUS
URALS
WESTERN SIBERIA
KAZAKHSTAN
OTHER REGIONS
CENTRAL ASIA
100
75
50
25
10
0
Per cent of Kazakh Grain Exports
200 0 400 800 1200
KILOMETERS
--- Boundaries of the Basic Economic Regions.
60°
50°
40°
30°
20°
70°
80°
90°

Fig. 34

tons of Kuznetsk coal to these regions in 1955 seems to reflect, at least in part, the imperfect substitutibility of Karaganda coal for the higher-grade coals of the Kuznetsk Basin.

Although, as Figure 34 points out, Central Asia received almost 11 per cent of the Kazakh grain exports in 1955, the absolute volume of this flow amounted to only an estimated 142,000 tons. The meager quantity of grain exported from Kazakhstan reflected the severe drought which devastated the wheat crop in the virgin lands in 1955. However, from 1955 to 1956, a bumper-harvest year, the grain loadings of the Kazakhs Republic jumped from 2.75 million tons to 10.60 million tons. If Central Asia had continued to receive the same share of the grain exports of the Kazakh in 1956 as in the previous year, or 10.7 per cent of total Kazakh grain exports, the volume of grain flowing from Kazakhstan to Central Asia would have been approximately 792,000 tons. This would have been slightly more than four times greater than a comparable 1955 figure. It seems improbable that this volume of grain movement could have been maintained in 1957 since, in that year, the virgin lands were again plagued by severe drought.

Although the Trans-Kazakhstan trunk-line has had a certain degree of success in re-orienting the interregional trade of Central Asia, the effectiveness of this route in creating considerably stronger trade links between Central Asia and Kazakhstan has been hindered by:

1. The decreasing relative dependence of Central Asia on imported coal which is reflected in comparatively small increments of coal imports. The continued flow of Kuznetsk coal to Central Asia also reduces the effectiveness of the Trans-Kazakhstan route in linking Central Asia more closely with Kazakhstan.

2. The great fluctuations in wheat harvests on the sprawling virgin and idle lands induced by recurrent droughts.

3. The lack of production in Kazakhstan which is complementary to the needs of Central Asia. As mentioned in the preceding chapter, the largest share of the total ton-kilometers involved in Central Asian terminations is contributed by lumber and other forest products. Kazakhstan, however, is also a region critically deficient in these commodities. The same may be said of a wide array of raw materials and manufactured articles.

Since the attempts to reduce the Central Asian average length of haul by developing closer sources of interregional supply have been only moderately successful, another method for reducing the extra real costs of transportation associated with the extremely long distances freight terminating in Central Asia moves, on the average, deserves study. This approach has attempted to reduce average lengths of haul by strengthening the degree of regional self-sufficiency or, to use the Soviet phrase, to increase the comprehensive development of regions.

Increasing the Degree of Regional Self-Sufficiency

The expansion of market-oriented industrial activity in Central Asia has been a persistent feature of the economic development of this region during the Soviet era, just as has the concomitant expansion of specialized agricultural production. The construction in Central Asia of huge mineral fertilizer plants and machinery industries producing equipment used in the production of raw cotton are examples of the types of industrial activity which have evolved in Central Asia primarily to serve the local agricultural market. Even though most of the cotton ginned in Central Asia is exported to other regions, approximately three-fourths of the rail freight originated in this region also terminates within it because of the close ties of many of the Central Asian manufacturing establishments and sites of mineral produc tion to their local, regional market. Despite the rapid expansion of market-oriented economic activity in Central Asia under the Five-Year Plans, this region has persistently increased its volume of interregional imports. In 1940, Central Asia imported 4.5 million tons of freight by rail while, in 1956, an estimated 18.1 million tons of freight flowed into the Central Asian market from supply areas located beyond the boundaries of this region (see Table 29, Appendix A). The rapid growth of interregional imports indicates that efforts to increase the degree of "comprehensive" economic development in Central Asia as a means of checking the absolute volume of rail imports have fallen far short of this goal.

However, a more important consideration is whether the expansion of market-oriented economic activity has reduced the relative dependence of the Central Asian market on the other basic economic regions of the Soviet Union. Although the development of local production to meet local Central Asian needs has been a persistent feature of the economic development of Central Asia under the Five-Year Plans, in examining the relative degree of self-sufficiency in this region particular attention will be paid to the changes since 1939. In that year, the Soviet Union began an intensive drive to reduce the average length of haul of bulk commodities, such as coal and lumber, and manufactured goods--including diversified machinery products--by attempting to strengthen the transport-saving, deglomerative forces in the Soviet regional economy. This program focused on the development of lower-grade deposits of raw materials and fuel located closer to existing centers of economic activity and, also, on the greater decentralization of manufacturing activity.[1]

Changes in the degree of regional self-sufficiency in the Soviet Union.--The best available measure of the changes in the degree of self-sufficiency in the basic economic regions of the Soviet Union since 1940 is a table in Khanukov[2] listing the percentage of locally originated freight in the total terminated freight volume of the basic regions in 1940 and 1952. These data are portrayed in map form in Figures 35 and 36 (also see Tables 34 and 35, Appendixes F and G). These maps indicate that the relative degree of self-sufficiency (the unshaded portions of the circles) increased in several of the basic economic regions from 1940 to 1952, such as the Center and Kazakhstan, while it declined in other regions, such as the Trans-Volga region and the Caucasus (including the Lower Don and Northern Caucasus). These were compensating changes, since the weighted average percentage of locally originated freight in the rail terminations of the basic economic regions was 67.8 per cent in 1952, as compared to 67.9 per cent in 1940. By 1954, the relative degree of self-sufficiency in these regions had returned exactly to the 1940 percentage of 67.9 per cent. Thus, the policy of intensifying the

---

[1]For further information on this subject see: Balzak, Vasyutin, and Feigin, pp. 160-66; Hunter, pp. 27-38; Yu. I. Koldomasov, Ratsionalizatsiya Perevozok na Zheleznodorozhnom Transporte (2d ed. rev.; Moscow: Transzheldorizdat, 1954), pp. 28-43; and The Land of Socialism Today and Tomorrow (Moscow: Foreign Languages Publishing House, 1939), pp. 124-36.

[2]P. 233.

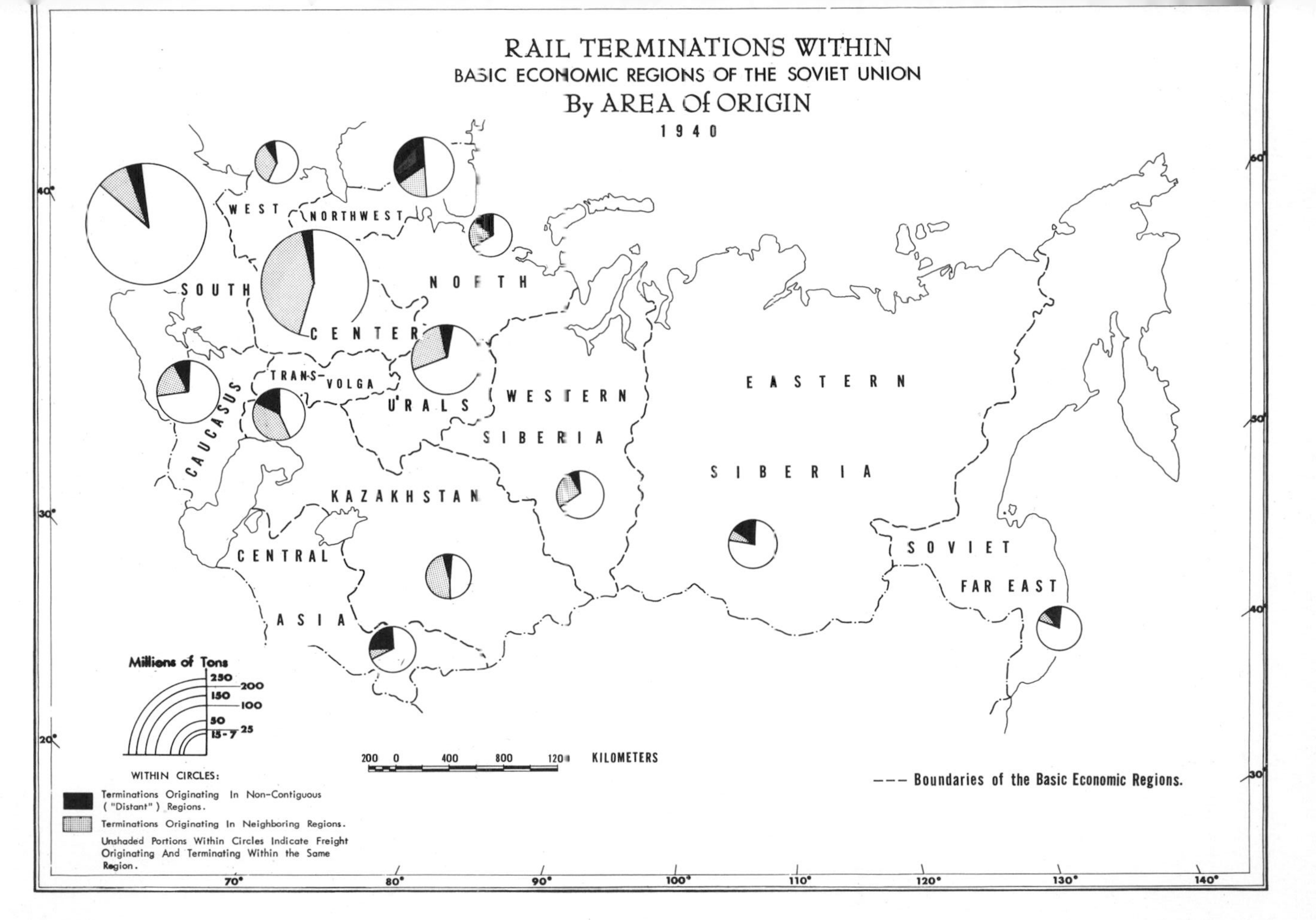
RAIL TERMINATIONS WITHIN
BASIC ECONOMIC REGIONS OF THE SOVIET UNION
By AREA Of ORIGIN
1940
WEST
NORTHWEST
SOUTH
NORTH
CENTER
TRANS-VOLGA
CAUCASUS
URALS
WESTERN SIBERIA
EASTERN SIBERIA
KAZAKHSTAN
CENTRAL ASIA
SOVIET FAR EAST
Millions of Tons
250
200
150
100
50
25
15-7
WITHIN CIRCLES:
Terminations Originating In Non-Contiguous ("Distant") Regions.
Terminations Originating In Neighboring Regions.
Unshaded Portions Within Circles Indicate Freight Originating And Terminating Within the Same Region.
200 0 400 800 1200 KILOMETERS
--- Boundaries of the Basic Economic Regions.
70°
80°
90°
100°
110°
120°
130°
140°
20°
30°
40°
50°
60°

Fig. 35

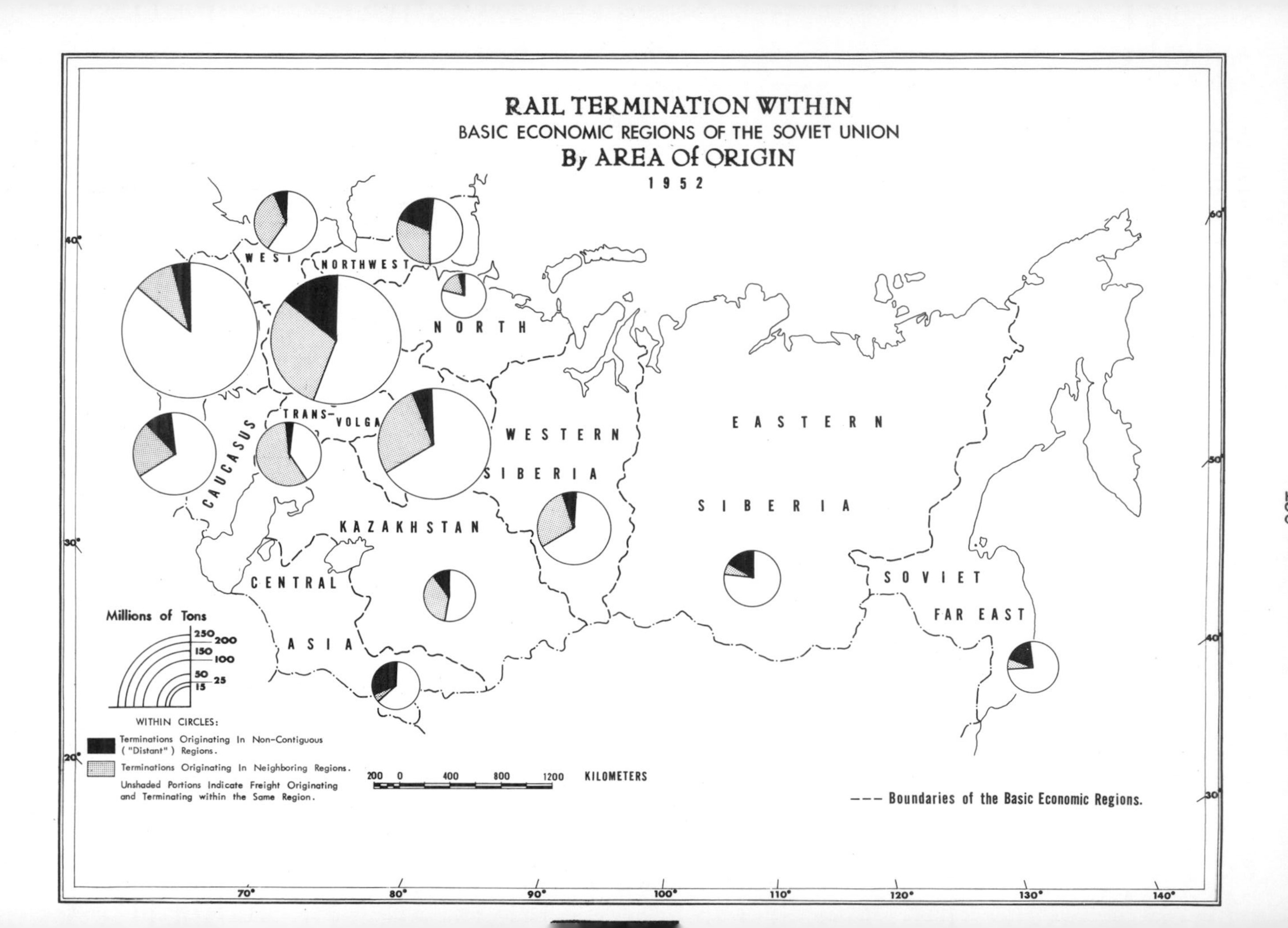
RAIL TERMINATION WITHIN
BASIC ECONOMIC REGIONS OF THE SOVIET UNION
By AREA Of ORIGIN
1952
WEST
NORTHWEST
NORTH
CAUCASUS
TRANS-VOLGA
WESTERN SIBERIA
EASTERN SIBERIA
KAZAKHSTAN
CENTRAL ASIA
SOVIET FAR EAST
Millions of Tons
250 200 150 100 50 25 15
WITHIN CIRCLES:
Terminations Originating In Non-Contiguous ("Distant") Regions.
Terminations Originating In Neighboring Regions.
Unshaded Portions Indicate Freight Originating and Terminating within the Same Region.
200 0 400 800 1200 KILOMETERS
--- Boundaries of the Basic Economic Regions.
70° 80° 90° 100° 110° 120° 130° 140°
20° 30° 40° 50° 60°

degree of "comprehensive" regional development in the Soviet Union did not measurably increase the relative degree of regional autarky.

But yet, from 1940 to 1952, the average length of haul on the Soviet rail net increased from 700 kilometers to 744 kilometers while, in 1954, the net-wide average distance of freight movement reached 757 kilometers. The primary reason for the persistent increases in the national average length of haul despite a stable degree of regional self-sufficiency can be seen by comparing Figures 35 and 36. The major source of the increased average length of haul in 1952 was the greater reliance of the basic economic regions on imports from "distant" (non-contiguous) regions at the expense of freight imports from neighboring, basic economic regions. From 1940 to 1952, the per cent of freight terminated from "distant" regions rose from 8.3 per cent to 10.3 per cent. Although the total tonnage of freight terminations from "distant" regions amounted to only 10.3 per cent of Soviet rail terminations in 1952, this movement accounted for approximately 40 per cent of the total ton-kilometer work of the Soviet rail net in that year. As Figures 35 and 36 reveal, the greatest single increase in the tonnage of "distant"-originated freight from 1940 to 1952 occurred in the Center; to a considerable degree, as a result of the increased flow of Siberian coal and lumber to this region. The importance of freight terminations from "distant" regions in determining the average length of haul is apparent not only for the basic economic regions as a whole but, also, for the regional average lengths of haul.

The closer correlation between the average distance of haul of individual economic regions and the per cent of their freight terminations originating in "distant" regions than between the regional average lengths of haul and the degree of regional self-sufficiency can be demonstrated by the use of Kendall's Coefficient of Rank Correlation. The Coefficient of Rank Correlation between the regional average lengths of haul--ranked from shortest to longest--and the degree of self-sufficiency--ranked from highest to lowest--in the basic economic regions is a negligible +.051, which is clearly non-significant, while the Coefficient of Rank Correlation between the regional average lengths of haul and the per cent of terminations in these regions originating in "distant" regions is +.538, which is significant at the .99 confidence level. Thus, attempts to reduce the average distance of freight movement to the basic economic regions of the Soviet

Union are more dependent upon the success in reducing the per cent of terminations coming from "distant" regions than on merely increasing the relative degree of self-sufficiency.

Since the middle 1950's, even the theory of Soviet regional planning has come to recognize the difficulties associated with the reduction of long-haul commodity flows in an enormous land mass characterized by pronounced regional inequalities in the scale and type of economic activity. For example, a Soviet regional planner, V. Kostennikov, asserted recently: "There have been and there will be long and inordinately long shipments, such as the shipments of lumber, if they are caused by the objective geographic division of labor."[1]

Changes in the degree of regional self-sufficiency in Central Asia.--The relative degree of self-sufficiency, expressed by the per cent of locally originated freight in total terminations, in Central Asia, declined from 67.9 per cent in 1940 to 63.0 per cent in 1952. This is a considerably greater decline than that of the basic economic regions of the Soviet Union as a whole, as can be seen in Table 28.

TABLE 28

RELATION OF CENTRAL ASIAN RAIL TERMINATIONS BY AREA OF ORIGINATION TO AVERAGE FOR BASIC ECONOMIC REGIONS[a]

Region	Per Cent of Terminations Originated Locally		Per Cent from Neighboring Regions		Per Cent from "Distant" Regions	
	1940	1952	1940	1952	1940	1952
National average for basic economic regions ...	67.9	67.8	23.8	21.9	8.3	10.3
Central Asia	67.3	63.0	7.3	6.5	25.4	30.5

[a]Khanukov, p. 233

The major transport implications of the decline in the degree of self-sufficiency in Central Asia by 1952, in comparison with 1940, is that this region had become increasingly dependent on "distant" supply regions to a degree which was considerably

---

[1]V. Kostennikov, Ob Ekonomicheskom Raionirovanii SSSR (Moscow: Gospolitizdat, 1957), p. 54.

greater than that of any of the other basic economic regions of the Soviet Union. Since 1952, Central Asia has become even less self-sufficient. In 1955, this region originated an estimated 57 per cent of its total rail terminations while, by 1956, this percentage dropped even further to an estimated 50 per cent (see n. c, Table 31, Appendix C). Even though the completion of the Trans-Kazakhstan trunk-line in 1953 has strengthened the role of Kazakhstan as a supply region for the Central Asian market--as of 1955, at least--most of the increase in the share of Kazakh-originated freight in Central Asian terminations filled the gap created by the decline in the relative degree of self-sufficiency since 1952. In 1955, although Kazakhstan supplied slightly over 14 per cent of Central Asian rail terminations, the estimated percentage of terminations originating in "distant" regions was still an extremely high 28.7 per cent, as compared to 30.5 per cent in 1952. By 1956, in contrast to 1955, the virgin lands of northern Kazakhstan had a bumper harvest of grain, which undoubtedly strengthened the relative position of the Kazakh Republic in the Central Asian market. However, the estimated decline in the relative degree of self-sufficiency in Central Asia from 57 per cent to 50 per cent lessened the effect of these closer trade ties on the reduction of terminations from "distant" regions; just as in the period from 1952 to 1955.

An examination of some of the reasons for the failure of efforts to reduce the Central Asian average length of haul for terminated freight should shed some light on the traffic effects of economic development in this region as well as in other outlying areas of the Soviet Union. Among these reasons are:

1. The development of specialized export activities based upon the unique natural and cultural endowment of this region in practice has persistently been given higher priority by Soviet planners than activities designed to reduce the regional average length of haul. The stronger desire to derive the benefits accruing from regional specialization than to reduce average lengths of haul through "comprehensive" regional development can perhaps best be seen by the "squeezing out" of grain crops from the productive, irrigated lands of Central Asia in the face of rising regional imports of grain. Central Asia could undoubtedly become self-sufficient in grain by reducing the acreage in cotton; but this would be too high a price to pay for a reduction in regional transport inputs.

2. Another fundamental reason for the continued long-haul flow of many bulk commodities to Central Asia is the lack of adequate reserves of natural resources which are in great local demand. This is a particular problem in the case of lumber and other forest products, since this commodity group accounts for over one-fourth of the ton-kilometers involved in Central Asian terminations and also because Kazakhstan is unable to supply Central Asia with forest products. The only effort undertaken thus far to check the complementary flow of lumber from the Siberian forests to the tree-sparse republics of Central Asia has been to expand local production of mineral building materials. But because of imperfect substitutability and an inadequate level of local production in relation to local demand, the rapid growth of building materials production in Central Asia in recent years has been accompanied by sharply rising increments of imported lumber. The imperfect substitution of the low-grade coals of Central Asia for higher-grade coal has resulted in at least a portion of the large volume of Central Asian coal imports.

3. In many fields where local production geared closely to the needs of Central Asian consumers has expanded rapidly, the volume of interregional imports has continued to grow because local consumption has increased even more rapidly, at least in absolute terms. Examples of this are provided by the expanding Central Asian minimum deficits of commodities such as mineral fertilizers, ferrous metals, building materials, and coal.

4. Another reason for the persistent growth of Central Asian interregional imports is the relatively limited assortment of locally produced manufactured goods in relation to local demand. This is caused not only by the complete absence of many types of industry but, also, by the inadequate consideration given the needs of the local market by several of the existing industries. The underemphasis of the local market in the planning of the ferrous metals, petroleum, and cotton-textile industries in Central Asia has led to a considerable volume of exports, in addition to the large-scale imports, of diversified products within these three broad commodity groupings.

5. Another factor contributing to the long regional average distance of haul has been the existence of irrational freight flows resulting from the complex system of freight planning. The decentralization of the functions of many of the enormous economic ministries centered in Moscow and the creation of Regional Economic Councils in the Central Asian Republics under the administra-

tive reform of the Soviet economy in 1957 is designed to remove the bureaucratic barriers to the rational planning of economic development and freight movement.[1]

[1]N. S. Krushchev, O Dal'neishem Sovershenstvovanii Organizatsii Upravleniya Promyshlennost'yu i Stroitel'stvom, Dokland na VII Sessii Verkhovnogo Soveta SSSR, May 7, 1957 (Moscow: Gospolitizdat, 1957), pp. 12-18.

CHAPTER VII

SUMMARY AND CONCLUSIONS

The major findings of this study may be grouped under the following three headings: the construction of the Central Asian rail pattern; the technical renovation of the rail pattern; and, commodity movement and regional economic development. The first two of these categories contain substantive conclusions about the construction and technical renovation of the rail pattern, while the third topic, which is also the most extensive, centers around an interpretation of the complex interrelationships between the rail pattern and the movement of commodities as they reflect the conflicting forces of specialization and self-sufficiency in the economic development of Soviet Central Asia.

The Construction of the Central Asian Rail Pattern

1. The rapid economic growth of the Central Asian republics has been associated with an ambitious program of railroad construction. This program has been designed to provide access to formerly isolated nodes of irrigated agriculture and mining and, also, to integrate this region more fully into the national economy as a specialized producer of cotton, for which this area has climatic resources lacking in other parts of the Soviet Union. The building of interregional rail lines, as well as the technical improvement of existing routes, has facilitated regional specialization by lowering the time and cost of commodity interchange. The construction of the Turk-Sib (Semipalatinsk-Arys') and the Trans-Kazakhstan (Karaganda-Chu) trunk-lines during the Soviet era has also promoted the expansion of specialized economic activity in Central Asia by redressing the previous inflexibility in the interregional trade orientation of this region. The completion of these lines has shifted the supply area of grain, lumber, and many other commodities imported by Central Asia from European Russia to Siberia and Kazakhstan. In contrast to the effect of the interregional rail lines on the direction of Central Asian economic development, the laying of numerous rail spurs to mining centers

producing coal, building materials, and other commodities for local consumption, has promoted the intensification of regional self-sufficiency.

2. One of the major weaknesses of the present interregional rail pattern is the extremely circuitous routing involved in the movement of commodities by rail between the western portions of Central Asia and European Russia. Primarily because of the high costs of transshipment and the vast distances separating Krasnovodsk from the major nodes of Central Asian economic activity, maritime routes via the Caspian Sea are unable to offer effective competition to the interregional trunk-lines in the movement of cotton and diversified freight. This is true despite the severe tariff penalties imposed on the movement of ginned cotton from Central Asia to the Moscow Region by rail during navigation season. Another possible remedy for the inefficient rail access of the western portions of Central Asia would be the linking of the Kungrad line (Chardzhou-Kungrad) directly to the rail net of European Russia. But evidently because of the higher priority attached by Soviet planners to the continuation through Kazakhstan of the Chinese-Soviet trunk-line via Sinkiang Province, the extension of the Kungrad line to the northwest has been deferred until some time after 1960.

The Technical Renovation of the Central Asian Rail Pattern

1. One of the most striking features of rail transportation in Central Asia up until the early 1950's was the ability of the rail lines of this region to handle a persistently expanding volume of traffic by relying on internal reserves associated with the more intensive use of existing plant and equipment. Perhaps the best example of this is provided by the rapid increases in the density of train movement made possible by the more intensive utilization of the relatively antiquated electric-staff method of signaling. Supplementing the policy of relying on internal reserves was the selection of the less expensive technical variants when improvements were required. This was demonstrated by the preference given the improvement of signaling rather than the more expensive technical alternative of double-tracking, even on the sections of track with an extremely high flow density. The success of the Soviets in reducing transport investment has important implications for capital-scarce underdeveloped countries.

2. Since the early 1950's, the unprecedented expansion of Central Asian rail traffic, resulting from sharply rising regional income and a declining degree of regional self-sufficiency, has necessitated a large-scale program of technical renovation which, in many respects, represents a distinct departure from the previous emphasis on restricting transport investment. Among the measures now being carried out are: the introduction of powerful Diesel-electric road locomotives on many of the rail lines serving Central Asia and the double-tracking of the sections of route where interregional traffic converges. In addition, the installation of advanced methods of signaling, such as centralized traffic control and automatic blocking, is now being carried out on all the interregional rail lines. The single most important method presently being employed to expand the traffic capacity of the rail net of Central Asia and its approaches is to increase train weights through the use of the newly constructed Diesel-electric locomotives.

3. At present, several important technical limitations impede the ability of the rail lines of Central Asia and Kazakhstan from handling traffic efficiently. One of these is the absence of second tracks on all but a small portion of this rail net, despite the recently launched program of double-tracking. Other problems are the lack of continuous Diesel traction on the main lines of this region and the widespread use of antiquated, coal-burning locomotives for yard switching work, even on sections where the main line is Dieselized. Central Asian rail planners, however, are calling for the Dieselization of all rail operations in this region by 1965.

Commodity Movement and Regional Economic Development

1. The construction of the Turk-Sib Railroad in 1930 was designed specifically to intensify the specialization of Central Asian agriculture on the production of cotton by supplying Siberian grain to compensate for the replacement of grain by cotton on the irrigated plains of the Central Asian republics. The expansion of irrigated cotton acreage in Central Asia was part of a Soviet drive in this period to make the nation self-sufficient in the production of cotton fiber. Contrary to the expectations of the builders of this line, the Turk-Sib played a negligible role in the achievement of national autarky in cotton fiber during the early 1930's, primarily because of the inability of the Siberian

grain lands and forests to produce surpluses for Central Asian consumption. By the start of World War II, however, this route had become the primary artery for the shipment of grain and lumber to Central Asia. At present, the Turk-Sib and the newer Trans-Kazakhstan trunk-line play an important role in the increasing cotton specialization of the irrigated lands of Central Asia by supplying this region with wheat from the virgin lands of Kazakhstan and Siberia, lumber from Siberian forests, and a wide variety of other commodities.

2. The vast increments of Central Asian interregional rail trade during the Soviet era have entailed a considerable volume of extra costs associated with the longer average distances the freight terminated in this region travels in comparison with the other railroads of the Soviet Union. The only railroads with an average haul longer than that of the Central Asian lines are those found in the eastern margin of Eastern Siberia and the Soviet Far East. The average distance of haul for commodities terminating in Central Asia in 1952 was almost twice as long as the national average. Expressed in different terms, an estimated 2.3 per cent of the total ton-kilometer work of the Soviet rail net would have been avoided if the average distance of terminated commodity movement in Central Asia were equal to that of the rest of the nation as a whole. Another, less important, type of extra freight cost is that associated with the pronounced imbalance of Central Asian interregional trade, which has resulted in the large-scale flow of empty freight cars over long distances from Central Asia to bulk commodity loading points in Siberia and Kazakhstan.

3. One of the approaches employed to reduce the extremely long regional average distance of haul has been the attempt to increase trade between Central Asia and the neighboring region of Kazakhstan through the completion of the Trans-Kazakhstan trunk-line in 1953. By strengthening the trade links between these two regions, Soviet planners hoped to alter the inverse distance relationships obtaining in 1952 in the interregional supply of commodities to the Central Asian republics. In that year, Central Asia received five times as much freight from "distant" (non-contiguous) regions as from the neighboring Kazakh Republic. Although attempts to reduce the average distance of haul in all the basic economic regions of the Soviet Union are dependent, to a considerable extent, on the reduction of commodity terminations from "distant" regions, these efforts are of even greater pertinence in Central Asia since the railroads of this region received approxi-

mately 30 per cent of their terminated tonnage in 1952 from "distant" regions. This percentage was considerably higher than a comparable figure for any of the other basic economic regions of the country.

By 1955, the Trans-Kazakhstan trunk-line had helped in strengthening the relative share of Kazakh-originated freight in the total tonnage of freight terminating in the Central Asian market to an estimated 14.3 per cent, as compared to 6.5 per cent in 1952. However, the completion of this line had by no means given Kazakhstan a pre-eminent position in the interregional supply of commodities to Central Asia primarily because of:

a. The lack of diversified production in Kazakhstan complementary to Central Asian demand.

b. The undependability of wheat production on the virgin lands of Kazakhstan.

c. The comparatively small increments of Central Asian coal imports is due to the rapid growth of local coal production. Although the Karaganda Basin has become the principal exporter of coal to Central Asia, the decreasing dependence of the latter region on coal imports and, to a lesser extent, the continued competition from the Kuznetsk Basin have diminished the effectiveness of this achievement.

4. A second approach designed to reduce the average length of haul of Central Asian rail terminations has centered around the intensification of the degree of self-sufficiency in this region. Since 1940, there have been vigorous efforts to increase the relative importance of market-oriented economic activity in Central Asia. Among other things, these efforts have resulted in a rapid expansion in the production of lignite, building materials, and mineral fertilizers. From 1940 to 1952, however, the relative degree of autarky in Central Asia actually declined considerably more than the national average for the basic economic regions. Even more important, a steeper decline in the relative self-sufficiency of Central Asia since 1952 has seriously diminished the effectiveness of the Trans-Kazakhstan trunk-line which, as mentioned above, was scheduled to reduce the volume of Central Asian terminations coming from "distant" regions by increasing the volume of trade between Kazakhstan and Central Asia.

Among the forces hindering attempts to reduce average distances of movement by trying to increase the degree of self-sufficiency in Central Asia, and also in other regions of the Soviet Union, are:

a. The unwillingness of Soviet planners to sacrifice the economies of scale accruing from the expansion of the specialized export activities associated with the natural and cultural endowment of this region, even when such activities have directly conflicted with the development of local, transport-saving economic activities. The squeezing out of grain from the irrigated fields of Central Asia despite the need for large-scale grain imports provides a clear example of this.

b. The lack of adequate reserves of natural resources, such as lumber, which are in great local demand. This is a problem intensified by the imperfect substitutability of local resources for regional imports from distant sources of supply.

c. The growing gap, in absolute terms, between the volume of local production and consumption of many commodities, despite sharply rising increments of local production.

d. The relatively limited assortment of locally-produced manufactured goods.

e. Occasionally inadequate planning of freight shipments. One of the major goals of the decentralization of much of the administration of the Soviet economy in 1957 was to stop "irrational" shipments resulting from the administrative complexity of the Soviet economy.

Future

The creation in 1957 of Regional Economic Councils in Central Asia, to a certain extent, will tend to strengthen the autarkic forces of economic development in this region. This, in turn, would tend to reduce the demand for interregional rail construction and renovation by encouraging greater cooperation between the industries located in the same administrative regions and, also, by promoting the more intensive utilization of local resources. Although this reform may result in a reduction of the average length of haul for certain commodities, such as building materials, it seems unlikely that it will be able to diminish the long-haul flow of commodities to and from Central Asia for the following reasons:

1. Specialized export activities in the administrative regions have been given high priority in this reform.

2. The planning of major commodity flows is still highly centralized.

3. Irrational freight shipments resulting from "provincialism" (the placing of local economic interests above national interests) thus far appear to be at least as frequent as those

under the former system of economic administration.

4. By far, the most important reason for the probable maintenance of an extremely long average length of haul in Central Asia is that the forces tending toward long-haul freight movement are deeply imbedded in the location, resources, and economy of this region, as well as in the other emerging regional economies east of the Urals-Caspian divide. As recent years have demonstrated, these forces are not easily overcome.

THE RAIL PATTERN OF CENTRAL
ASIA AND APPROACHES
K A Z A K H
S. S. R.
U Z B E K
S. S. R.
T U R K M E N
S. S. R.
K I R G H I Z
S. S. R.
T A D Z H I K
S. S. R.
CASPIAN
SEA
ARAL
SEA
LAKE
BALKHASH
KHOREZM
OASIS
Ural'sk
Alexsandrov-Gai
Chkalov
Orsk
Aktyubinsk
Khrom-Tau
Kandagach
Makat
Gur'yev
Koschagyl
Akmolinsk
Karaganda
Zharyk
Atasuskiy
Marganets
Baikonur
Karsakpai
Dzhezkazgan
Mointy
Kounradskiy
Balkhash
Aktogai
Gosgranitsa
Semipalatinsk
Lokot
Aleisk
Leninogorsk
Ust-Kamenogorsk
Zyryanovsk
Taldy-Kurgan
Tekeli
Alma-Ata
Chu
Frunze
Rybach'e
Kazalinsk
Dzhusaly
Chiili
Achisai
Borisovka
Chulak-Tau
Dzhambul
Arys'
Burnoye
Chimkent
Lenger
Lugovaya
Chirchik
Tashkent
Almalyk
Angren
Andizhan
Syr-Darinskiy
Kokand
Dzhalal-Abad
Dzhizak
Ursat'yevskaya
Samarkand
Bukhara
Kagan
Muinak
Kungrad
Krasnovodsk
Nebit
Dag
Vyshka
Kyzyl-Arvat
Ashkhabad
Chardzhou
Mary
Karshi
Kitab
Samsonovo
Stalinabad
Kurgan-Tyube
Kulyab
Termez
Nizhniy Pyandzh
MOSCOW
U S S R
50 0 100 200 MILES
LEGEND
Double Track
Single Track
Narrow Gauge
Double Track Under Constr.
Narrow Gauge Under Constr.
Single Track Under Constr.
Boundary of the USSR
Boundary of the Republics
Capitals of the Republics
Cities
1958

Fig. 37

DATE OF COMPLETION OF THE RAIL LINES OF CENTRAL ASIA AND APPROACHES

KAZAKH S. S. R.

UZBEK S. S. R.

TURKMEN S. S. R.

KIRGHIZ S. S. R.

TADZHIK S. S. R.

CASPIAN SEA

ARAL SEA

LAKE BALKHASH

Chkalov 1918 Orsk 1940 1906 1944 Kandagach 1942 Gur'yev 1906 Kazalinsk 1934 1913 Arys' 1934 1954 1906 Tashkent 1944 1898 1913 Ursat'yevskaya 1933 Samarkand 1888 Kagan Bukhara 1907 Chardzhou 1915 1924 Samsonovo 1931 Stalinabad 1941 1935 Mary 1896 Kushka Ashkhabad 1888 Kyzyl-Arvat 1881 1933 Krasnovodsk Kungrad 1956

Karsakpai Dzhezkazgan 1940 Karaganda 1931 1953 1939 1953 1924 1944 1953 1915 Semipalatinsk 1939 Leninogorsk 1953 Zyryanovsk 1931 Aktogai Gosgranitsa Tekeli 1943 Alma-Ata 1931 Chu 1931 1946 Lugovoya 1924 Frunze 1942 Bystrovka 1950

1937 1928 1916 1924 1916 1928 1931

MOSCOW U S S R

LEGEND

- Double Track
- Single Track
- Narrow Gauge
- Double Track Under Constr.
- Narrow Gauge Under Constr.
- Single Track Under Constr.
- Pre-Revolutionary Line.
- 1958 Number Indicates Year Line Placed In Permanent Operation.
- Boundary of the USSR
- Boundary of the Republics
- Capitals of the Republics
- Cities

50 0 100 200 MILES

1958

Fig. 38

APPENDIX A

TABLE 29

ESTIMATED PERCENTAGE OF TERMINATIONS ON INDIVIDUAL RAILROADS IN UNION REPUBLICS[a]

Republic and Railroad	Per Cent of Terminations
Uzbek SSR	100
Tashkent Railroad[b]	83
Ashkhabad Railroad[c]	17
Turkmen SSR	100
Ashkhabad Railroad	100
Tadzhik SSR	100
Tashkent Railroad[d]	39
Ashkhabad Railroad[e]	61
Kirghiz SSR	100
Tashkent Railroad[f]	40
Turk-Sib Railroad[g]	60

[a]The per cent of terminations is equal to the per cent of the urban population of the oblasts served by individual railroads in the union republics, on the basis of population data appearing in Narodnoye Khozyaistvo SSR v Godu. Fortunately, there was almost no overlap between railroad and oblast boundaries.

[b]Includes Andizhan, Namangan, Samarkand, Fergana, and Tashkent oblasts.

[c]Includes Bukhara, Kashka-Darya, Surkhan-Darya, and Khorezm oblasts and, also, Kara-Kalpak ASSR.

[d]Includes Leninabad oblast.

[e]Includes all of Tadzhikstan, with the exception of Leninabad Oblast.

[f]Includes Dzhalal-Abad and Osh oblasts.

[g]Includes Issyk-Kul', Tyan'-Shan, and Frunze oblasts.

APPENDIX B

TABLE 30

AVERAGE LENGTH OF HAUL OF TERMINATED COMMODITIES ON RAILROADS WITHIN BASIC ECONOMIC REGIONS, 1952[a]

Region	Kilometer
North	
Northern	840
Pechora	550
Average	695
Northwest	
Kirov	1,150
October	890
Average	1,020
West	
Belorussian	530
Minsk	700
Average	615
Center	
Moscow-Circular	800
Yaroslavl	720
Moscow-Ryazan	660
Moscow-Kursk	630
Average	703
South	
Yuzhnaya	515
Severo-Donets	430
Stalinsk	470
Southwest	610
Odessa	695
Average	545
Caucasus	
North Caucasus	565
Azerbaidzhan	900
Transcaucasus	975
Average	813
Trans-Volga	
Ryazan-Ural'sk	780
Stalingrad	515
Kuibyshev	920
Average	738
Urals	
Perm	515
Sverdlovsk	630
Yuzhno-Ural'sk	855
Average	667
Kazakhstan[b]	
Karaganda	830
Average	830
Central Asia	
Tashkent	1,410
Ashkhabad	1,460
Turk-Sib	1,450
Average	1,440
Western Siberia	
Omsk	1,075
Tomsk	720
Average	898
Eastern Siberia[c]	
Krasnoyarsk	980
East-Siberian	965
Average	973
Far East	
Far-Eastern	1,880
Primor'ye	2,170
Trans-Baikal	2,010
Average	2,020
National Average	749

[a]Khanukov, pp. 237-38.

[b]Turk-Sib Railroad data are grouped under the regional heading of Central Asia.

[c]The Trans-Baikal Railroad average distance of haul is placed under the heading of Far East.

APPENDIX C

TABLE 31

INTERREGIONAL RAIL TRADE OF CENTRAL ASIA[a]
(Millions of Tons)

Type of Trade	1940[b]	1952[b]	1956 (Estimate)[c]
Rail imports	4.5	9.2	18.1
Rail exports	3.6	7.2	8.4
Total interregional trade	8.1	16.4	26.5

[a]Derived from information in Khanukov, pp. 230-31; and Transport i Svyaz' SSSR, p. 67.

[b]The volume of interregional trade in 1940 and 1952 was obtained by first converting the per cent of Central Asian rail terminations originating locally into tonnage figures. These figures were then subtracted from the tonnage of Central Asian rail terminations and originations to arrive at the volume of rail imports and exports, respectively.

[c]The volume of Central Asian imports in 1956, estimated at 8.4 million tons, was arrived at by increasing the 1952 export tonnage by the per cent increase in total Central Asian rail originations from 1952 to 1956. If the resulting export figure obtained in 1956, it can be determined that Central Asia would have imported 50 per cent of its total rail terminations in that year. This figure of 50 per cent probably does not overestimate the actual per cent of non-local freight in total terminations because if Central Asia were to export only as much freight in 1956 as in 1952, the per cent of locally-originated freight in total terminations could not have exceeded 53 per cent. Thus, the volume of rail exports in 1956 was arrived at by multiplying the tonnage of Central Asian terminations in that year by 50 per cent. The same method applied to 1955 Central Asian termination, incidentally, yields an estimate of 57 per cent for the relative share of locally-originated freight in the total terminated freight of this region.

APPENDIX D

TABLE 32

RAIL EXPORTS OF THE KAZAKH REPUBLIC IN 1952 AND 1955[a]

Year	Total	Central Asia	Trans-Volga	Urals	West Siberia	Other
Rail exports in 1952						
Per cent	100.0	7.0	12.4	58.5	13.4	8.7
Est. tonnage (millions)[b]	24.19	1.69	3.00	14.16	3.24	2.10
Rail exports in 1955						
Per cent	100.0	10.6	11.0	56.1	13.6	8.7
Est. tonnage (millions)[c]	42.90	4.50	4.72	24.07	5.83	3.78

[a]Percentage data for 1952 taken from Khanukov, p. 228; percentage data for 1955 taken from Kazakhskaya SSR, p. 166.

[b]Total tonnage of rail exports in 1952 was arrived at by first determining the per cent of Kazakh terminations originated locally from Table 33. This percentage was converted into an absolute figure and then subtracted from the tonnage of Kazakh originations in 1952 to determine the tonnage of rail exports.

[c]The total tonnage of Kazakh rail exports in 1955 was arrived at by multiplying total Kazakh rail originations in that year by 74 per cent. The use of the latter figure is based upon the following statement on p. 115 of Kazakhskaya SSR, ". . . a little more than one fourth of the originated goods are shipped within the republic, and about three fourths shipped beyond her boundaries."

APPENDIX E

TABLE 33

RAIL EXPORTS OF GRAIN FROM KAZAKHSTAN, 1955[a]

Commodity	Total	Central Asia	Trans-Volga	Urals	West Siberia	Other
Grain						
Per cent of exports	100.0	10.7	8.4	14.7	3.3	62.9
Est. tonnage (thousands)[b]..	1,330	142	112	195	44	837

[a]Derived from Kazkhskaya SSR, p. 116.

[b]The total tonnage of Kazakh grain exports was arrived at by multiplying the per cent of these commodities in the total rail exports of the republic by the estimated total tonnage of Kazakh rail exports (see Table, p. 90).

APPENDIX F

TABLE 34

PER CENT OF LOCAL ORIGINATIONS IN THE TOTAL TERMINATED RAIL TONNAGE OF THE BASIC ECONOMIC REGIONS, 1940 AND 1952[a]

Region	Per Cent of Local Freight Originations in Total Terminated Tonnage[b]		Changes in Percentages from 1940 to 1952
	1940	1952	
National average .	67.9	67.8	- 0.1
Central Asia	67.3	63.0	- 4.3
North	62.5	79.5	17.0
Northwest	49.9	48.0	- 1.9
West	57.9	64.3	6.4
Center	54.4	59.4	5.0
South	86.3	85.8	- 0.5
Caucasus	72.0	66.9	- 5.1
Trans-Volga	44.0	39.6	- 4.4
Urals	67.4	66.9	- 0.5
Kazakhstan	46.7	53.6	6.9
Western Siberia ..	70.0	68.3	- 1.7
Eastern Siberia ..	79.3	76.4	- 2.9
Far East	77.7	78.2	- 0.5

[a]Derived from Khanukov, p. 233.

[b]Although the use of value instead of tonnage relationships might reveal a far different degree of self-sufficiency than the above data indicate, the use of tonnage figures is more pertinent to the goals of the present study.

APPENDIX G

TABLE 35

PER CENT OF TERMINATIONS FROM NEIGHBORING AND "DISTANT" REGIONS IN THE TERMINATED RAIL TONNAGE OF THE BASIC ECONOMIC REGIONS, 1940 AND 1952[a]

Region	Per Cent of Terminations from Neighboring Basic Economic Regions		Per Cent of Terminations from "Distant" Basic Economic Regions	
	1940	1952	1940	1952
National average	23.8	21.9	8.3	10.3
Central Asia ..	7.3	6.5	25.4	30.5
North	23.4	16.2	14.1	4.3
Northwest	17.6	31.0	32.5	21.0
West	37.4	29.3	4.7	6.4
Center	43.0	27.0	2.6	13.6
South	9.1	9.1	4.6	5.1
Caucasus	22.0	20.4	6.0	12.7
Trans-Volga ...	38.5	57.2	17.5	3.2
Urals	28.0	25.7	4.6	7.4
Kazakhstan	45.7	36.5	7.6	9.9
Western Siberia	23.7	25.0	6.3	6.7
Eastern Siberia	6.3	7.3	14.4	16.3
Far East	8.1	6.1	14.2	15.7

[a]Khanukov, p. 233

APPENDIX H

CHANGES SINCE 1958

The Regional and Historical Setting of Rail Transportation in Central Asia

The Regional Economy

Agriculture.--The recently launched drive to increase the production of synthetic fibers in the Soviet Union has not been associated with a decreased emphasis on the growing of cotton in the irrigated plains of Central Asia. By 1965, the end of the Seven-Year Plan, the Soviet Union hopes to be harvesting 5.7 to 6.1 million tons of raw cotton annually.[1] This would represent a 30 to 40 per cent increase over the 4.4 million tons produced in 1958.

As in the past, the expansion of cotton production will be achieved through increasing both the acreage of irrigated cotton land and yields per acre. During the Seven-Year Plan, however, considerably more stress will be laid upon extending the irrigated cotton area than upon increasing average yields per acre. In the Uzbek Republic, for example, approximately 450,000 to 500,000 hectares of previously uncultivated land will be brought into crop production by irrigative-meliorative measures.[2] If this program is implemented, the amount of irrigated land in the republic will increase by roughly 30 per cent. The projected increases in average cotton yields per hectare in the Uzbek Republic are on a considerably more modest scale. By 1965, Uzbekistan is slated to obtain an average of 25 to 26 centners of cotton per hectare, as compared to an average yield of 22 centners per hectare in 1956.[3]

---

[1] Vneocherednoy XXI S'yezd Kommunisticheskoy Partii Sovetskogo Soyuza: Stenograficheskiy Otchet, II (Moscow: Gospolitizdat, 1959), 496.

[2] S. K. Ziyadullayev, Sovetskiy Uzbekistan v Semiletke (Tashkent: Gosizdat Uzbekskoy SSR, 1959), p. 70.

[3] Ibid., p. 65.

Industry.--The Seven-Year Plan calls for the rapid growth of industry in the Central Asian republics, with particular emphasis on the industrial expansion of the Uzbek Republic. Included in the numerous industrial projects scheduled to be carried out in this period are: the reconstruction of 28 of the 46 machine-building plants in the Uzbek Republic; the expansion of non-ferrous metal production, particularly lead, zinc and copper; and the completion of a second oil refinery in the Fergana Basin, at the town of Fergana. The most striking change in the industrial economy of Central Asia, however, will be the intensive exploitation of the recently discovered deposits of natural gas in the vicinity of Bukhara. The major deposit of natural gas is at Gazli, 110 kilometers northwest of Bukhara. The Gazli reserves are estimated to be largest deposits in the Soviet Union, even though the total gas reserves of the Uzbek Republic are considerably less than those of the RSFSR.

In 1958, the Uzbek Republic produced only 172 million cubic meters of natural gas, which constituted less than 1 per cent of national production. By 1965, however, natural gas production in Uzbekistan is scheduled to reach 18.3 billion cubic meters, or one-eighth of the total planned production in the USSR.[1] According to tentative estimates, the Uzbek Republic will be producing almost 60 billion cubic meters of natural gas annually by 1973.[2] No less impressive than the planned increases in the production of natural gas are the plans to pipe the natural gas of the Bukhara region to the Urals and, also, to the major urban centers of Central Asia and southern Kazakhstan. A pipeline is scheduled to be laid over the 1,800 kilometers separating Gazli from the Urals industrial center of Chelyabinsk by 1963, while two years later, a parallel 2,100 kilometer pipeline is slated to be in operation between the Gazli fields and the city of Sverdlovsk in the Urals. By 1965, additional pipelines will have been laid from other gas fields near Bukhara to Tashkent, the Fergana Basin, Alma-Ata, Stalinabad, and intermediate points.[3]

The intensive development of local natural gas is associated with ambitious plans to expand the chemical industries of Central Asia. For example, huge nitrogen fertilizer plants, using natural gas as their primary raw material, will be constructed at Fergana and Navoi, a village approximately 100 kilometers west of

---

[1] Ibid., p. 27. [2] Ibid. [3] Ibid., p. 28.

Bukhara which is being transformed into a major industrial complex. A major effect of the increased utilization of natural gas in Central Asia, and particularly in the Uzbek Republic, will be a radical shift in the sources of power for the generation of electricity, as Table 36 reveals:

TABLE 36

SOURCES OF ELECTRICITY IN THE UZBEK REPUBLIC[a]

Source	Per Cent of Electricity Production	
	1958	1965 (Planned)
Natural gas	1.1	42.6
Coal	28.1	33.0
Hydropower	62.6	22.7
Petroleum	8.2	1.7

Source: Ziyadullayev, p. 31.

[a]Table 5, p. 26, shows the overall energy balance of the Uzbek Republic in 1955 and includes guza-paya- the stems of the cotton plant.

The planned increase in the relative share of natural gas in the generation of electricity, from a little over 1 per cent in 1958 to almost 43 per cent in 1965, will play the major role in the scheduled expansion of electricity production in Uzbekistan to 11.7 billion kilowatt-hours in 1965, as compared to 4.6 billion kilowatt-hours generated at the start of the Seven-Year Plan.[1] Several large, thermal-power stations based on natural gas are scheduled to come into operation during the Seven-Year Plan. One of these plants is located in the new industrial complex at Navoi. By 1965, the Uzbek Republic will consume approximately 6 billion cubic meters of natural gas, or one-third of its scheduled production.[2] This, of course, means that two-thirds of Uzbek natural gas production in 1965 will be piped to the Urals, southern Kazakhstan, and adjacent Central Asian republics. As Table 36 points out, the planned increase in the relative importance of natural gas in the generation of electricity will be accomplished at the expense of hydropower and, to a lesser extent, petroleum. Coal is actually scheduled to increase in importance as a source of Uzbek electricity

[1]*Ibid.*, pp. 40-41. [2]*Ibid.*, p. 31.

by the end of the Seven-Year Plan. This is reflected in the sharp increase envisaged in the production of Uzbek coal, primarily from the Angren lignite mines, from 3.6 million tons in 1958 to 6.2 million tons in 1965.[1] Approximately one-half of the Uzbek coal mined in the latter year is scheduled to be used by the power plant at Angren, which will have a capacity of 600,000 kilowatts.

The Interregional Rail Pattern

Flow Densities

The relative importance of the three interregional rail lines linking Central Asia with the rest of the Soviet Union is clearly shown on a general diagram of freight density (in the "freight direction" or toward Central Asia) on the railroads of Kazakhstan for the year 1955 which recently appeared in the journal *Geografiya i Khozyaistvo*.[2] The heavy volume of traffic handled by the single-track Kazalinsk route is one of the most striking features of the diagram of flow densities. This route had an average freight density of 10 to 20 million tons (presumably per kilometer of route) from Kandagach down to Tashkent, except for a 448 kilometer stretch between Aral'skoye, on the northern shore of the Aral Sea, to Kzyl-Orda which had an average southbound flow density of 5 to 10 million tons. The second major interregional rail line, the Turk-Sib, had a traffic density of 10 to 20 million tons from Novosibirsk to Semipalatinsk. The average density of movement on this route declined to somewhere between 5 and 10 million tons from Semipalatinsk southwards to the junction with the Trans-Kazakhstan trunk-line at Chu, while the freight density from Chu to the rail hub of Arys' was once again in the category of 10 to 20 million tons. The light traffic load of the Mointy-Chu line contrasted sharply with the volume of freight shipped on the neighboring interregional rail lines. From Karaganda southwards to Mointy, the Trans-Kazakhstan route handled from 5 to 10 million tons of freight, but from Mointy to Chu, the average density of freight movement was only from 1 to 5 million tons. This latter density figure was also

---

[1] *Ibid.*, p. 33.

[2] I. V. Nikol'skiy, "Geografiya Transporta Kazakhstana," *Geografiya i Khozyaistvo*, I (December, 1958), 48.

found on most of the branch-lines of the interregional routes.[1] The only branch lines with a freight density less than 1 million tons were the line from the Turk-Sib to the mining center of Tekeli and the new line in the Altay mining region from Ust'-Kamenogorsk to Zyryanovsk. Both of these lines had average traffic densities ranging from 500,000 tons to 1 million tons.

The prospects of diminishing the traffic burden of the Kazalinsk route in the Seven-Year Plan are hardly encouraging. The frequently discussed extension of the Chardzhou-Kungrad line to Makat and, eventually, to Aleksandrov-Gay was not included in the Seven-Year Plan. In fact, the only rail lines scheduled to be constructed in Central Asia and its approaches from 1958 to 1965 are the line between Gur'yev and Astrakhan and the long-awaited rail route from Malinovoye Ozero to Rubtsovsk, which is designed to provide more direct rail access between the Altay region and markets and sources of supply located to the west.[2]

Caspian Sea Routes

The role of routes via the Caspian Sea as arteries of interregional trade will apparently have a relatively minor effect on interregional rail traffic, except in the movement of petroleum. The competitive weaknesses of Caspian Sea routes from Central Asia can perhaps best be demonstrated by the example of cotton fiber shipments. In 1955, only 13,000 tons of cotton fiber were shipped from the port of Krasnovodsk--an amount equal to 13 per cent of the estimated interregional rail exports.[3] Perhaps the most striking characteristic of the maritime exports of cotton fiber from Central Asia is the insignificant role of the all-water Caspian-Volga route. The port of Astrakhan handled only 12,000 tons of baled cotton in 1955, or less than one-tenth of the

---

[1]In this category are the following branch lines: Gur'yev-Kandagach; Zharyk-Dzhezkazgan; Mointy-Balkhash; Lokot'-Leninogorsk; and, Dzhambul-Chulak Tau.

[2]S. I. Bagayev, "Novoye Zheleznodorozhnoye Stroitel'stvo Snizheniye ego Stoimosti i Povysheniye Kachestva," *Zheleznodorozhnyy Transport*, XXXXI (February, 1959), 16.

[3]Tsentral'nyy Nauchno-Issledovatel'skiy Institut Ekonomiki i Ekspluatatsii Vodnogo Transporta Ministerstva Rechnogo Flota, *Voprosy Ekonomiki Smeshanykh Zheleznodorozhno-Vodnykh Perevozok* (Moscow: Ministerstvo Rechnogo Flota, 1958), p. 156. Cited hereafter as *Voprosy Ekonomiki Smeshanykh Zheleznodorozhno-Vodnykh Perevozok*.

Krasnovodsk cotton loadings. The port of Makhach-Kala, by contrast, unloaded a little over 70,000 tons of Central Asian cotton, while about 48,000 tons were shipped across the Caspian to Baku.[1]

Among the reasons frequently cited for the under-utilization of the Caspian Sea routes are the long delays and high costs of shipping goods via these routes. For example, the average delay between the arrival and departure of cotton fiber at the port of Krasnovodsk (October, 1955) is 17 days, while some rail arrivals of cotton fiber have to wait two to three months before being loaded into Caspian Sea vessels.[2] The necessity of handling all loading-unloading operations at the river port of Astrakhan manually, to say nothing of the other problems associated with the use of this port, considerably increases the time and costs of shipments via the Caspian-Volga route. Not only do the transshipments required for the shipment of goods by way of the Caspian Sea directly increase the costs and time of movement, but they also have a pronounced negative effect on the quality of shipments. For one thing, a sizable percentage of the cotton bales arriving by rail at the port of Krasnovodsk break open during transshipment.[3] For these and other reasons, Central Asian cotton ginneries try to avoid using the Caspian Sea for the movement of cotton fiber to the textile mills of European Russia.[4]

The high costs of cotton shipments via the Caspian Sea are reflected in the general tariffs. For example, the freight charges for the shipment of one ton of baled cotton from Kagan' to Moscow by an all-rail route is 116 rubles, while a corresponding tariff for the Caspian-Volga route is 150 rubles.[5] Thus, only when the 50 per cent penalty on the shipment of cotton fiber to European Russia by rail during the navigation season is applied are the freight charges for the Caspian-Volga route less than the all rail traffic. But the resulting differential of 24 rubles (174 - 150) apparently does not compensate for the inferior freight service provided by the Caspian-Volga route. The 1955 rail tariffs eliminated the 50 per cent penalty on the all-rail shipment of cotton fiber to European Russia for originating points on the Tashkent railroad, while retaining this

---

[1] Ibid. [2] Ibid., p. 158. [3] Ibid., p. 159.
[4] Ibid., p. 162. [5] Ziyadullayev, pp. 164-165.

penalty for points served by the Ashkhabad railway.[1]

Plans for a rail ferry between Krasnovodsk and Baku have recently been revived. The most recent suggestion is for a passenger-freight train ferry with a capacity of 300 passengers and 30 four-axle freight cars to shuttle between these two ports.[2] Even if this plan were implemented, it could scarcely provide more than a partial remedy to the problems of Caspian Sea transportation.

The Technical Renovation of the Rail Pattern

Signaling

The major change in signaling on the rail pattern of Central Asia is the extension of automatic block signaling from Ursat'yevskaya westward to Samarkand and eastward to the gateway of the Fergana Basin--Leninabad.[3]

Dieselization

According to the Seven-Year Plan, diesel traction will be introduced on the entire route of the Turk-Sib south of Barnaul; on the Trans Caspian line from Ziyadin to Ursat'yevskaya; and, the sections of the Kazalinsk route which were not dieselized as of 1957.[4] Thus, by 1965, every mainline route in Central Asia and its approaches will be dieselized. Even in that year, however, many of the branch lines in the region under study will still be relying upon steam locomotives.[5] The failure to install diesel traction on these lines during the Seven-Year Plan presumably reflects the major delaying factor of dieselization in the Soviet Union--a shortage of diesel-electric locomotives.

---

[1] U.S.S.R., Ministerstvo Putey Soobshcheniy SSSR, Tarifnoye Rukovodstvo No. 1 (Moscow: Transzheldorizdat, 1957), p. 62. Cited hereafter as Tarifnoye Rukovodstvo No. 1.

[2] B. B. Sushkov and Yu. Yu. Siryy, "Zheleznodorozhnyy Parom dlya Kaspiiskogo Morya," Zheleznodorozhnyy Transport, XXXXI (April, 1959), 56-57.

[3] Ziyadullayev, p. 74.

[4] "Elektricheskaya i Teplovoznaya Tyaga," Zheleznodorozhnyy Transport, Vol. XXXXI (February, 1959), inset map.

[5] Among these lines are: Rubtsovsk-Altay Complex; Lugovaya-Frunze-Rybach'ye; Zharyk-Dzhezkazgan; Mointy-Balkhash, Ursat'yevskaya-Fergana Basin; Karshi-Stalinabad; and, Mary-Kushka.

Even though diesel traction will not be found on every rail line of Central Asia and its approaches through Kazakhstan by 1965, the dieselization of the main lines should aid considerably in handling the projected traffic volume of that year.

Interregional Trade

Exports

Even if the goal set by the Seven-Year Plan to expand cotton production is achieved, the increased volume of cotton fiber exports from Central Asia would not make a significant contribution to a narrowing of the gap between the volume of regional imports and exports. Little help in this respect can be expected from Central Asian petroleum. The role of the railroad in exporting Turkmen petroleum is severely handicapped by existing tariffs. A 50 per cent penalty is levied on all rail shipments of crude oil from stations on the Ashkhabad railroad to any area not served by the Ashkhabad, Tashkent, or Turk-Sib railroads.[1] The same penalty applies to the rail movement of gasoline, diesel fuel and tractor kerosene from the port and refinery at Krasnovodsk; although the 50 per cent penalty on tractor kerosene is in effect only during navigation season.[2] These tariffs, incidentally, seem to have had a greater effect on Caspian Sea movement than the 50 per cent penalty levied on cotton fiber rail shipments. A regional export which someday might rank with cotton fiber in terms of value is natural gas. But the railroad is not competitive with the pipeline in the movement of this commodity.

Imports

The major change envisaged by the Seven-Year Plan in the predominant, southbound flow of bulk commodities to the Central Asian republics is the complete halting of all Karaganda coal movement to the Central Asian market.[3] As mentioned in the text, the Karaganda coal mines supplied approximately 1.9 million tons of coal to Central Asia and southern Kazakhstan. The flow of Kuzbass coal west of Alma-Ata apparently will also be of negligible

---

[1] Tarifnoye Rukovodstvo No. 1, pp. 92-95.

[2] Ibid.

[3] Vneocherednoy XXI S'yezd Kommunisticheskoy Partii, II, 515.

importance. In fact, there is a 50 per cent tariff penalty on the shipment of Kuzbass coal west of Alma-Ata.[1] But yet, as seen earlier in this appendix, the relative share of coal in the generation of electricity in Uzbekistan, the major industrial region of Central Asia, is scheduled to increase from 28 per cent to 33 per cent during the Seven-Year Plan. This means that the planned increases in local coal production (including lignite) will enable Central Asia to meet expanding local demand as well as to become self-sufficient in coal--a long sought-after goal of uncertain economic merit.

There are no indications that the enormous regional imports of bulk commodities, such as grain and lumber, will not continue to increase during the Seven-Year Plan. In this connection it might be mentioned that the dominance of Siberia in supplying lumber to Central Asia is strengthened by a 25 per cent penalty which is levied on the rail movement of forest products from the Urals to the Central Asian republics.[2]

Attempts to Reduce the Average Distance of Haul of Rail Freight Terminations in Central Asia

If successful, the plan to eliminate Karaganda coal from the Central Asian market would debilitate even further the trade ties between Kazakhstan and Central Asian republics. Inasmuch as Karaganda coal would be replaced by local coal, this would tend to reduce the regional average distance of haul. This effect, however, could be more than counterbalanced by the rapid growth of long haul, bulk-commodity imports, which could also actually decrease the degree of regional self-sufficiency. Still another consequence of the elimination of Karaganda coal from the Central Asian energy balance would be a sharp decline in the already weak role of the Trans Kazakhstan route as an interregional trunk-line.

---

[1] Tarifnoye Rukovodstvo No. 1, p. 88.

[2] Ibid., p. 74.

APPENDIX I

MAP AND PHOTOGRAPH SOURCES

Figure	Map Sources
1	Freikin, p. 206 (map). Narzikulov and Ryazantsev, p. 91 (map). Cherdantsev, pp. 246, 291, 327 (maps). Geograficheskiy Atlas SSSR: dlya 7-go i 8-go Klassov Sredney Shkoly (Moscow: Glavnoye Upravleniye Geodezii i Kartografii pri Sovete Ministrov SSSR, 1951), pp. 56-57 (maps).
2	Atlas SSSR (2d ed.; Moscow: Glavnoye Upravleniye Geodezii Kartografii pri Sovete Ministrov SSSR, 1955), map Nos. 49-56. Suslov, pp. 576-78.
3	Geograficheskiy Atlas SSSR, p. 7 (map). B. P. Alisov, Klimat SSSR (Moscow: Izdatel'stvo Moskovskogo Universiteta, 1956), Inset map No. 8.
14	Atlas SSSR, map No. 57. Uzbekskaya SSR, pp. 245-46. Narzikulov and Ryazantsev, p. 129. Gudok, July 19, 1956.
17	Atlas SSSR, map Nos. 47-48.
18	Gudok, September 30, 1956 (map). Tulyaganov, Zheleznodorozhnyy Transport, XXXVIII (September, 1957), 6. Mulyukin, Zheleznodorozhnyy Transport, XXXVIII (July, 1957), 10. Petrov and Tsenin, Zheleznodorozhnyy Transport, XXXVII (October, 1956), 45 (map).
19	Distances taken from Ofitsial'nyy Ukazatel' Passazhirskikh Soobshcheniy: Leto 1957 Goda.
20	Gudok, March 31, 1956. Gudok, July 19, 1956. Kulak, Zheleznodorozhnyy Transport, XXXVIII (October, 1957), 79.
21	Ofitsial'nyy Ukazatel' Passazhirskikh Soobshcheniy: Leto 1957 Goda, pp. 477-95, 632-44, 646, 661.
22	Orobinskiy, Zheleznodorozhnyy Transport, XXXVII (September, 1956), 18. Kulak, Zheleznodorozhnyy Transport, XXXVIII (October, 1957), 78-79. Kolyada, Zheleznodorozhnyy Transport, XXXVII (September, 1956), 73.

Figure	Map Sources
23	Zaglyadimov, Petrov, and Sergeyev, inset map. Beskrovnyy and Belen'kiy, Zheleznodorozhnyy Transport, XXXVII (November, 1956), 16. "Rabota Zheleznodorozhnogo Transporta v 1957 g.," Zheleznodorozhnyy Transport, XXXIX (February, 1958), 26. Kulak, Zheleznodorozhnyy Transport, XXXVIII (October, 1957), 79. Osyannikov and Larin, Zheleznodorozhnyy Transport, XXXVIII (July, 1957), 67.
25	Railroad boundaries taken from Ofitsial'nyy Ukazatel' Passazhirskikh Soobshcheniy: Leto 1957 Goda.
26	Transport i Svyaz' SSSR, p. 67.
27	Ibid.
28	Ibid.
29	Ibid.
30	Ibid., pp. 70-74.
31	Ibid.
32	Khanukov, pp. 237-38.
33	Ibid., p. 228.
34	Kazakhskaya SSR, p. 116.
35	Khanukov, p. 233.
36	Ibid.
37	Atlas SSSR, map Nos. 47-58. Uzbekskaya SSR, pp. 245-46. Narzikulov and Ryazantsev, p. 129. Gudok, July 19, 1956. Kazkakhskaya SSR, pp. 218-21. Zhelezorudnaya Baza Chernoi Metallurgii SSSR, p. 367.
38	Gudok, April 9, 1957. Uzbekskaya SSR, pp. 245-46. Vol'fson, Ledovskoi, and Shil'nikov, pp. 506-507. Aziatskaya Rossiya, II, 545-50.

Photograph Sources

13	Tadzhikskaya SSR, inset photographs.
16	Kazakhskaya SSR, inset photograph.
24	Courtesy of V. V. Zvonkov.

All other photographs used in this text were taken by the author in July, 1957.

BIBLIOGRAPHY

Government Publications

Russia. Pereselencheskago Upravleniye Glavnago Upraveniya Zemleustroistva i Zemledeliya. *Aziatskaya Rossiya.* 2 vols. Saint Petersburg: Izdaniye Pereselencheskago Upravleniya Glavnago Upravleniya Zemleustroistva i Zemledeliya, 1914.

U.S. Interstate Commerce Commission. *Sixty-Eighth Annual Report on Transport Statistics in the United States for the Year Ended December 31, 1954.* Washington: Government Printing Office, 1955.

U.S.S.R. Gosplan pri Sovete Narodnykh Komissarov SSSR. *Osnovnyye Ob'yekty Kapital'nogo Stroitel'stvo vo Vtorom Pyatiletii.* Moscow: Partizdat, 1934.

________. *Proyekt Vtorogo Pyatiletnego Plana Razvitiya Narodnogo Khozyaistvo SSSR: (1933-1937 gg.).* 2 vols. Moscow: Partizdat, 1934.

U.S.S.R. Komitet Sodeistviya Postroiki Turkesano-Sibirskoi Zheleznoi Dorogi pri SNK, RSFSR. *Turkestano-Sibirskaya Magistral': Sbornik Statey.* Moscow, 1929.

U.S.S.R. Ministerstvo Putey Soobshcheniya SSSR. Glavnoye Passazhirskoye Upravleniye. *Ofitsial'nyy Ukazatel' Passazhirskikh Soobshcheniy: Leto 1957 Goda.* Moscow: Transzheldorizdat, 1957.

U.S.S.R. Ministerstvo Ugol'noi Promyshlennosti. *Ugol'naya Promyshlennost' SSSR: Statisticheskiy Spravochnik.* Moscow: Ugletekhizdat, 1957.

U.S.S.R. Narodnyy Komissariat Putey Soobshcheniya. *Materialy po Statistike Putey Soobshcheniya.* Vols. CV, CXXXI, and CXXXIX. Moscow: Transzheldorizdat, 1935.

________. *Ofitsial'nyy Ukazatel' Zheleznodorozhnykh, Vodnykh, i Drugikh Passazhirskikh Soobshcheniy: Zimneye Dvizheniye--1934-35 Godu.* Moscow: Transzheldorizdat, 1957.

U.S.S.R. Statisticheskoye Upravleniye Kazakhskoi SSR. *Narodnoye Khozyaistvo Kazakhskoi SSR: Statisticheskiy Sbornik.* Alma-Ata: Kazakhskoye Gosudarstvennoye Izdatel'stvo, 1957.

U.S.S.R. Tsentral'noye Statisticheskoye Upravleniye. *Mezhraionniy Gruzooborot na Zheleznodorozhnykh i Vodnykh Putyakh za 1926-27 i 1927-28 gg.* Moscow: Statizdat, 1930.

U.S.S.R. Tsentral'noye Statisticheskoye Upravleniye pri Sovete Ministrov SSSR. *Narodnoye Khozyaistvo SSSR v 1956 Godu: Statisticheskiy Yezhegodnik.* Moscow: Gosstatizdat, 1957.

________. *Promyshlennost' SSSR: Statisticheskiy Sbornik.* Moscow: Gosstatizdat, 1957.

________. *Transport i Svyaz' SSSR: Statisticheskiy Sbornik.* Moscow: Gosstatizdat, 1957.

Books and Pamphlets

Akademiya Nauk SSSR, Institut Geografii. Povolzh'ye: Ekonomiko-Geograficheskaya Kharakteristika. Moscow: Geografgiz, 1957.

Akademiya Nauk SSSR, Institut Geografii, and Akademiya Nauk Kazakhskoi SSR. Kazakhskaya SSR: Ekonomiko-Geograficheskaya Kharakteristika. Moscow: Geografgiz, 1957.

Akademiya Nauk SSSR, Sovet po Izucheniyu Prirodnikh Resursov Turkmenskoi SSR. Problemy Turkmenii. Vol. I: Trudy Pervoi Konferentsii po Izucheniyu Proizvoditel'nykh Sil Turkmenskoi SSR. Leningrad: Izdatel'stvo Akademiya Nauk SSSR, 1934.

Akademiya Nauk Uzbekskoi SSR, Institut Ekonomiki. Voprosy Ekonomiki Promyshlennosti Uzbekskoi SSR. Tashkent: Izdatel'stvo Akademii Nauk Uzbekskoi SSR, 1957.

Alisov, B. P. Klimat SSSR. Moscow: Izdatel'stvo Moskovskogo Universiteta, 1956.

Arkhipov, N. P. Sredne-Aziatskiye Respubliki. Moscow: Gosizdat, 1956.

Balzak, S., Vasyutin, V., and Feigin, Ya. (eds.) Economic Geography of the USSR. American edition edited by Chauncy D. Harris. New York: The Macmillan Company, 1949.

Beshchev, B. P. Zheleznodorozhnnyy Transport SSSR v Shestoi Pyatiletke. Moscow: Transzheldorizdat, 1957.

Cherdantsev, G. N., Nikitin, N. P., Tutykhin, B. A. (eds.) Ekonomicheskaya Geografiya SSSR: Rossiiskaya Sovetskaya Federativnaya Sotsialisticheskaya Respublika. Moscow: Uchpedgiz, 1956.

Chernomordik, D. I. Zheleznodorozhnyye Gruzovyye Tarify SSSR. Moscow: Izdatel'stvo Akademii Nauk SSSR, 1953.

Clark, M. Gardner. The Economics of Soviet Steel. Cambridge: Harvard University Press, 1956.

Curzon, George N. Russia in Central Asia. London: Longmans, Green, and Company, 1889.

Freikin, Z. G. Turkmenskaya SSR: Ekonomiko-Geograficheskaya Kharakteristika. Moscow: Geografgiz, 1957.

Gaister, A. E. (ed.) Srednyaya Aziya. Vol. VII: Trudy Pervoi Vsesoyuznoi Konferentsii po Razmeshcheniyu Proizvoditel'nykh Sil Soyuza SSR. Moscow: Izdatel'stvo Obshchestva Izucheniya Sovetskoi Azii, 1933.

Galitskiy, A. E. Planirovaniye Perevozok. Moscow: Gosplanizdat, 1939.

Gibshman, A. E. et al. Osnovy Proyektirovaniya Zheleznykh Dorog. Moscow: Transzheldorizdat, 1954.

Hunter, Holland. Soviet Transportation Policy. Cambridge: Harvard University Press, 1957.

Khachaturov, T. S. Zheleznodorozhnyy Transport SSSR. Moscow: Transzheldorizdat, 1952.

Khanukov, E. D. Transport i Razmeshcheniye Proizvodstva. Moscow: Transzheldorizdat, 1956.

Khrushchev, N. S. O Dal'neishem Sovershenstvovanii Organizatsii Upravleniya Promyshlennost'yu i Stroitel'stvom. Doklad na VII Sessii Verkhovnogo Soveta SSSR, May 7, 1957. Moscow: Gospolitizdat, 1957.

Koldomasov, Yu. I. Ratsionalizatsiya Perevozok na Zheleznodorozhnom Transporte. 2d ed. rev. Moscow: Transzheldorizdat, 1954.

Kostennikov, V. Ob Ekonomicheskom Raionirovanii SSSR. Moscow: Gospolitizdat, 1957.

Kovalyev, I. V. Zheleznodorozhnyy Transport v Novoi Stalinskoi Pyatiletke. Moscow: Transzheldorizdat, 1957.

Livshits, R. S. Razmeshcheniye Promyshlennosti v Dorevolutsionnoi Rossii. Akademiya Nauk SSSR, Institut Ekonomiki. Moscow: Izdatel'stvo Akademii Nauk SSSR, 1955.

Lorimer, Frank. The Population of the Soviet Union: History and Prospects. Geneva: League of Nations, 1946.

Lyashchenko, Peter I. History of the National Economy of Russia: To the 1917 Revolution. Translated by L. M. Herman. New York: The Macmillan Company, 1949.

Naporko, A. G. Ocherki Razvitiya Zheleznodorozhnogo Transporta SSSR. Moscow: Transzheldorizdat, 1954.

Narzikulov, I. K., and Ryazantsev, S. N. (eds.) Tadzhikskaya SSR: Ekonomiko-Geograficheskaya Kharakteristika. Akademiya Nauk Tadzhikskoi SSR and the Institut Geografii, Akademii Nauk SSR. Moscow: Geografgiz, 1956.

Ob Oroshenii i Osvoyenii Golodnoi Stepi: Sbornik Materialov. Tashkent: Gosizdat, Uzbekskoi SSR, 1956.

Onika, D. T. Ugol'naya Promyshlennost' SSSR v Shestoi Pyatiletke. Moscow: Ugletekhizdat, 1956.

Osnovnyye Voprosy Pyatiletnego Plana Vosstanovleniya i Razvitiya Zheleznodorozhnogo Transporta na 1946-1950 gg.: Sbornik Statey. Edited by B. I. Levin. Moscow: Transzheldorizdat, 1947.

Ostrovskiy, Z. The Great Trunk-Line. Moscow: Centrizdat, 1931.

Shaposhnikov, A. S. Astrakhan': Geograficheskiy Ocherk. Moscow: Geografgiz, 1956.

Shimkin, Demitri. Minerals: A Key to Soviet Power. Cambridge: Harvard University Press, 1953.

Sredneaziatskiy Gosudarstvennyy Universitet imeni V. I. Lenin, Geograficheskiy Fakul'tet. Uzbekskaya SSR. Moscow: Geografgiz, 1956.

Stuart, A. Les Traces du Chemins de Fer Central-Asiatique Projetes par Mm. F. de Lesseps et Cotard. Paris: Aux Bureaux de L'Exploreteur, 1875.

Suslov, S. P. Fizicheskaya Geografiya SSSR: Aziatskaya Chast'. 2d ed. rev. Moscow: Uchpedgiz, 1954.

The Land of Socialism Today and Tomorrow. Moscow: Gospolitizdat, 1939.

Umnyakov, I. I., Aleskerov, Yu. N., and Mikhailov, K. M. Samarkand: Kratkiy Spravochnik-Putevoditel'. Tashkent: Gosizdat Uzbekskoi SSR, 1956.

Vernadsky, George. A History of Russia. 3d ed. rev. New Haven: Yale University Press, 1944.

Vol'fson, L. Ya., Ledovskoi, V. I., and Shil'nikov, N. S. Ekonomika Transporta. Moscow: Transzheldorizdat, 1941.

Voprosy Ratsionalizatsii Perevozok Vazneishikh Gruzov. Edited by V. P. Potapov and B. I. Shafirkin. Moscow: Transzheldorizdat, 1957.

Yakobi, A. Zheleznyye Dorogi SSSR v Tsifrakh. Moscow: Tsunkhu Gosplana SSSR, 1935.

Yezhegodnik Bol'shoi Sovetskoi Entsiklopeii: 1957. Edited by B. A. Vvedenskiy. Moscow: Gosnaukizdat, 1957.

Zaglyadimov, D. P., Petrov, A. P., and Sergeyev, E. S. Organizatsiya Gruzovogo Dvizheniya. 3d ed. rev. Moscow: Transzheldorizdat, 1956.

Zhelezorudnaya Baza Chernoi Metallurgii SSSR. IX. Zhelezorudnyye Mestorozhdeniya SSSR. Edited by I. P. Bardin. Moscow: Izdatel'stvo Akademii Nauk SSSR, 1957.

Articles and Periodicals

Ballod, K. A. "Na Putyakh k Osvoyeniyu Krupneishey Mednoi Bazy SSSR," Sotialisticheskiy Transport, No. 11 (November, 1934), pp. 72-79.

________. "Perspektivy Razvitiya Seti Zheleznykh Dorog v Kazakhskoi SSR," Sotsialisticheskiy Transport, No. 7 (July, 1937), pp. 75-81.

Belen'kiy, N. P., and Vasil'yev, N. P. "Udlineniye Priyemo-Otpravochnykh Putey--Vazhneisheye Zveno Rekonstruktsii Stantsii," Zheleznodorozhnyy Transport, XXXVII (August, 1956), 37-41.

Beskrovnyy, I. G., and Belen'kiy, M. N. "Effektivnost' Primeneniya Teplovoznoi Tyagi na Dorogakh Sredney Azii i Kazakhstana," Zheleznodorozhnyy Transport, XXXVII (November, 1956), 18-22.

Bochkarev, N. G. "Novoye Zheleznodorozhnoye Stroitel'stvo i Razvitiye Transportnikh Svyazyei," Zheleznodorozhnyy Transport, XXXVII (February, 1956), 30-37.

Chernomordik, D. "Rol' Transporta v Razvitii Proizvoditel'nykh Sil Strany," Zheleznodorozhnyy Transport, XXVIII (December, 1947), 23-31.

Erlikh, D. "Ekonomicheskiye Problemy Razvitiya Sistemy Mashin v Khlopkovodstve," Voprosy Ekonomiki, XI (January, 1958), 47-56.

Fedorov, M. I. "Puti Rekonstruktsii Zheleznodorozhnykh Vykhodov iz Sredney Azii," Sotsialisticheskiy Transport, No. 1 (January, 1945), pp. 57-67.

Firsov, B. "Za Novyy Pod'yem Sovetskogo Khlopkovodstva," Planovoye Khozyaistvo, No. 3 (March, 1958), pp. 49-61.

Gel'fman, M. M. "Novoye Zheleznodorozhnoye Stroitel'stvo vo Vtorom Pyatiletke," Sotsialisticheskiy Transport, No. 11 (December, 1934), pp. 56-79.

Gudok. 1953-1957.

Khachaturov, Tigran S. "The Organization and Development of Railway Transport in the U.S.S.R.," International Affairs, XXI (April, 1945), 220-35.

Khodzhayev, G. "Zheleznaya Doroga Chardzhou--Kungrad," Zheleznodorozhnyy Transport, XXVIII (July, 1947), 17-21.

Kolyada, G. I. "Ob Effektivnosti Primeneniya i Tempakh Stroitel'stva Avtomatiki i Telemekhaniki," Zheleznodorozhnyy Transport, XXXVII (September, 1956), 72-76.

Kosorotov, N. G. "Tekhniko-Ekonomicheskaya Effektivnost' Vnedreniya Dispetcherskoi Tsentralizatsii," Zheleznodorozhnyy Transport, XL (April, 1958), 65-68.

Kulak, V. S. "Turkestano-Sibirskaya Zheleznaya Doroga--Pervenets Pyatiletok," Zheleznodorozhnyy Transport, XXXI (October, 1957), 76-80.

Maksimovich, B. M., and Fel'dman, E. D. "Effektivnoye Ispol'zovaniye Sredstv Uvelicheniya Propusknoi Sposobnosti," Zheleznodorozhnyy Transport, XXXVII (January, 1956), 12-18.

Mulyukin, F. P. "Neotlozhnyye Voprosy Povysheniya Effektivnosti Kapitalovlozheniy," Zheleznodorozhnyy Transport, XXXVIII (July, 1957), 8-14.

Naumov, A. N. "Perspektivy Usileniya Puti i Mekhanizatsii Putevykh Rabot," Zheleznodorozhnyy Transport, XXXVII (February, 1956), 9-16.

Orobinskiy, G. D. "Vazhnyye Voprosy Povysheniya Effektivnosti Ekspluatatsii Teplovozov," Zheleznodorozhnyy Transport, XXXVII (September, 1956), 13-17.

Osyannikov, V. N., and Larin, V. N. "Vysokoproisvoditel'noye Ispol'zovaniye Teplovozov," Zheleznodorozhnyy Transport, XXXVIII (July, 1957), 66-69.

Petrov, V. I., and Tsenin, S. S. "Razvitiye Ekonomiki Vostochnykh Rainov i ikh Transportnoye Osvoyeniye," Zheleznodorozhnyy Transport, XXXVII (October, 1956), 42-48.

"Rabota Zheleznodorozhnogo Transporta v 1957 g.," Zheleznodorozhnyy Transport, XXXIX (February, 1958), 29-34.

Romanovskiy, K. "Paromnyye Perepravy," Zheleznodorozhnyy Transport, XXI (October, 1940), 52-58.

Troitskiy, A. P. "Opyt Vnedreniya Teplovoznoi Tyagi na Tashkentskoi Doroge," Zheleznodorozhnyy Transport, XXXVII (May, 1956), 32-35.

Tulyaganov, U. "Zheleznyye Dorogi i Razvitiye Ekonomiki Respublik Sredney Azii," Zheleznodorozhnyy Transport, XXXVIII (September, 1957), 3-6.

Atlases

Atlas SSSR. 2d ed. Moscow: Glavnoye Upravleniye Geodezii Kartografii pri Sovete Ministrov SSSR, 1955.

Geograficheskiy Atlas SSSR: dlya 7-go i 8-go Klassov Sredney Shkoly. Moscow: Glavnoye Upravleniye Geodezii i Kartografii pri Sovete Ministrov SSSR, 1951.

Interviews

Chicago and Northwestern Railway. Interview with Mr. Harold Lenske, Director of Public Relations, June 7, 1958.

Samarkand Silk-weaving Factory. Interview with the Manager, July 10, 1957.

Tashkent Textile Combine. Interview with an official, July 12, 1957.

THE UNIVERSITY OF CHICAGO
DEPARTMENT OF GEOGRAPHY
RESEARCH PAPERS (Planographed, 6 × 9 Inches)

(Available from Department of Geography, Rosenwald Hall 24, University of Chicago, Chicago 37, Illinois. Price: four dollars each; by series subscription, three dollars each.)

1. GROSS, HERBERT HENRY. *Educational Land Use in the River Forest–Oak Park Community (Illinois)*
   September, 1948. 173 pp. 7 maps in pocket.
2. EISEN, EDNA E. *Educational Land Use in Lake County, Ohio*
   December, 1948. 161 pp. 2 maps in pocket.
3. WEIGEND, GUIDO GUSTAV. *The Cultural Pattern of South Tyrol (Italy)*
   June, 1949. 198 pp. (out of print)
4. NELSON, HOWARD JOSEPH. *The Livelihood Structure of Des Moines, Iowa*
   September, 1949. 140 pp. 3 folded maps. (out of print)
5. MATTHEWS, JAMES SWINTON. *Expressions of Urbanism in the Sequent Occupance of Northeastern Ohio*
   September, 1949. 179 pp.
6. GINSBURG, NORTON SYDNEY. *Japanese Prewar Trade and Shipping in the Oriental Triangle*
   September, 1949. 308 pp. (out of print)
7. KEMLER, JOHN H. *The Struggle for Wolfram in the Iberian Peninsula, June, 1942—June, 1944: A Study in Political and Economic Geography in Wartime*
   September, 1949. 151 pp.
8. PHILBRICK, ALLEN K. *The Geography of Education in the Winnetka and Bridgeport Communities of Metropolitan Chicago*
   September, 1949. 165 pp. 1 folded map.
9. BRADLEY, VIRGINIA. *Functional Patterns in the Guadalupe Counties of the Edwards Plateau*
   December, 1949. 153 pp.
10. HARRIS, CHAUNCY D., and FELLMANN, JEROME DONALD. *A Union List of Geographical Serials*
    June, 1950. 144 pp. (out of print)
11. DE MEIRLEIR, MARCEL J. *Manufactural Occupance in the West Central Area of Chicago*
    June, 1950. 264 pp. (out of print)
12. FELLMANN, JEROME DONALD. *Truck Transportation Patterns of Chicago*
    September, 1950. 120 pp. 6 folded maps. (out of print)
13. HOTCHKISS, WESLEY AKIN. *Areal Pattern of Religious Institutions in Cincinnati*
    September, 1950. 114 pp.
14. HARPER, ROBERT ALEXANDER. *Recreational Occupance of the Moraine Lake Region of Northeastern Illinois and Southeastern Wisconsin*
    September, 1950. 184 pp. 3 folded maps. (out of print)
15. WHEELER, JESSE HARRISON, JR. *Land Use in Greenbrier County, West Virginia*
    September, 1950. 192 pp.
16. McGAUGH, MAURICE EDRON. *The Settlement of the Saginaw Basin*
    December, 1950. 432 pp.
17. WATTERSON, ARTHUR WELDON. *Economy and Land Use Patterns of McLean County, Illinois*
    December, 1950. 164 pp. (out of print)
18. HORBALY, WILLIAM. *Agricultural Conditions in Czechoslovakia, 1950*
    June, 1951. 120 pp. 1 map in pocket.
19. GUEST, BUDDY ROSS. *Resource Use and Associated Problems in the Upper Cimarron Area*
    June, 1951. 148 pp. 2 maps in pocket.
20. SORENSEN, CLARENCE WOODROW. *The Internal Structure of the Springfield, Illinois, Urbanized Area*
    June, 1951. 204 pp. 5 maps in pocket.
21. MUNGER, EDWIN S. *Relational Patterns of Kampala, Uganda*
    September, 1951. 178 pp. 3 folded maps. (out of print)
22. KHALAF, JASSIM M. *The Water Resources of the Lower Colorado River Basin*
    December, 1951. Volume I, 248 pp.; Volume II, 15 maps in pocket.
23. GULICK, LUTHER H. *Rural Occupance in Utuado and Jayuya Municipios, Puerto Rico*
    June, 1952. 268 pp.
24. TAAFFE, EDWARD JAMES. *The Air Passenger Hinterland of Chicago*
    August, 1952. 176 pp. 1 folded map
25. KRAUSE, ANNEMARIE ELISABETH. *Mennonite Settlement in the Paraguayan Chaco*
    December, 1952. 160 pp. 4 maps in pocket.
26. HAMMING, EDWARD. *The Port of Milwaukee*
    December, 1952. 172 pp. 1 folded map.
27. CRAMER, ROBERT ELI. *Manufacturing Structure of the Cicero District, Metropolitan Chicago*
    December, 1952. 192 pp. 2 maps in pocket.
28. PIERSON, WILLIAM H. *The Geography of the Bellingham Lowland, Washington*
    March, 1953. 172 pp. 3 maps in pocket. (out of print)
29. WHITE, GILBERT F. *Human Adjustment to Floods: A Geographical Approach to the Flood Problem in the United States*
    June, 1942. 236 pp.
30. OSBORN, DAVID G. *Geographical Features of the Automation of Industry*
    August, 1953. 120 pp.

31. THOMAN, RICHARD S. *The Changing Occupance Pattern of the Tri-State Area, Missouri, Kansas, and Oklahoma*
August, 1953. 152 pp. 1 folded chart. (out of print)

32. ERICKSEN, SHELDON D. *Occupance in the Upper Deschutes Basin, Oregon*
December, 1953. 152 pp.

33. KENYON, JAMES B. *The Industrialization oj the Skokie Area*
July, 1954. 144 pp.

34. PHILLIPS, PAUL GROUNDS. *The Hashemite Kingdom of Jordan: Prolegomena to a Technical Assistance Program*
March, 1954. 208 pp.

35. CARMIN, ROBERT LEIGHTON. *Anápolis, Brazil: Regional Capital of Agricultural Frontier*
December, 1953. 184 pp.

36. GOLD, ROBERT N. *Manufacturing Structure and Pattern of the South Bend–Mishawaka Area*
June, 1954. 224 pp. 6 folded inserts. 2 maps in pocket.

37. SISCO, PAUL HARDEMAN. *The Retail Function of Memphis*
August, 1954. 176 pp. 2 folded inserts.

38. VAN DONGEN, IRENE S. *The British East African Transport Complex*
December, 1954. 184 pp. 3 maps in pocket.

39. FRIEDMANN, JOHN R. P. *The Spatial Structure of Economic Development in the Tennessee Valley*
March, 1955. 204 pp.
(Published jointly as Research Paper No. 1, Program of Education and Research in Planning, The University of Chicago.)

40. GROTEWOLD, ANDREAS. *Regional Changes in Corn Production in the United States from 1909 to 1949*
June, 1955. 88 pp.

41. BJORKLUND, E. M. *Focus on Adelaide—Functional Organization of the Adelaide Region, Australia*
December, 1955. 144 pp. 2 folded inserts. 1 map in pocket.

42. FORD, ROBERT N. *A Resource Use Analysis and Evaluation of the Everglades Agricultural Area*
June, 1956. 128 pp. 1 folded insert.

43. CHRISTENSEN, DAVID E. *Rural Occupance in Transition: Sumter and Lee Counties, Georgia*
June, 1956. 172 pp.

44. GUZMÁN, LOUIS E. *Farming and Farmlands in Panama*
December, 1956. 148 pp.

45. ZADROZNY, MITCHELL G. *Water Utilization in the Middle Mississippi Valley*
December, 1956. 132 pp.

46. AHMED, G. MUNIR. *Manufacturing Structure and Pattern of Waukegan–North Chicago*
February, 1957. 132 pp.

47. RANDALL, DARRELL. *Factors of Economic Development and the Okovango Delta*
December, 1956. 282 pp.
(Published jointly as Research Paper No. 3, Program of Education and Research in Planning, The University of Chicago.)

48. BOXER, BARUCH. *Israeli Shipping and Foreign Trade*
April, 1957. 176 pp.

49. MAYER, HAROLD M. *The Port of Chicago and the St. Lawrence Seaway*
May, 1957. 304 pp. 2 folded maps. Cloth $5.00. University of Chicago Press.

50. PATTISON, WILLIAM D. *Beginnings of the American Rectangular Land Survey System, 1784-1800*
December, 1957. 260 pp.

51. BROWN, ROBERT HAROLD. *Political Areal-Functional Organization: With Special Reference to St. Cloud, Minnesota*
December, 1957. 130 pp.

52. BEYER, JACQUELYN. *Integration of Grazing and Crop Agriculture: Resources Management Problems in the Uncompahgre Valley Irrigation Project*
December, 1957. 131 pp.

53. ACKERMAN, EDWARD A. *Geography as a Fundamental Research Discipline*
July, 1958. 40 pp. $1.00.

54. AL-KHASHAB, WAFIQ HUSSAIN. *The Water Budget of the Tigris and Euphrates Basin*
December, 1958. 113 pp.

55. LARIMORE, ANN EVANS. *The Alien Town: Patterns of Settlement in Busoga, Uganda*
August, 1958. 210 pp.

56. MURPHY, FRANCIS C. *Regulating Flood-Plain Development*
November, 1958. 216 pp.

57. WHITE, GILBERT F., *et al. Changes in Urban Occupance of Flood Plains in the United States*
November, 1958. 256 pp.

58. COLBY, MARY MCRAE. *The Geographic Structure of Southeastern North Carolina*
December, 1958. 242 pp.

59. MEGEE, MARY CATHERINE. *Monterrey, Mexico: Internal Patterns and External Relations*
December, 1958. 122 pp.

60. WEBER, DICKINSON. *A Comparison of Two Oil City Business Centers* (Odessa-Midland, Texas)
November, 1958. 256 pp.

61. PLATT, ROBERT S. *Field Study in American Geography*
July, 1959. 408 pp.

62. GINSBURG, NORTON, editor. *Essays on Geography and Economic Development*
1960. 196 pp.

63. HARRIS, CHAUNCY D., and FELLMANN, JEROME DONALD. *International List of Geographical Serials*
1960.

64. TAAFFE, ROBERT N. *Rail Transportation and the Economic Development of Soviet Central Asia*
1960. 186 pp.